MW01164776

DESIGN RESEARCH IN SOCIAL STUDIES EDUCATION

This edited volume showcases work from the emerging field of design-based research (DBR) within social studies education and explores the unique challenges and opportunities that arise when applying the approach in classrooms. Usually associated with STEM fields, DBR's unique ability to generate practical theories of learning and to engineer theory-driven improvements to practice holds meaningful potential for the social studies. Each chapter describes a different DBR study, exploring the affordances and dilemmas of the approach. Chapters cover such topics as iterative design, using and producing theory, collaborating with educators, and the ways that DBR attends to historical, political, and social context.

Beth C. Rubin is Professor of Education at the Graduate School of Education, Rutgers University, USA.

Eric B. Freedman is Assistant Professor of Teacher Education and Secondary Social Studies at Sacred Heart University, USA.

Jongsung Kim is Assistant Professor of Social Studies Education at the Graduate School of Education, Hiroshima University, Japan.

DESIGN RESEARCH IN SOCIAL STUDIES EDUCATION

Critical Lessons from an Emerging Field

Edited by Beth C. Rubin, Eric B. Freedman and Jongsung Kim

Routledge
Taylor & Francis Group

NEW YORK AND LONDON

First published 2019
by Routledge
52 Vanderbilt Avenue, New York, NY 10017

and by Routledge
2 Park Square, Milton Park, Abingdon, Oxon, OX14 4RN

Routledge is an imprint of the Taylor & Francis Group, an informa business

© 2019 Taylor & Francis

The right of Beth C. Rubin, Eric B. Freedman, and Jongsung
Kim to be identified as the authors of the editorial material, and
of the authors for their individual chapters, has been asserted in
accordance with sections 77 and 78 of the Copyright, Designs and
Patents Act 1988.

Library of Congress Cataloging-in-Publication Data
A catalog record for this title has been requested

ISBN: 978-0-367-11024-6 (hbk)
ISBN: 978-0-367-11025-3 (pbk)
ISBN: 978-0-429-02438-2 (ebk)

Typeset in Bembo
by Swales & Willis Ltd, Exeter, Devon, UK

CONTENTS

FOREWORD

Much of the research in social studies focuses, quite laudably, on practice. Many researchers in the field began their careers as classroom teachers and experienced both the joy of teaching and the complexities of the work. The questions they encountered daily in their classrooms were varied and challenging. Why do some students resonate with and learn from a particular pedagogical approach, while others are resistant or bored? What perspectives should be given time in the curriculum and why? What do I want students to learn in my classroom—and who else should have a say in determining the outcomes that matter? More broadly, what should the aims of social studies be? And should those aims be the same for all students, or should they be rooted in students' differing cultural contexts? Teachers regularly grapple with how to make decisions about these important dilemmas, and the list of questions they ask themselves is as long as it is varied.

Social studies researchers have addressed some of these questions more adequately than they have others. Many of the questions come about because teachers are tinkerers, always in search of more effective approaches. Whether they are creating curriculum and teaching strategies from whole cloth, or using those designed by others, the most exciting and effective teachers are continually assessing what their students are learning and why—and making adaptations along the way.

For some teachers, the questions they pose cause them to enter doctoral programs, where they are formally prepared as researchers whose careers will begin to address them. Along the way, some recognize that many important questions can't really be addressed unless they create a new approach to teaching. Or conversely, they create a new approach—an innovation—and they find that using it generates even more questions they had not previously considered.

The systematic combination of design and inquiry is an important building block of design-based research. But because it is almost unheard of to design a new program so perfect on its first attempt that it needs no improvement, another critical building block is iteration: Begin by designing something (e.g., a new simulation or a new unit on a controversial perennial issue), try it out, rigorously and systematically investigate what students are learning and why—and then go back to the drawing board to make changes based on what you learned, and try it again in as many iterations as needed. Along the way, design researchers address important questions, create theory, and hopefully produce high-quality approaches to teaching and learning. The quality of these approaches—and their usefulness to others—lies not only in the clarity of the initial design but also in the rigor of iterative processes of testing and revision.

Although the processes at the core of design-based research have undoubtedly been going on for many years, until recently there has been little attempt to systematically analyze the methodology's use in social studies or disseminate its results. There has been no "go to" source in the field that clearly describes what design-based research is, outlines its history and potential, or provides varied examples of such research in social studies. *Design Research in Social Studies Education: Critical Lessons from an Emerging Field* fills this void in a way that is impressively thorough and incredibly interesting. The introductory chapter—about the history, methodology, and promise of design-based research in social studies—is rich, clear, and comprehensive. The nine chapters that follow, with examples of such research, are detailed, varied, and unfailingly interesting. One important takeaway: There is no single "right way" to execute a design-based research project. At its core, design-based research relies on inquiry, innovation, and iteration to achieve its goals, and this means that the methodology must be expansive enough to accommodate various approaches. The final chapter takes a helpful step out of the details of designed-based research in order to analyze how the approach can and should be used toward socially transformative ends.

This important book is a must-read for anyone who wants to better understand design-based research in social studies education. Like all methods of inquiry, it is not a panacea. But because it provides a way to inquire about important questions, to innovate, and to move systematically toward improvement—often in deep collaboration and partnership with classroom teachers—design-based research has particular power and promise to improve social studies education.

Diana E. Hess

PREFACE

In 1992, learning scientist Ann Brown described classroom life as "synergistic," in that "aspects of it that are often treated independently . . . actually form part of a systemic whole" (pp. 142–143). This notion, that classrooms are complex and dynamic systems that should be examined holistically, was novel to a field dominated by laboratory approaches to the study of learning. Brown and others (e.g., Collins, 1992) proposed that researchers collaborate with educators to try out new approaches in classroom settings, and then examine, revise, and re-implement in an ongoing cycle of innovation—an iterative approach to the study of teaching and learning called *design-based research*, or DBR (Cobb, Confrey, diSessa, Lehrer, & Schauble, 2003; Collins, Joseph, & Bielaczyc, 2004; McKenney & Reeves, 2012).

Perhaps due to its roots in the learning sciences, the majority of design-based research has occurred in science, technology, and mathematics education (Anderson & Shattuck, 2012; Kelly, Lesh, & Baek, 2008). Yet DBR holds equal promise for the social studies. The small but increasing number of DBR projects in that field reveal the methodology's unique ability both to generate practical theories of learning and to engineer theory-driven improvements to practice. While some DBR projects in the social studies follow Brown's original model, others draw more directly on sociocultural and critical frameworks. For that reason, this emerging body of work holds important implications both for social studies scholarship and for DBR across the content areas.

This volume, which originated from a symposium held during the 2017 Annual Conference of the College and University Faculty Assembly of the National Council for the Social Studies in San Francisco, showcases how a design-based approach can be applied to pressing questions in social studies education. It explores the opportunities and challenges the methodology poses and considers the implications of social studies DBR for the learning sciences community, particularly in relation to the sociocultural, historical, and political dimensions of the methodology. This book is meant for educational researchers wishing to learn more about DBR in the social studies, for learning scientists in the STEM fields who may know little of the methodology's use in the social studies, and for curriculum developers and research organizations seeking ways to iteratively improve their products based on evidence.

Before describing the book's contents, a note on terminology: Some scholars use Brown's original term, "design experiment" (e.g., Cobb, Confrey, diSessa, Lehrer, & Schauble, 2003), while others prefer "design study" or "educational design research" (e.g., McKenney & Reeves, 2012; van den Akker, Gravemeijer, McKenney, & Nieveen, 2006) to avoid conflation with controlled experiments. We use "design-based research" (DBR) for this same reason and to follow with convention. Occasionally we use "design research," as in the book's title, to refer to DBR along with its variants such as design-based implementation research (DBIR) and design-based action research (DBAR).

In the introductory chapter, Freedman and Kim describe the DBR methodology, including its unique aims, features, affordances, and constraints. The chapter also provides a historical review of DBR's use in the social studies. The authors then describe the promise the methodology offers for the future of social studies research. The main body of the book consists of four parts, each focusing on a different aspect of the method: iterative design, use and production of theory, collaboration with practitioners, and the social and political context of design, although individual chapters may touch on more than one of these aspects.

Part I, "Improving Practice through Iterative Design," highlights the ways that DBR's iterative approach allows researchers to work with educators to develop and improve upon new instructional practices for the social studies. In Chapter 2, Monte-Sano, Hughes, and Thomson describe a design-based project that aimed to integrate inquiry practices into history courses in Grades 6 through 8. The middle school teachers with whom they worked hoped to better support the learning and achievement of their African-American, English-Learner, and low-income student populations, whose test scores lagged significantly behind their peers'. The chapter highlights the importance of collaborating with practitioners, conducting multiple iterations, and using various sources of data in DBR.

In the next chapter, Stoddard and Rodriguez report on a project called "PurpleState Solutions," a virtual online internship that places students in the role of interns at a strategic communications firm. In the simulation, students learn core concepts in political communications and develop skills and habits to inquire into controversial issues. The chapter focuses on how iterative design allowed the developers to increase access and engagement in the simulation. After analyzing data from early iterations, they revised materials to make the simulation more accessible, developed scaffolding for participants and their online mentors, refined discussion models and automated scripts, and clarified the teacher's role in helping students succeed.

In the final chapter in this section, Day and Bae describe their journey to construct authentic performance assessments for an elementary classroom "mini-economy" simulation. The chapter illustrates how DBR can be used to respond to state mandates, spotlights the need to "iterate fast" in the initial stages of the research and development process, and underscores the importance of involving teachers in each step of the process. While most DBR has sought to illuminate the core components of effective designs, this chapter reflects on the design process itself.

Part II, "Using and Producing Theory," focuses on the ways that DBR researchers in social studies education both draw upon and generate theory when engaging in design. Burke describes a design-based study of a unit on gender created using the principles of anti-bias education (Derman-Sparks & Edwards, 2010). The fluid nature of DBR enabled Burke to make split-second decisions to alter lessons based on student discourse and allowed for insight into student and teacher thinking that could have been missed in a clinical setting. Through discourse analysis, she realized that despite her intention to interrupt the rigid gender binary, she was inadvertently reinforcing it. This project highlights the ability of DBR to employ theory (gender binarism) to inform the design of instruction (anti-bias education).

In the next chapter, Freedman describes how DBR methodology allowed him to discover new ways to characterize forms of history teaching and learning. In DBR, researchers often code the data inductively (similar to grounded theory), which allows them to notice unanticipated patterns in the data. Using this technique while field-testing a 13-week, inquiry-based history curriculum, Freedman noticed that despite the curriculum's intentions to foster "critical historical reasoning," the students ended up practicing something more akin to "positivistic historical reasoning" (see Freedman, 2015). Traditional experimental approaches that define constructs prior to field-testing would not have facilitated this "ontological innovation" (diSessa & Cobb, 2004), or on-the-fly invention of useful theoretical constructs.

Part III, "Collaborating with Practitioners," focuses on the nature of the working relationships with teachers and school personnel that undergird design-based projects in the social studies. Obenchain, Pennington, and Bardem examine the evolving relationship between themselves as researchers and their teacher-collaborator in designing and implementing a "Critical Democratic Literacy" (CDL) unit for elementary students. As the unit progressed, the classroom teacher began to rely on the researchers for professional advice and advocacy, which placed her in a tenuous space due to the constraints of the school's newly mandated curriculum. At times, the collaborative nature of their relationship grew threatened. The authors suggest that the relations between constituents are a critical aspect of DBR that has not always received the scholarly attention it deserves.

In the following chapter, Lo, Adams, Goodell, and Nachtigal showcase an example of design-based implementation research (DBIR), an extension to DBR that addresses concerns over scalability (Fishman, Penuel, Allen, Cheng, & Sabelli, 2013). They present data from a four-year, longitudinal case study of a teacher who participated in a DBIR study that tested a project-based learning (PBL) approach to teaching Advanced Placement U.S. Government. Results from the case study suggest that the iterative nature of DBIR can facilitate teachers' long-term professional growth.

Part IV, "Contextualizing DBR Historically, Socially, and Politically," aims to illuminate the ways that DBR projects are deeply and productively embedded in particular contexts. Rubin describes a study in which teachers and university researchers built a new approach to teaching U.S. History upon critical, sociocultural theories of civic learning, rooted in the issues and concerns of students living amid historical and structural inequalities. Starting with design principles attentive to the social and political context of civic learning (Rubin, 2007), the team developed a thematic curriculum undergirded by enduring civic questions and enacted through student-centered pedagogies focusing on discussion, engagement, and inquiry. The project highlights the necessity of understanding learning contexts as situated amid the historical, social, and political dimensions of community, state, and nation.

In the next chapter, Kim describes a design-based study problematizing current territorial education in South Korea and Japan. Using a framework called "authentic communication" (Kim, 2017), he worked with students in both countries to "make a better textbook" on the Dokdo/Takeshima island dispute. Kim's approach involved having the students trade their ideas for revision back and forth in an iterative cycle. This cross-national communication led the students to reevaluate their own country's official discourse surrounding the island, and to recognize the issue as controversial and open to multiple interpretations. The chapter considers the ways that national context affects the design of classroom instruction, as well as the ways that DBR can be adapted in international settings.

In a concluding chapter, Rubin reflects on the significance of the body of work described in the book. She maps out three dimensions of an approach to "socially transformative design" (Gutiérrez, 2016) that might be used for DBR in the social studies, and perhaps beyond. Rubin suggests that those employing DBR consider the ways that structural inequality shapes the contexts surrounding their projects, that they think through how power imbalances figure into their collaborative work with participants, and that they ask hard questions about the goals of their projects: Do they expand transformative learning possibilities for young people or reinforce existing hierarchies? Researchers in the learning sciences have begun to grapple with the social, cultural, historical, and political dimensions of design work (e.g., Nasir, Rosebery, Warren, & Lee, 2014). Social studies researchers are well situated to help this community think more carefully about the possibilities of a socially transformative approach to this promising methodology.

Beth C. Rubin
Eric B. Freedman
Jongsung Kim
Editors

References

Anderson, T., & Shattuck, J. (2012). Design-based research: A decade of progress in education research? *Educational Researcher, 41*(1), 16–25.

Brown, A. L. (1992). Design experiments: Theoretical and methodological challenges in creating complex interventions in classroom settings. *Journal of the Learning Sciences, 2*(2), 141–178.

Cobb, P., Confrey, J., diSessa, A., Lehrer, R., & Schauble, L. (2003). Design experiments in educational research. *Educational Researcher, 32*(1), 9–13.

Collins, A. (1992). Toward a design science of education. In E. Scanlon & T. O'Shea (Eds.), *New directions in educational technology* (pp. 15–22). New York, NY: Springer.

Collins, A., Joseph, D., & Bielaczyc, K. (2004). Design research: Theoretical and methodological issues. *Journal of the Learning Sciences, 13*(1), 15–42.

Derman-Sparks, L., & Edwards, J. O. (2010). *Anti-bias education for young children and ourselves.* Washington, DC: National Association for the Education of Young Children.

diSessa, A. A., & Cobb, P. (2004). Ontological innovation and the role of theory in design experiments. *Journal of the Learning Sciences, 13*(1), 77–103.

Fishman, B. J., Penuel, W. R., Allen, A.-R., Cheng, B. H., & Sabelli, N. (2013). Design-based implementation research: An emerging model for transforming the relationship of research and practice. *National Society for the Study of Education, 112*(2), 136–156.

Freedman, E. B. (2015). "What happened needs to be told": Fostering critical historical reasoning in the classroom. *Cognition and Instruction, 33*(4), 357–398. DOI:10.1080/0 7370008.2015.1101465

Gutiérrez, K. D. (2016). Designing resilient ecologies: Social design experiments and a new social imagination. *Educational Researcher, 45*(3), 187–196. DOI:10.3102/00131 89X16645430

Kelly, A. E., Lesh, R. A., & Baek, J. Y. (Eds.). (2008). *Handbook of design research methods in education: Innovations in science, technology, engineering, and mathematics learning and teaching.* New York, NY: Routledge.

Kim, J. (2017). Jiko to tasha no "Sinseinataiwa" nimotozuku nikkan kankeisi kyouiku: Nikkan no kodomo o syutai tosita "Yoriyoi nissin/nichiro sensou no kyoukasyo zukuri" o jireini (Teaching history of Japan-Korea relations based on "Authentic Communication" between the self and others: A case for "Making a Better History Textbook as relates to the Sino-Japanese War and Russo-Japanese War" by Japanese and Korean students). Shakaika Kyouiku Kennkyu (The Journal of Social Studies), 130, 1–12.

McKenney, S. E., & Reeves, T. C. (2012). *Conducting educational design research.* New York, NY: Routledge.

Nasir, N. S., Rosebery, A. S., Warren, B., & Lee, C. D. (2014). Learning as a cultural process: Achieving equity through diversity. In R. K. Sawyer (Ed.), *The Cambridge handbook of the learning sciences* (Second ed., pp. 686–706). New York, NY: Cambridge University Press.

Rubin, B. C. (2007). "There's still not justice": Youth civic identity development amid distinct school and community contexts. *Teachers College Record, 109*(2), 449–481.

van den Akker, J., Gravemeijer, K., McKenney, S., & Nieveen, N. (Eds.). (2006). *Educational design research.* New York, NY: Routledge.

CONTRIBUTORS

Carol M. Adams teaches literacy and instructional planning courses at Seattle University. She earned her M.Ed. in Language and Literacy from the Harvard Graduate School of Education and her Ph.D. in Curriculum and Instruction from the University of Washington with a focus on secondary literacy. She served as research scientist on the *Knowledge in Action* project, which investigated how project-based learning can be applied to rigorous high school courses to promote deep and adaptive learning. Her current research interests include the intersection between literacy and content learning, research-practice collaboration, and teaching for deeper learning.

Christine L. Bae is Assistant Professor of Educational Psychology at the Virginia Commonwealth University, School of Education, in Richmond, VA. Her research explores the role of cognition and motivation in educational contexts, focused particularly on STEM learning. Her work has appeared in journals such as *Learning and Instruction, Research in Science Education*, and *Learning and Individual Differences*.

Maricela Bardem (pseudonym) is an elementary school teacher who began her career 20 years ago as a special education teacher, after receiving her Bachelor of Science degree in Elementary and Special Education. She then pursued her Master of Education in Literacy Studies while teaching 2nd grade. Maricela currently teaches in a diverse, multi-grade classroom.

Jennifer Burke is Assistant Professor at Millersville University, in Lancaster County, Pennsylvania. Twelve years of teaching in a diverse public elementary school in central New Jersey fostered her profound interest in the possibility for social justice through education. Her current research explores how elementary children engage with critical curricula designed to encourage them to examine the role race and gender play in their daily lives.

Stephen Day is Assistant Professor and director of the Center for Economic Education at Virginia Commonwealth University in Richmond, VA. His research focuses on economic education, inquiry learning, and iterative methodologies, such as DBR. His published work has appeared in *Social Education, Social Studies Review,* and the *Journal of Consumer Education.* He was also co-editor of *Teaching the C3 Framework*, Vol. 1.

Eric B. Freedman is Assistant Professor of Teacher Education at Sacred Heart University's Farrington College of Education in Fairfield, CT, where he teaches courses in social studies methods, educational psychology, and the social foundations of education. His research explores the teaching of history and the design of anti-oppressive curriculum, and has appeared in the journals *Cognition and Instruction* and *Harvard Educational Review.*

Alexandra Goodell is a Curriculum Designer, Professional Learning Specialist, and School Partnerships Coordinator at Educurious, after completing her doctoral work in Learning Sciences at the University of Washington. Her research focuses on student identity and engagement in project-based classes. She has a professional background in both special education and gifted education, with an emphasis on inclusion. As a Program Director at the University of Washington's Robinson Center for Young Scholars, she supported teachers' development and enactment of inquiry-based classes that incorporated PBL, differentiated instruction for diverse students, and maintained intellectual rigor.

Ryan E. Hughes is a Ph.D. Candidate in Teaching and Teacher Education and a former elementary school teacher. He researches how K-5 students learn history through inquiry instruction. He earned his M.A.T. from Teachers College, Columbia University, teaching certification from the Bay Area Teacher Training Institute, and B.A. in History from the San Francisco State University.

Jongsung Kim is Assistant Professor of Social Studies Education at Hiroshima University, Japan, where he teaches social studies methods courses and runs international research projects and student exchange programs. He is interested in designing interventions that support students to overcome the national discourse gap between countries and achieve mutual understanding. His work also relates to peace education, history education, and controversial issues education in international settings. Dr. Kim has published his research in Korean, Japanese, and English-language journals.

Jane C. Lo is Assistant Professor of Social Science Education in the School of Teacher Education at Florida State University. Her research focuses on civic education. Specifically, she is interested in the political engagement of youth, social studies curriculum development, and the development of youth civic identity. Her methodological expertise includes mixed-methods designs, design-based implementation research, interview and survey methods, and advanced correlational techniques. She teaches undergraduate and graduate courses in social studies methods. Her work has appeared in *Theory & Research in Social Education* and *Democracy & Education.*

Chauncey Monte-Sano is Associate Professor of Educational Studies at the University of Michigan. A former high school history teacher and National Board Certified teacher, she currently prepares novice teachers for social studies classrooms, works with veteran social studies teachers through a variety of professional development programs, and works with novice teacher educators. She has received research grants from the Braitmayer Foundation, the Institute of Education Sciences, the Library of Congress, the McDonnell Foundation, and the Spencer Foundation. Her research examines how students learn to reason with evidence in writing, and how their teachers learn to teach such historical thinking.

Sara Nachtigal is a Curriculum Designer and Program Manager at Educurious, a Seattle-based non-profit that designs and supports project-based learning (PBL) instruction with the goal of making learning meaningful, relevant, and rigorous. She works in partnership with community organizations, districts, schools, and teachers. Her research focuses on secondary literacy across content areas and ways to support teacher learning in PBL contexts.

Kathryn M. Obenchain is Professor of Social Studies Education and Associate Dean for Learning, Engagement, and Global Initiatives in the College of Education at Purdue University in West Lafayette, Indiana, USA. Her research centers on democratic citizenship education in the U.S. and emerging democracies. She is particularly interested in how teachers structure the environment to promote democratic knowledge, skills, and dispositions, which includes examining the civic identities of teachers. Her work also explores how K–12 students understand civic life, and their own roles as citizens. Dr. Obenchain has published extensively in domestic and international journals.

Julie L. Pennington is a professor of literacy studies at the University of Nevada, Reno. She has focused on the areas of literacy and diversity throughout her career as a classroom teacher and literacy intervention teacher for 14 years and currently as a teacher educator and researcher. Her research interests include the use of autoethnography in teacher education and the pursuit of questions related to how teachers approach literacy instruction in linguistically and culturally diverse settings.

Kimberly S. Rodriguez is a doctoral candidate of the Educational Policy, Planning, and Leadership program at the College of William and Mary in Williamsburg, VA, where she specializes in Curriculum and Educational Technology. Her current research explores the nature of computational thinking in higher education students learning to code. As a graduate assistant, she taught a master's level course on educational technology integration, and was a graduate assistant for the PurpleState online learning simulation platform project. She is currently completing her dissertation.

Beth C. Rubin is Professor at the Graduate School of Education at Rutgers, The State University of New Jersey. She uses school-based, ethnographic study to explore how young people come to see themselves as citizens and as learners amid the nested contexts of classroom, school, community, and society, with particular attention to how civic identity takes shape within local contexts marked by historical and contemporary inequalities. Her work appears in journals such as the *American Educational Research Journal, Teachers College Record, Harvard Educational Review, Curriculum Inquiry, Social Education*, the *Journal of Teacher Education*, and has been supported by the Spencer Foundation, the Fulbright Foundation, and CIRCLE, among other organizations.

Jeremy D. Stoddard is Associate Professor in the Department of Curriculum & Instruction at the University of Wisconsin—Madison, where he teaches courses in social studies pedagogical methods and graduate courses in media and democratic education. His research explores the role of media in teaching and learning democratic education, with a particular focus on teaching difficult historical and controversial contemporary issues. His research has appeared in *Teachers College Record, Curriculum Inquiry*, and *Learning, Media, and Technology*. He is also co-editor of *Teaching Difficult History Through Film* (Routledge, 2017).

Sarah Thomson is a Ph.D. candidate in Teaching and Teacher Education at the University of Michigan. She taught middle school in North Carolina before joining U-M. Sarah is interested in the teaching practices and curriculum supports that promote literacy learning for culturally and linguistically diverse learners. She earned her M.Ed. and teaching certification from the University of Maryland, and a B.A. in International Studies from the University of North Carolina at Chapel Hill.

Introduction

1

DESIGN RESEARCH IN THE SOCIAL STUDIES

History, Methodology, and Promise

Eric B. Freedman and Jongsung Kim

If one wished to design a better form of education than what school-age students typically experience, how would one go about it? For many teachers the answer is clear: try something new in their classroom and see what happens. The two of us can certainly relate. Each year our courses slightly improve, as we learn to explain a concept more clearly or eliminate a boring reading. Burkhardt (2006) calls this the "craft-based" approach to educational reform, in which "innovation comes from a few people pushing the boundaries of good practice, trying something new and seeing if it works—for them" (p. 122). Undoubtedly, much benefit accrues from this—a thousand teachers in a thousand schools, all refining their pedagogy year after year.

As a systematic means of improving instruction, though, the craft-based approach falls short. Some teachers share their hard-earned wisdom at professional conferences or, in rare cases, in published work (e.g., Bain, 2006). Others attract a researcher's attention and are featured in a journal article (e.g., Monte-Sano, 2011; Schweber, 2003). Yet the bulk of teachers' accumulated knowledge rarely disseminates beyond each one's circle of acquaintances. The frenetic work lives of teachers also prevent most of them from keeping pace with the latest theory and research on learning. Hence, their innovations are more likely to build upon existing practice than to test a radically new idea.

Moreover, trusting the efficacy of teachers' everyday experimentation requires a small leap of faith. As Burkhardt puts it, craft-based innovation "lacks systematic evaluation of effectiveness in well-defined circumstances: for who, what, and when, does it *work*, and with what range of outcomes?" (p. 123, emphasis in original). This critique equally applies to the majority of curricular materials on the market. Each year at the Annual Meeting of the

National Council for the Social Studies, dozens of organizations peddle their wares in a giant exhibit hall, yet only a small fraction go through rigorous field-testing.

Perhaps controlled experiments, then, are a better way to establish which innovations merit widespread use. Since the early 2000s, the National Research Council has championed the randomized controlled trial (RTC) as the highest standard for testing whether a given innovation works. Yet therein lies the problem: Controlled trials offer a means of assessing the efficacy of reforms, not of designing them. In fields such as pharmaceutical medicine, the RTC represents the final stage of a multiyear process of research and development. As Collins, Joseph, and Bielaczyc (2004) put it, controlled experiments fail to "provide the kind of detailed picture needed to guide the refinement of a design" (p. 21). RTCs also can underestimate the complexity of learning ecologies, in which changing one set of variables may transform the entire system. Moreover, why should we assume that educational researchers can devise better forms of instruction than teachers can? Though armed with rigorous theory and methodology, most of us spend so little time in schools or with the young people who reside there, that it is hard to imagine we could outperform seasoned practitioners in this regard.

Enter design-based research (DBR). At its core, DBR mimics the progressive tinkering that so many teachers already undertake, yet infuses into it a greater concern for careful measurement and the use and production of theory. The best examples involve teams of teachers and researchers sharing their varied expertise and working collaboratively to attack educational problems of mutual concern.

The idea dates back to the likes of John Dewey in the early twentieth century, yet DBR did not emerge as a formal research methodology until much later. In 1992, Collins asserted, "in aeronautics the goal is to elucidate how different designs contribute to lift, drag, maneuverability, etc. Similarly, a design science of education must determine how different designs of learning environments contribute to learning, cooperation, motivation, etc." (p. 15). In this way, Collins likened educational reform to the field of engineering, where the act of tinkering with designs until they work as intended yields theories about how and why they work.

In that same year, educational psychologist Ann Brown (1992) published a seminal article that described her 20-year evolution from traditional laboratory experiments to school-based design research. "My training," she writes, "was that of a classic learning theorist prepared to work with 'subjects' (rats, children, sophomores), in strictly controlled laboratory settings" (p. 141). Yet as theories of human learning grew more complex, Brown found that lab experiments stripped away too much of the complexity that characterizes learning in natural contexts. As she put it, "The lion's share of my current research program is devoted to the study of learning in the blooming, buzzing confusion of inner-city classrooms" (p. 141).

Granted, other research methodologies have long sought to capture this "blooming, buzzing confusion," or at least account for it. Ethnographies describe the cultural systems that arise in schools and classrooms (e.g., Eckert, 1989), while "models of wisdom" studies document the work of exceptional teachers within these contexts (e.g., Hess, 2002; Ladson-Billings, 1994; Wineburg & Wilson, 1988). Yet these approaches describe what currently exists; they do not envision or test out novel approaches. That job traditionally has fallen to experimental interventions, which, as we have seen, do better at testing than at envisioning (see Kelly, 2003).

DBR documents the conception, development, assessment, and revision of educational innovations so that others may learn from these design narratives (Barab, Baek, Schatz, Scheckler, & Moore, 2008). In one sense its goals are eminently practical: to yield a usable product or approach, tested and refined with real kids in real schools. Yet DBR also aims to generate theory. As Brown (1992) put it, "I attempt to engineer interventions that not only work by recognizable standards but are also based on theoretical descriptions that delineate why they work, and thus render them reliable and repeatable" (p. 143).

In a special issue of *Educational Researcher* devoted to the methodology of design-based research, Cobb, Confrey, diSessa, Lehrer, and Schauble (2003) delineated its main elements as follows:

1. First, the purpose of design experiments is to develop a class of theories about both the process of learning and the means that are designed to support that learning. . .
2. Design studies are typically test-beds for innovation. The intent is to investigate the possibilities for educational improvement by bringing about new forms of learning in order to study them. . .
3. Design studies create the conditions for developing theories yet must place these theories in harm's way [i.e. by testing them empirically]. . .
4. As conjectures are generated and perhaps refuted, new conjectures are developed and subjected to test. The result is an iterative design process featuring cycles of invention and revision. . .
5. [D]esign experiments tend to emphasize an intermediate theoretical scope . . . that is located between a narrow account of a specific system (e.g., a particular school district, a particular classroom) and a broad account that does not orient design to particular contingencies.

(pp. 9–11)

In the first book-length treatment of the subject, McKenney and Reeves (2012) depicted DBR in similar terms, as a genre of research in which the iterative development of solutions to practical and complex educational problems also provides the context for empirical investigations, which yields theoretical understanding that can inform the work of others. Its goals and method are rooted in, and not cleansed of, the complex variation of the real world.

(p. 7)

DBR has been championed by learning scientists in science, technology, engineering, and math (STEM) education but is far less common in the social studies (Anderson & Shattuck, 2012; cf. McKenney & Reeves, 2013). Our aim in this chapter is to show what benefits the approach might hold for that field. We begin by explaining the steps involved in conducting DBR and by considering some critiques launched against it. We then review examples of DBR in social studies education. We end with thoughts on how this emerging body of work can inform curriculum and teaching in the social studies and beyond.

Design-Based Research Methodology

In their book, McKenney and Reeves (2012) lay out a generic model for conducting design research in education (Figure 1.1). The model specifies three phases, or micro-cycles: (a) analysis and exploration, (b) design and construction, and (c) evaluation and reflection. A DBR project typically involves multiple roundtrips through these phases, with each trip called a meso-cycle or, more commonly, an iteration—allowing for what Collins et al. (2004) call the "progressive refinement" (p. 18) of the educational innovation. Each successive iteration brings the designed artifact closer to readiness for use beyond

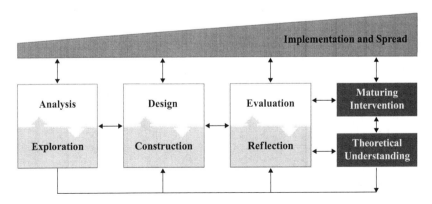

FIGURE 1.1   Generic Model for Conducting Design Research in Education.
Source: McKenney & Reeves, 2012, p. 77.

the research site—a feature of the methodology McKenney and Reeves (2012) call "[planning for] implementation and spread" (p. 80). Each iteration also informs a theoretical understanding of why the artifact does or does not work as intended (see Stoddard & Rodriguez, this volume).

The point of the *analysis and exploration* phase is to ascertain the problem space before devising a solution. As McKenney and Reeves (2012) put it, DBR should address "legitimate problems versus solutions in search of problems" (p. 88). Cobb et al. (2003) similarly advocate for determining the "intellectual and social starting points" (p. 11) of the students, teachers, and other stakeholders involved. These starting points might include the students' background knowledge and skills, cultural traits, and interests, as well as prevalent teaching practices, the school-wide culture, and the broader social and political context (see Kim, this volume; Rubin, this volume). Thus, in addition to the standard literature review, McKenney and Reeves (2012) recommend site visits, observations, focus groups, questionnaires, review of policy documents, and interviews with site personnel. Pre-tests also can occur during this phase to establish baseline measures of knowledge and skills in the targeted area.

Equally important in this initial phase is to delineate the research goals. Cobb et al. (2003) mention three different kinds of goals, which can often work in tandem. First, researchers might develop "an alternative conception of a domain" (p. 11)—for example, history learning as discovery versus recitation of facts. Second, they might hope to emerge from the study with a newly tested educational artifact—for example, a curriculum, piece of computer software, or professional development program. Finally, researchers might want to prompt new kinds of student "performances" that are "indicative of deep understanding" (p. 11; see Day & Bae, this volume). The analysis and exploration phase results in a detailed description of the problem space, a long-range goal or vision statement, a set of initial design propositions that specify what the solution might entail, and a list of requirements and constraints on that design (McKenney & Reeves, 2012).

The second phase in McKenney and Reeves's model, *design and construction*, involves developing the intervention itself. After reviewing previous designs in the literature, the team brainstorms, plans, and builds a prototype, creating "models, mock-ups, sketches, and stories as their vocabulary" to flesh out ideas (p. 115). Findings from phase one guide the prototype's development, to "ensure that revisions reflect responsive evolution (e.g., redesign to better meet the stated goals) and not 'mission creep' (e.g., redesign changes goals without realizing it)" (p. 130).

Some degree of testing and revision naturally occurs during phase two, but the bulk occurs during the third phase in McKenney and Reeves's (2012) model: *evaluation and reflection*. This is when the intervention is tested in a live setting, "with the aim of refining (theoretical) understanding about if, how, and why intervention features work" (p. 133). The team employs both formative and summative evaluation, often concurrently. The latter primarily determines the extent to which the intervention is working or not, while the former identifies possible reasons why. In this sense, DBR typically employs mixed-methods designs, with qualitative and quantitative data yielding formative and summative insights, respectively. As Brown (1992) remarked:

> We have records of student portfolios, including individual and group long-term projects. . . . Ethnographic observations . . . are taken routinely, together with extensive video and audio taping of individuals, groups, and whole classroom settings. In fact, we have no room to store all the data, let alone time to score it.
>
> *(p. 152)*

A hallmark of DBR is to collect these data not only at the beginning and end of the study, but also during each iteration. This way, it becomes clearer which modifications yielded which outcomes (Collins et al., 2004).

In describing their model, McKenney and Reeves (2012) draw on theoretical distinctions between different forms of curriculum: ideal (as intended by designers), formal (as written), perceived (as by teachers and administrators), operational (as enacted in classrooms), experiential (as experienced by students), and attained (as measured by what students have learned). The successive iterations of a DBR project follow this trajectory: Alpha testing typically examines the soundness and feasibility of the initial design (ideal curriculum), beta testing examines the viability of the design in a live setting but often with unsustainably high levels of scaffolding (operational curriculum), while gamma testing examines how the now finely tuned intervention impacts learning outcomes (attained curriculum). While impact on learning can be tracked throughout, it typically gains greater prominence in later iterations to allow for addressing initial flaws in design (see Monte-Sano, Hughes, & Thomson, this volume).

Many DBR projects, though, never shed the scaffolds erected during beta testing. These supports can include selecting only exceptional teachers to participate, providing extensive professional development, or even having designers co-teach the curriculum. McKenney and Reeves (2012) caution, "Designing for actual use takes into consideration the fact that any such scaffolds will fade over time" (p. 170). Along these lines, Fishman, Marx, Blumenfeld, Krajcik, and Soloway (2004) express concern that "much design-based research focuses on a designed product or resultant theory and not the system variables that impact the scaling potential of the work beyond the sites where the research was carried out" (p. 69). In response, Fishman and his colleagues propose a variant of DBR called "design-based implementation research" (DBIR) that attends to matters of sustainability and scalability by asking "What works when, for whom, and under what conditions?" and "How can we make this innovation work under a wide range of conditions?" (Fishman, Penuel, Allen, Cheng, & Sabelli, 2013, p. 146; see also Penuel, Fishman, Cheng, & Sabelli, 2011). DBIR aligns with McKenney and Reeves's (2012) notion of planning for "implementation and spread" (p. 80) beyond the initial research site.

As a final suggestion, numerous authors recommend working collaboratively with school personnel from the earliest planning stages through the final analysis of data (see Obenchain, Pennington, & Bardem, this volume). McKenney and Reeves (2012), for instance, delineate the benefits of a "clinical partnership" over the more typical "data extraction agreement" (p. 18). As the point of design-based research is to improve educational practice, diverse stakeholders should help define the kinds of improvements they wish to see (see Freedman, 2007).

Design-Based Research: Science or Sorcery?

Some commentators have questioned whether DBR methodology yields valid and reliable scientific knowledge. For example, Shavelson, Phillips, Towne, and Feuer (2003) point out that reports of it often take the form of a narrative describing what the researchers did and what students learned as a presumable result. "Some narratives will inevitably (perhaps unknowingly) make causal claims (e.g. we did x and it produced y). But narratives lacking more traditional controls on extraneous variables will not be able to warrant the causal claim" (p. 27). Shavelson et al. then ask, "To what extent can rival narrative accounts of the same action be ruled out? To what extent would another narrator replicate the account? To what extent does the narrative generalize to other times and places?" (p. 27). Such a critique could be leveled against nearly all qualitative research, but DBR is particularly vulnerable since it aims to develop causal theories linking interventions to learning outcomes.

Dede (2004) raises additional concerns. At what point in the iterative process, he asks, should a design "be considered too ineffective to merit further scholarly investment?" Furthermore, what differentiates "a design from its 'conditions for success'?" Failure to arrive at consensus answers to these questions "can easily lead to situations in which DBR presents unfalsifiable propositions, with failures always attributable to defects in implementation rather than flaws in the theory-based design itself" (p. 108). Too often, Dede observes, design researchers collect massive amounts of data to arrive at common-sense conclusions—exerting an "elephantine effort that resulted in the birth of mouse-like insights in their contribution to educational knowledge" (p. 107). Other times, the designed intervention is too costly or difficult to implement under normal circumstances. "Put bluntly," writes Dede, "neither policymakers nor practitioners want what the DBR community is selling right now" (p. 114).

Design researchers have long recognized these potential shortcomings. Brown (1992) warned against the "tendency to romanticize research of this nature and rest claims of success on a few engaging anecdotes or particularly exciting transcripts" (p. 173). The Design-Based Research Collective (2003) cautioned that design researchers "regularly find themselves in the dual intellectual roles of advocate and critic" (p. 7). Yet there are ways to mitigate these concerns. As noted earlier, the division of progressive refinement into distinct iterations, with consistent assessments at the end of each one, increases the validity of causal claims (Collins et al., 2004). Others suggest that as part of the overall study, researchers conduct controlled experiments when two or more alternative explanations could both account for the outcomes observed (Shavelson et al., 2003). Along these lines, McCandliss, Kalchman, and Bryant (2003) propose that design researchers work collaboratively with laboratory experimenters, sharing theories and comparing results. DBR also can employ randomized controlled trials in the final iteration.

Concerns about design studies' validity and generalizability point to an inherent tension, however. In one sense, the goal is to construct a usable product. As Sloane and Gorard (2003) put it, "From the simplest paper clip to the Space Shuttle, inventions are successful only to the extent that their developers properly anticipate how a device can fail to perform as intended" (p. 30). They suggest that DBR's proper aim is to "obviate failure" rather than "to produce unbiased estimators in support of robust theory" (p. 31). On the other hand, design researchers have been reluctant to abandon theory-construction altogether. Cobb et al. (2003) argue succinctly, "Design experiments are conducted to develop theories, not merely to empirically tune 'what works'" (p. 9). The tension between these two strands suggests an inherent trade-off between too much tinkering (which could yield a better product) versus too many controls (which could yield better-validated theory).

Some commentators have argued instead that DBR's purpose is not to validate theory, but rather to generate it (see Freedman, this volume). As Edelson (2002) explains, "The practical process of applying a theory to construct a design naturally exposes inconsistencies" (p. 118) and underspecified elements within the theory. Sifting through the qualitative data generated during field-testing—what Edelson calls "retrospective analysis" (p. 116)—yields new theoretical insights. He delineates three kinds of theories towards which DBR can contribute in this manner: *domain theories* "about learners and how they learn, teachers and how they teach, or learning environments and how they influence teaching and learning"; *design frameworks* (or design principles) that "describe the characteristics that a designed artifact must have to achieve a particular set of goals in context"; and *design methodologies* that describe "(a) a process for achieving a class of designs, (b) the forms of expertise required, and (c) the roles to be played by the individuals representing those forms of expertise" (pp. 113–115; see Day and Bae, this volume).

DiSessa and Cobb (2004) further note that many useful theories (e.g., the germ theory of disease) contain constructs that are undetectable (e.g., germs) unless the observer knows how and where to look for them—thus necessitating a process the authors call "bootstrapping" (p. 84). In this sense, DBR holds close affinity to grounded theory approaches that seek to discover new constructs through meticulous coding and comparison of observed phenomena (see Glaser, 1978). What makes DBR unique is that this inductive analysis is undertaken within a designed as opposed to a natural setting, positioning DBR as an "interventionist ethnography" (Dede, 2004, p. 111). We agree that design-based research functions more effectively at generating than at validating theory. Unlike randomized controlled trials that describe only the finished product, DBR produces a detailed narrative documenting what transpired when design features were added, modified, or removed (Barab et al., 2008). By reflecting on these design narratives, analysts can discover new facets of human learning and the scaffolds that support it.

Design-Based and Interventionist Research in the Social Studies

A systematic review spanning the years 2002–2011 found that the vast majority of DBR occurred in the fields of science, mathematics, and educational technology (Anderson & Shattuck, 2012). Although some have questioned the review's methodology (McKenney & Reeves, 2013), the point still stands that design research is rare in the social studies. We compiled a comprehensive list of DBR in that field through searches on ERIC and Education Research Complete, cross-referenced articles, and communication with colleagues.[1] Table 1.1 lists the most prominent results of our search—that is, the studies appearing in the widest-read outlets and that uphold DBR's methodological criteria to the fullest extent.

In reviewing this work, we wish to tell two simultaneous stories. The first considers the designs introduced, the similarities and differences between them, and the vision they represent for transforming social studies curriculum and instruction. The second story considers the research methods employed, the extent to which they match the DBR approach described above, and the affordances and constraints these methods have brought.

Experimental Research

Designing and testing new forms of social studies instruction long predates the formal articulation of DBR methodology. In the 1960s, Oliver and Shaver (1966) developed a two-year curriculum for Grades 7 and 8 that taught an elaborate method for analyzing public issues, which involved breaking them into definitional, factual, and value-based disputes. Based on post-treatment one-on-one interviews and student-led discussions, the authors found that the curriculum effectively taught students to employ the method, as compared to three control schools employing a standard curriculum (although gains were strongest in the first year). Two other early intervention studies were the Amherst History Project (Committee on the Study of History, 1969) and the Schools Council Project "History 13–16" in Great Britain (Shemilt, 1983). Like Oliver and Shaver's, though, these studies did not provide the detailed design narrative over multiple iterations typical of DBR.

Intervention studies enjoyed a resurgence in the 1990s and 2000s, as part of the domain-specific turn in educational research (see Stevens, Wineburg,

TABLE 1.1 Select Examples of Interventionist and Design-based Research in the Social Studies

Study	Artifact / Intervention	Research Design	Multiple Iterations?	Theoretical Contribution
Oliver and Shaver (1966)	Harvard Social Studies Project (two-year public issues curriculum)	Quantitative pre/post with control group	Somewhat (multiple implementations but no design narrative)	Jurisprudential framework for analyzing public issues
Britt and Aglinskas (2002)	Sourcer's Apprentice (computer-based tutoring environment for analyzing sources)	Quantitative pre/post with control group	No (multiple uses of the tool but little evidence of progressive refinement)	Effect of a computer-based tutoring environment at promoting use of history-thinking heuristics
VanSledright (2002a, 2002b, 2002c)	Yearlong 5th-grade curriculum on historical investigation	Mixed methods, but without statistical analysis	No (refinement in between units but only one implementation overall)	Effect of an inquiry-based curriculum on students' knowledge of and skill at historical investigation
* Saye and Brush (2004, 2007)	Decisions Point! (online environment promoting problem-based historical inquiry, PBHI)	Mixed methods	Yes	Effects of hard and soft scaffolding on students' PBHI
Kohlmeier (2006)	Teacher-led discussions on primary sources in a middle-school classroom	Qualitative action research	No (little evidence of progressive refinement between implementations)	Effect of teacher-led discussions on students' historical empathy

Bain (2006)	Inquiry-based unit on the bubonic plague in a 9th-grade classroom	Qualitative action research	No (progressive refinement of unit not described)	Strategies for building students' sense of authority to critique textbook and teacher
Freedman (2009, 2015)	12-week inquiry-based curriculum on recent American history	Mixed methods, but without pre/post data or statistical analysis	Somewhat (refinement between first and third-periods, but only one implementation overall)	Critical historical reasoning; framing
Reisman (2012a, 2012b, 2015)	Reading Like a Historian (collection of 83 single-day inquiry lessons)	Mixed methods with control group	No	Efficacy of "Document-based Lesson" model for teaching historical thinking
Rubin (2012)	U.S. History II course organized around civic themes and practices	Qualitative	No	Role of students' social world in structuring their civic reasoning and engagement
*Halvorsen et al. (2012)	Project-based 2nd-grade social studies curriculum	Mixed methods with control group	Yes	Efficacy of project-based curriculum at narrowing the achievement gap
Herrenkohl and Cornelius (2013)	Comparative, inquiry-based curriculum in science and history	Mixed methods, but without pre/post data or statistical analysis	No	Effect of inquiry-based curriculum on students' epistemic understanding of history and science

(continued)

TABLE 1.1 *(continued)*

Study	Artifact / Intervention	Research Design	Multiple Iterations?	Theoretical Contribution
* Parker et al. (2011); Parker et al. (2013); Parker and Lo (2016); (Parker et al., 2018)	Knowledge in Action (KIA) (project-based AP government curriculum)	Mixed methods with control group (HLM)	Yes	Effect of PBL on students' AP test scores and deeper learning; student beliefs about PBL in AP courses
*De La Paz et al. (2014); Monte-Sano et al. (2014); De La Paz et al. (2017)	18-day, middle-school curriculum on historical writing	Mixed methods with control group (HLM)	Yes	Efficacy of a cognitive apprenticeship approach to teaching historical writing
Duhaylongsod et al. (2015)	Social Studies Generation (SoGen) (six one-week disciplinary literacy units for sixth grade)	Qualitative	Somewhat (progressive refinement is implied but not documented)	Tensions between disciplinary authenticity and student engagement in an inquiry-based curriculum
Kim (2016, 2017, 2018)	Let's Make a Better Social Studies Textbook (cross-national, collaborative textbook writing project)	Qualitative	Somewhat (progressive refinement but without a detailed design narrative)	Efficacy of authentic communication at fostering critical evaluation of national discourses

Note: * = Incorporates all of the following methodological components of DBR. The components are: 1) Designed artifact tested in a field setting; 2) Progressive refinement over multiple iterations; and 3) Mixed-methods design with retrospective analysis.

Herrenkohl, & Bell, 2005). Unlike projects of the 1960s and 1970s, this newer work could draw on studies of disciplinary expertise—particularly those of Sam Wineburg (1991), who identified heuristics that historians employ when interpreting accounts of past events (e.g., sourcing, contextualization, and corroboration) (see also Carretero & Voss, 1994; Leinhardt, Beck, & Stainton, 1994; Leinhardt & Young, 1996; Rouet, Favart, Britt, & Perfetti, 1997; Stearns, Seixas, & Wineburg, 2000; Wineburg, 2001). Early applications of Wineburg's work examined if students could learn to employ these heuristics given various types of instruction or scaffolding (Rouet, Britt, Mason, & Perfetti, 1996; Stahl, Hynd, Britton, McNish, & Bosquet, 1996), yet this research placed little emphasis on the intricacies of the instructional design.

Later work devoted considerably more attention to design characteristics. Britt and Aglinskas (2002) developed a computer-based tutoring environment called the "Sourcer's Apprentice" to foster use of historical-thinking heuristics. The environment presented competing viewpoints on a series of historical controversies, e.g., "To what extent was Carnegie responsible for breaking the union at Homestead?" (p. 499), along with primary sources pertaining to each viewpoint. It prompted students to answer sourcing questions about each document (providing hints for incorrect responses) and then to write an essay taking a position on the controversy. In three controlled studies, students improved in their ability to employ sourcing on a transfer task after working with the Sourcer's Apprentice for just one 40-minute class period.

While Britt and Aglinskas examined a technological tool, other work has focused on the design of classroom instruction (e.g., De La Paz, 2005; De La Paz & Felton, 2010; Ferretti, MacArthur, & Okolo, 2001; Hynd, Holschuh, & Hubbard, 2004; Nokes, Dole, & Hacker, 2007; Wissinger & De La Paz, 2016). Reisman (2012a) built off this work to design a series of inquiry-based lessons in American history called "Reading Like a Historian" (RLH). Each one posed a historical question and then presented 10 minutes of background information through lecture or video, followed by 30 minutes of guided historical inquiry, and ending with 10 minutes of whole-class discussion. Reisman (2012b) enlisted teachers at five high schools to devote at least half their instructional time to these lessons over a six-month period. Compared to control classrooms at each school, Reisman found that students experiencing the lessons improved in their historical-thinking ability, mastery of content knowledge, general reading comprehension, and even their ability to transfer their newfound skills to contemporary issues. However, despite a four-day summer training and a pair of three-hour follow-up workshops, teacher fidelity to the intervention was low, suggesting that they needed more support than she gave them to implement it fully.

These experimental studies incorporated some elements of DBR methodology (see Table 1.1). Each assessed the performance of a designed intervention in a real-world setting. However, none included multiple iterations or a retrospective analysis of modifications across them—and aside from Reisman

(2015), who analyzed whole-class discussions occurring during hers, none looked at qualitative data indicating not just *whether* the interventions worked, but *how* and *why*.

Action Research and Self Study

In other cases, teacher–scholars have studied innovations in their own practice (see Burke, this volume; Kim, this volume). For example, Kohlmeier (2006) investigated whether consistently engaging students in discussions of primary sources improved their historical empathy. She recorded class discussions and collected student essays at the middle school where she taught. Kohlmeier found that that over the course of three teacher-led discussions, students improved in their ability to explain the perspective of the source's author, to distinguish that perspective from those of others living at the time, and to defend their analysis with historical evidence. Students showed more difficulty recognizing how the past differs from the present (i.e., contextualization).

Another example is Bain's (2006) retrospective account of a unit he taught on the bubonic plague. Seeking to undercut their reliance on the textbook, Bain provided his ninth-grade students with models and scaffolds for interpreting 40 primary sources on the plague's outbreak in medieval Afro-Eurasia. Then at the end of the unit, he had them use the knowledge gained in their investigations to analyze their textbook's treatment of the plague. In this way, Bain helped his students to develop the expertise, confidence, and motivation to critique the textbook—and even their teacher. Like Kohlmeier, though, Bain reported no class-wide quantitative data, making it difficult to assess the magnitude of the effects he observed, and neither scholar offered a design narrative cataloguing the progressive refinement of their instructional approach over multiple years.

Design-Based Research

VanSledright (2002a, 2002b, 2002c) was the first to apply the ideas of Wineburg's generation in a full-fledged DBR project. He examined whether a semester-long curriculum that he designed and taught improved students' understanding of historical investigation. Working with a diverse class of 23 fifth graders, VanSledright employed various instructional techniques that placed them in the role of the historian, exploring questions such as who was responsible for the "starving time" in the early colonial Jamestown settlement. He videotaped each session, kept a detailed journal, and retained copies of student work. At the beginning and end of the project, he also interviewed students on what a historian's job entails and assessed their ability to analyze multiple sources through a think-aloud task. Results of the study were mixed. Many students retained what VanSledright (2002c) called an "encyclopedia epistemology" (p. 72) that assumes that the answer to historical questions lies waiting in the textbook. Data from the interviews and think-aloud, though, indicated that students improved in their knowledge of what historians do and in their ability to corroborate sources— although he did not perform statistical tests on this data. VanSledright modified the curriculum as he taught it based on observation, but his project did not involve multiple iterations.

Saye and Brush (2004, 2007) undertook a much longer DBR project spanning several years. They worked with teachers to create a technology-enhanced learning environment called "Decision Point!" that aimed to promote what they call "problem-based historical inquiry," or PBHI. The environment functioned as "an interactive database of multimedia civil rights content resources, and scaffolding tools for collecting, analyzing, and evaluating historical evidence and presenting conclusions" (Saye & Brush, 2004, p. 354). Through iterative design, implementation, analysis, and reflection on data including classroom observations, student and teacher interviews, student artifacts and presentations, and paper-and-pencil tests, Saye and Brush (2007) found that the learning environment yielded higher levels of student engagement, empathy, complex reasoning, and decision-making, and also led teachers to endorse inquiry-oriented pedagogy.

However, Saye and Brush (2007) found that students' proposed solutions to the historical problems tended to be superficial. The authors reasoned that inadequate support from teachers—what they call "soft scaffolding," in comparison to the "hard scaffolding" provided by the technology itself—helped account for this shortcoming. They concluded:

> Although curriculum designers can examine expert thinking and develop general strategic models for approaching a problem, the ill-structured nature of social problems invites multi-logical reasoning paths and raises varied conceptual challenges for diverse individuals that cannot be predicted in advance. Skilled teachers must diagnose and address those difficulties as they arise.
>
> *(p. 215)*

In response to this challenge, Callahan, Saye, and Brush (2015) turned their focus to teacher professional development (PD). They found that supplementing the technology-enhanced learning environment with opportunities for teachers to discuss and co-plan inquiry-based instruction with their peers (e.g., through Lesson Study) helped the teachers learn to enact elements of PBHI, though none learned to practice it in full.

In contrast to much of this work, Rubin's (2012) DBR project prioritized civic over disciplinary goals. Concerned that students find the study of history alienating and disconnected from their own experiences, she worked with teachers at three different high schools to reimagine the 11th-grade U.S. History survey course. Together they aimed at "making connections between the curriculum and what young people do know about civic life from their daily experiences as citizens, rather than the more common objective of 'filling in' what they *do not know*" (Rubin, 2016, p. 19, emphasis in original). The team reorganized the course around five civic themes, each focused on an essential question (e.g., "What is a good American citizen?" for the government theme). They also foregrounded four student-centered teaching strategies: discussion, writing and expression, current events, and civic action research. Rubin's project involved just one iteration and did not track student gains quantitatively. Yet it illustrated how design principles could be translated into curricular and instructional strategies, and it offered rich descriptions of the varied ways that students from different backgrounds connected with the curricular content (see Rubin, this volume).

In another DBR project, Halvorsen et al. (2012) sought to narrow the achievement gap in second-grade social studies and content literacy between students of high and low socio-economic status (SES). The team conducted three iterations of two project-based units, "Producers and Producing in Our Community" and "Children, Citizenship, and Community," revising them based on classroom observations, teacher interviews, and assessments of learning gains among low-SES students (compared to a high-SES benchmark). The authors found that their project-based approach actively engaged students and effectively eliminated the achievement gap.

In perhaps the most extensive social studies design project to date, Parker and colleagues (Parker et al., 2011; Parker et al., 2013; Parker & Lo, 2016; Lo, 2017; Parker, Valencia, & Lo, 2018) worked with a multidisciplinary team of political scientists, teachers, and district personnel to remake the Advanced Placement U.S. Government (APGOV) course. Like Rubin, Parker's team reorganized the course around five thematic units. At the center of each stood a multi-week project or simulation, for example, a mock election or moot court—hence the project's name, "Knowledge in Action" (KIA). The student projects provided the impetus for learning high-level content tested on the AP exam—although in later years the team added additional supports (e.g., "learning from text" strategies) to help them more easily grasp that content (Parker et al., 2018).

The KIA project employed a mixed-methods design. Hierarchical linear modeling (HLM) analyses in four suburban schools and 12 classrooms in years one and two (not counting an initial planning year) found that students receiving the curriculum scored at least as well on the AP test as those in control classrooms receiving traditional instruction, but outperformed them on a test of deeper learning (Parker et al., 2013). However, qualitative data showed that many students questioned the purpose of the curriculum's interactive simulations and actually yearned for straightforward test-prep as in other AP courses. For project years three through six, the design team ported the curriculum to two urban districts and achieved similar quantitative results (Parker et al., 2018). Throughout the project's duration, Parker and his colleagues analyzed how teachers took up or adapted the curriculum under varied conditions, qualifying KIA as design-based implementation research (DBIR), one of the few such examples in the social studies (see Lo, Adams, Goodell, & Nachtigal, this volume).

De La Paz, Monte-Sano, Felton, and colleagues (De La Paz et al., 2014; Monte-Sano, De La Paz, & Felton, 2014; De La Paz et al., 2017) conducted a similarly extensive project in middle-school history, with a focus on historical writing. (Although they do not frame it as such, we consider their project DBR, as it satisfies all our criteria.) Building on the work of Reisman (2012a, 2012b) and others, they designed a curriculum consisting of six investigations, each following a sequence similar to hers but stretched out over three days, with the final day devoted to planning and composing an essay. The authors developed two scaffolds to support students' work: IREAD, which prompted them to "Identify the author and dates, Read the whole document, Earmark phrases that clued you into the author's perspective, Assess the setting, and Detail your evaluation in the margins"; and H2W (How to Write Your Essay), which listed components of an introductory paragraph, two supporting paragraphs, rebuttal paragraph, and conclusion (Monte-Sano et al., 2014, pp. 567, 570). Participating teachers received 88 hours of PD over 11 full-day sessions (earning them six graduate credits). During these sessions, the authors "modeled and discussed the differences between simply telling students what to do and actually performing the practice and externalizing the thinking that goes into using [it] . . . in a way that directions alone cannot [accomplish]" (De La Paz et al., 2017, p. 36).

Through these extensive supports, De La Paz, Monte-Sano, Felton, and colleagues managed to achieve respectable levels of teacher fidelity that had eluded Reisman and others. An HLM analysis of the curriculum's impact in eight teachers' classrooms at the end of year one showed significant gains in students' historical argumentation and essay length but not in overall essay quality, as compared to six control classrooms (De La Paz et al., 2014). The authors then revised the curriculum for years two and three, overhauling their PD and adding increased emphasis on general writing strategies on top of the discipline-specific strategies already in place. They also studied how teachers adapted the curriculum to fit students' needs, and they incorporated some of these adaptations into the formal curriculum and PD for year three (Monte-Sano et al., 2014). A final HLM analysis of 22 teachers employing the curriculum in years two and three showed gains on all three outcome measures, as compared to 14 teachers in a control condition, after controlling for gender, ethnicity, and reading proficiency (De La Paz et al., 2017). The more faithfully teachers adhered to the curriculum, the greater students' gains.

Several other recent projects employ DBR, but on a smaller scale. Herrenkohl and Cornelius (2013) designed a fifth- and sixth-grade curriculum that promoted inquiry practices in history and science. The authors examined how students conceived of the epistemic differences between the two subjects. Kim (2016, 2017, 2018) designed a project called "Let's Make a Better Social Studies Textbook" that created opportunities for students in South Korea and Japan to witness the other country's national discourse on specific historical and political topics, and then to communicate back and forth to find middle ground (see Kim, this volume). Duhaylongsod, Snow, Selman, and Donovan (2015) describe the dilemmas they faced in designing a middle-school curriculum that adhered to standards of historical literacy while catering to students of varied reading ability. For example, they rewrote primary sources in simpler language and illustrated historical concepts through contemporary analogies, a practice Wineburg (2001) has cautioned against. Finally, Freedman (2009, 2015) designed a 12-week curriculum on recent American history that positioned students to ask of historical narratives, not only "Does it align with the evidence?" but also "Whose experiences does it highlight or ignore? Whose interests does it serve?" (see Freedman, this volume). By extending or challenging Wineburgian conceptions of historical thinking, these studies open new avenues for future research. None, though, conducted statistical analysis of learning outcomes.

Summary and Conclusion

What has this body of design-based and interventionist research in the social studies taught us? One thread running through it is that students from elementary to college age can engage in complex historical and social analysis when given proper modeling and supports. In short, a cognitive apprenticeship approach works in the social studies just as it does in literacy, science, and math (see Collins, Brown, & Newman, 1989). The research reviewed here also supports Engle and Conant's (2002) theory that students grow most productively engaged in disciplinary work when the learning environment problematizes the content, gives them intellectual authority, holds them accountable to disciplinary norms, and provides relevant resources. At the same time, several of these studies highlight the "gatekeeping" role that teachers play in relation to educational innovation (see Thornton, 2005). The well-designed interventions of Reisman (2012b) and Saye and Brush (2007) faltered when teachers lacked the expertise or motivation to fully enact them. By contrast, the extensive PD provided by Parker et al. (2013) and De La Paz et al. (2017) proved essential to their projects' success.

We also observe that the field of history looms large in this body of work, eclipsing that of economics, geography, or civics—and that one perspective on history education, that of disciplinary literacy (e.g., De La Paz et al., 2017; Duhaylongsod et al., 2015; Reisman, 2012b), has garnered more attention than have competing frameworks (see Barton & Levstik, 2004; Freedman, 2015; Rubin, 2012). Interventions grounded in this disciplinary perspective have emphasized forms of reasoning over the historical content students will reason about. As Parker et al. (2018) assert, "so rarely in the current era is content selection the object of curriculum scholarship that curriculum designers are left to their own devices. Meanwhile, the vacuum is filled by other communities with other interests" (p. 271). Future work could address these imbalances that privilege history over other fields, disciplinary over other perspectives, and skills over content.

Disciplinary approaches also fall victim to the critique that they lack a true social purpose. Ellsworth (1989) recalls that when she would inform students of her desire to develop their capacity for "critical" analysis, they would often express confusion. "Critical of what?" they would ask her. "From what position, to what end?" (p. 299). The academic disciplines, history included, can be put to a great many social purposes, from exposing patterns of oppression to celebrating nationalist and exclusionary practices. As Rubin reiterates in the Conclusion of this volume, design studies in history and the social sciences must determine whose goals they aim to serve and at whose expense.

Turning now to questions of methodology, we note that despite the growth in social studies interventionist research over the past 20 years, most of it has not incorporated all the elements of DBR (see Table 1.1). In fact, we could locate only four that did: Saye and Brush (2007), Halvorsen et al. (2012), Parker et al. (2013), and De La Paz et al. (2017). Each of these projects involved the development and field-testing of an educational artifact, progressive refinement over multiple iterations, and mixed methods of data analysis that yielded both practical and theoretical contributions.

VanSledright (2002c), Reisman (2012b), Rubin (2012), Herrenkohl and Cornelius (2013), Freedman (2015), and Kim (2016, 2017, 2018) incorporated most of these components but did not conduct multiple iterations, and of these studies only Reisman's involved statistical analysis of learning outcomes. Other studies were conceived as traditional field experiments (e.g., De La Paz & Felton, 2010; Nokes et al., 2007) and did not include a retrospective analysis of qualitative data. On the flip side, Kohlmeier (2006), Bain (2006), and Duhaylongsod et al. (2015) report only qualitative findings. While all these studies hold important implications in their own right, they miss out on some of DBR's affordances. Working across multiple iterations allows for progressive refinement of the intervention and provides opportunities to generate theory. Mixed-methods designs allow for retrospective analysis of the reasons why certain modifications yielded certain results. To fully capitalize on DBR's strengths, future work could incorporate more (or all) of its methodological features.

Twenty years ago, few could say whether disciplinary expertise in history and social science could effectively be taught. Now that we know it can be, where does that leave the field? Sputnik-era reform initiatives also proved effective in their day, but had small impact on the way social studies has since been taught in most schools and classrooms (see Evans, 2004). The pervading question of the next generation of DBR scholarship will be whether our innovations can transfer beyond the greenhouse settings where they originated and become standard practice in social studies classrooms.

This volume seeks to contribute to that endeavor. The studies it contains lend fresh focus to matters of student agency and curricular purpose (Rubin, Chapter 9), to the constraints placed on learning by pervasive national discourses (Kim, Chapter 10), and to ways of making social studies relevant in the current political climate (Stoddard & Rodriguez, Chapter 3). The studies reveal insights gained from field-testing over multiple iterations (Monte-Sano, Hughes, & Thomson, Chapter 2), from collaborating closely with practitioners (Obenchain, Pennington, & Bardem, Chapter 7), and from sifting through data in search of new theoretical constructs (Freedman, Chapter 6). While all were undertaken at a relatively small scale, the studies attend to the ways that design principles (Burke, Chapter 5) and design processes (Day and Bae, Chapter 4) influence intervention outcomes, as well as to the long-term effects of design work on teachers' professional growth (Lo, Adams, Goodell, & Nachtigal, Chapter 8). Together, these projects present a varied and innovative set of designs for social studies learning, tested and refined in real classrooms with real kids. They illustrate the potential of design-based research to fashion a better form of education than what school-age students typically experience.

Note

1 We conducted the following keyword search in the EBSCOhost search engine: ("design-based research" OR "design experiment" OR "design study" OR "design research") AND ("social studies" OR "social science" OR "history" OR "geography" OR "economics" OR "civic"). We also consulted the abstracts of all articles published in *Theory and Research in Social Education* from 2000–2018.

References

Anderson, T., & Shattuck, J. (2012). Design-based research: A decade of progress in education research? *Educational Researcher, 41*(1), 16–25.

Bain, R. B. (2006). Rounding up unusual suspects: Facing the authority hidden in the history classroom. *Teachers College Record, 108*(10), 2080–2114.

Barab, S. A., Baek, E.-O., Schatz, S., Scheckler, R., & Moore, J. (2008). Illuminating the braids of change in a web-supported community: A design experiment by another name. In A. E. Kelly, R. A. Lesh, & J. Y. Baek (Eds.), *Handbook of design research methods in education: Innovations in science, technology, engineering, and mathematics learning and teaching* (pp. 320–352). New York, NY: Routledge.

Barton, K. C., & Levstik, L. S. (2004). *Teaching history for the common good.* Mahwah, NJ: Lawrence Erlbaum.

Britt, M. A., & Aglinskas, C. (2002). Improving students' ability to identify and use source information. *Cognition and Instruction, 20*(4), 485–522.

Brown, A. L. (1992). Design experiments: Theoretical and methodological challenges in creating complex interventions in classroom settings. *Journal of the Learning Sciences, 2*(2), 141–178.

Burkhardt, H. (2006). From design research to large-scale impact: Engineering research in education. In J. van den Akker, K. Gravemeijer, S. McKenney, & N. Nieveen (Eds.), *Educational design research* (pp. 121–150). New York, NY: Routledge.

Callahan, C., Saye, J., & Brush, T. (2015). Supporting in-service teachers' professional teaching knowledge with educatively scaffolded digital curriculum. *Contemporary Issues in Technology & Teacher Education, 15*(4), 568–599.

Carretero, M., & Voss, J. F. (1994). *Cognitive and instructional processes in history and the social sciences.* Hillsdale, NJ: Lawrence Erlbaum.

Cobb, P., Confrey, J., diSessa, A., Lehrer, R., & Schauble, L. (2003). Design experiments in educational research. *Educational Researcher, 32*(1), 9–13.

Collins, A. (1992). Toward a design science of education. In E. Scanlon & T. O'Shea (Eds.), *New directions in educational technology* (pp. 15–22). New York, NY: Springer.

Collins, A., Brown, J. S., & Newman, S. E. (1989). Cognitive apprenticeship: Teaching the crafts of reading, writing, and mathematics. In L. B. Resnick (Ed.), *Knowing, learning, and instruction: Essays in honor of Robert Glaser* (pp. 453–494). Hillsdale, NJ: Lawrence Erlbaum.

Collins, A., Joseph, D., & Bielaczyc, K. (2004). Design research: Theoretical and methodological issues. *Journal of the Learning Sciences, 13*(1), 15–42.

Committee on the Study of History. (1969). *The Amherst Project: Final Report.* Retrieved from Amherst, MA: https://files.eric.ed.gov/fulltext/ED066378.pdf

De La Paz, S. (2005). Effects of historical reasoning instruction and writing strategy mastery in culturally and academically diverse middle school classrooms. *Journal of Educational Psychology, 97*(2), 139–156.

De La Paz, S., Felton, M., Monte-Sano, C., Croninger, R., Jackson, C., Deogracias, J. S., & Hoffman, B. P. (2014). Developing historical reading and writing with adolescent readers: Effects on student learning. *Theory and Research in Social Education, 42*(2), 228–274.

De La Paz, S., & Felton, M. K. (2010). Reading and writing from multiple source documents in history: Effects of strategy instruction with low to average high school writers. *Contemporary Educational Psychology, 35*(3), 174–192.

De La Paz, S., Monte-Sano, C., Felton, M., Croninger, R., Jackson, C., & Piantedosi, K. W. (2017). A historical writing apprenticeship for adolescents: Integrating disciplinary learning with cognitive strategies. *Reading Research Quarterly, 52*(1), 31–52. DOI:10.1002/rrq.147

Dede, C. (2004). If design-based research is the answer, what is the question? A commentary on Collins, Joseph, and Bielaczyc; diSessa and Cobb; and Fishman, Marx, Blumenthal, Krajcik, and Soloway in the JLS special issue on design-based research. *Journal of the Learning Sciences, 13*(1), 105–114. DOI:10.1207/s15327809jls1301_5

Design-Based Research Collective. (2003). Design-based research: An emerging paradigm. *Educational Researcher, 32*(1), 5–8.

diSessa, A. A., & Cobb, P. (2004). Ontological innovation and the role of theory in design experiments. *Journal of the Learning Sciences, 13*(1), 77–103.

Duhaylongsod, L., Snow, C. E., Selman, R. L., & Donovan, M. S. (2015). Toward disciplinary literacy: Dilemmas and challenges in designing history curriculum to support middle school students. *Harvard Educational Review, 85*(4), 587–608.

Eckert, P. (1989). *Jocks and burnouts: Social categories and identity in the high school.* New York, NY: Teachers College Press.

Edelson, D. C. (2002). Design research: What we learn when we engage in design. *Journal of the Learning Sciences, 11*(1), 105–121. DOI:10.1207/S15327809JLS1101_4

Ellsworth, E. (1989). Why doesn't this feel empowering? Working through the repressive myths of critical pedagogy. *Harvard Educational Review, 59*(3), 297–324.

Engle, R. A., & Conant, F. R. (2002). Guiding principles for fostering productive disciplinary engagement: Explaining an emergent argument in a community of learners classroom. *Cognition and Instruction, 20*(4), 399–483.

Evans, R. W. (2004). *The social studies wars: What should we teach the children?* New York, NY: Teachers College Press.

Ferretti, R. P., MacArthur, C. D., & Okolo, C. M. (2001). Teaching for historical understanding in inclusive classrooms. *Learning Disability Quarterly, 24*(1), 59–71.

Fishman, B. J., Marx, R. W., Blumenfeld, P., Krajcik, J., & Soloway, E. (2004). Creating a framework for research on systemic technology innovations. *Journal of the Learning Sciences, 13*(1), 43–76. DOI:10.1207/s15327809jls1301_3

Fishman, B. J., Penuel, W. R., Allen, A.-R., Cheng, B. H., & Sabelli, N. (2013). Design-based implementation research: An emerging model for transforming the relationship of research and practice. *National Society for the Study of Education, 112*(2), 136–156.

Freedman, E. B. (2007). Is teaching for social justice undemocratic? *Harvard Educational Review, 77*(4), 442–473. DOI:10.17763/haer.77.4.hm13020523406485

Freedman, E. B. (2009). *Inquiry and ideology: Teaching everyday forms of historical thinking.* (Doctoral dissertation), University of Wisconsin, Madison, WI.

Freedman, E. B. (2015). "What happened needs to be told": Fostering critical historical reasoning in the classroom. *Cognition and Instruction, 33*(4), 357–398. DOI:10.1080/0 7370008.2015.1101465

Glaser, B. G. (1978). *Theoretical sensitivity: Advances in the methodology of grounded theory.* Mill Valley, CA: Sociology Press.

Halvorsen, A.-L., Duke, N. K., Brugar, K. A., Block, M. K., Strachan, S. L., Berka, M. B., & Brown, J. M. (2012). Narrowing the achievement gap in second-grade social studies and content area literacy: The promise of a project-based approach. *Theory and Research in Social Education, 40*(3), 198–229.

Herrenkohl, L. R., & Cornelius, L. (2013). Investigating elementary students' scientific and historical argumentation. *Journal of the Learning Sciences, 22*(3), 413–461. DOI:10. 1080/10508406.2013.799475

Hess, D. (2002). Discussing controversial public issues in secondary social studies classrooms: Learning from skilled teachers. *Theory and Research in Social Education, 30*(1), 10–41.

Hynd, C. R., Holschuh, J. P., & Hubbard, B. P. (2004). Thinking like a historian: College students' reading of multiple historical documents. *Journal of Literacy Research, 36*(2), 141–176.

Kelly, A. (2003). Research as design. *Educational Researcher, 32*(1), 3–4.

Kim, J. (2016). "Taihwagata" kokusairikaikyouiku eno cyousen: Nikkan no kodomo o syutai tosita "Yoriyoi shakaika kyoukasyo zukuri" jissen o jireini (The challenge for "Communication-Based" international education: A case for "Making a Better Textbook" with South Korean and Japanese students as the main agents). *Shakaika Kennkyu* (Journal of Educational Research on Social Studies), *84*, 49–60.

Kim, J. (2017). Jiko to tasha no "Sinseinataiwa" nimotozuku nikkan kankeisi kyouiku: Nikkan no kodomo o syutai tosita "Yoriyoi nissin/nichiro sensou no kyoukasyo zukuri" o jireini (Teaching history of Japan-Korea relations based on "Authentic Communication" between the self and others: A case for "Making a Better History Textbook as relates to the Sino-Japanese War and Russo-Japanese War" by Japanese and Korean students). *Shakaika Kyouiku Kennkyu (The Journal of Social Studies), 130*, 1–12.

Kim, J. (2018). "Shinseinataiwa" nimotodsuku sougourikaikyouiku: Nikkann no kodomo niyoru shakaika kyoukasyo zukuri no akusyonrisachi (Mutual Understanding Education based on "Authentic Communication": An Action Research of "Making a Better

Social Studies Textbook" Between Japanese and South Korean Students as Agents of Authorship) (Ph.D. doctoral dissertation), Hiroshima University, Japan.

Kohlmeier, J. (2006). "Couldn't she just leave?": The relationship between consistently using class discussions and the development of historical empathy in a 9th grade world history course. *Theory and Research in Social Education*, *34*(1), 34–57.

Ladson-Billings, G. (1994). *The dreamkeepers: Successful teachers of African American children.* San Francisco, CA: Jossey-Bass.

Leinhardt, G., Beck, I. L., & Stainton, C. (Eds.). (1994). *Teaching and learning in history.* Hillsdale, NJ: Lawrence Erlbaum.

Leinhardt, G., & Young, K. M. (1996). Two texts, three readers: Distance and expertise in reading history. *Cognition and Instruction*, *14*(4), 441–486.

Lo, J. C. (2017). Adolescents developing civic identities: Sociocultural perspectives on simulations and role-play in a civic classroom. *Theory & Research in Social Education*, *45*(2), 189–217. DOI:10.1080/00933104.2016.1220877

McCandliss, B. D., Kalchman, M., & Bryant, P. (2003). Design experiments and laboratory approaches to learning: Steps toward collaborative exchange. *Educational Researcher*, *32*(1), 14–16.

McKenney, S. E., & Reeves, T. C. (2012). *Conducting educational design research.* New York, NY: Routledge.

McKenney, S. E., & Reeves, T. C. (2013). Systematic review of design-based research progress: Is a little knowledge a dangerous thing? *Educational Researcher*, *42*(2), 97–100.

Monte-Sano, C. (2011). Beyond reading comprehension and summary: Learning to read and write in history by focusing on evidence, perspective, and interpretation. *Curriculum Inquiry*, *41*(2), 212–249.

Monte-Sano, C., De La Paz, S., & Felton, M. (2014). Implementing a disciplinary-literacy curriculum for US history: Learning from expert middle school teachers in diverse classrooms. *Journal of Curriculum Studies*, *46*(4), 540–575. DOI:10.1080/00220272.2014.904444

Nokes, J. D., Dole, J. A., & Hacker, D. J. (2007). Teaching high school students to use heuristics while reading historical texts. *Journal of Educational Psychology*, *99*(3), 492–504.

Oliver, D. W., & Shaver, J. P. (1966). *Teaching public issues in the high school.* Logan, UT: Utah State University Press.

Parker, W. C., Lo, J., Yeo, A. J., Valencia, S. W., Nguyen, D., Abbott, R. D., Nolen, S. B., Bransford, J. D., & Vye, N. J. (2013). Beyond breadth-speed-test: Toward deeper knowing and engagement in an advanced placement course. *American Educational Research Journal*, *50*(6), 1424–1459. DOI:10.3102/0002831213504237

Parker, W. C., & Lo, J. C. (2016). Reinventing the high school government course. *Democracy & Education*, *24*(1), 1–10.

Parker, W. C., Mosborg, S., Bransford, J., Vye, N., Wilkerson, J., & Abbott, R. (2011). Rethinking advanced high school coursework: Tackling the depth/breadth tension in the AP "US government and politics" course. *Journal of Curriculum Studies*, *43*(4), 533–559.

Parker, W. C., Valencia, S. W., & Lo, J. C. (2018). Teaching for deeper political learning: A design experiment. *Journal of Curriculum Studies*, *50*(2), 252–277. DOI:10.1080/00220272.2017.1343386

Penuel, W. R., Fishman, B. J., Cheng, B. H., & Sabelli, N. (2011). Organizing research and development at the intersection of learning, implementation, and design. *Educational Researcher*, *40*(7), 331–337.

Reisman, A. (2012a). The "Document-Based Lesson": Bringing disciplinary inquiry into high school history classrooms with adolescent struggling readers. *Journal of Curriculum Studies, 44*(2), 233–264.

Reisman, A. (2012b). Reading like a historian: A document-based history curriculum intervention in urban high schools. *Cognition and Instruction, 30*(1), 86–112.

Reisman, A. (2015). Entering the historical problem space: Whole-class text-based discussion in history class. *Teachers College Record, 117*(2), 1–44.

Rouet, J.-F., Britt, M. A., Mason, R. A., & Perfetti, C. A. (1996). Using multiple sources of evidence to reason about history. *Journal of Educational Psychology, 88*(3), 478–493.

Rouet, J.-F., Favart, M., Britt, M. A., & Perfetti, C. A. (1997). Studying and using multiple documents in history: Effects of discipline expertise. *Cognition and Instruction, 15*(1), 85–106.

Rubin, B. C. (2012). *Making citizens: Transforming civic learning for diverse social studies classrooms.* New York, NY: Routledge.

Rubin, B. C. (2016). *Making citizens: Using design-based research to transform civic learning.* Paper presented at the Research Methodology Seminar at Hiroshima University, Japan.

Saye, J. W., & Brush, T. (2004). Scaffolding problem-based teaching in a traditional social studies classroom. *Theory and Research in Social Education, 32*(3), 349–378.

Saye, J. W., & Brush, T. (2007). Using technology-enhanced learning environments to support problem-based historical inquiry in secondary school classrooms. *Theory and Research in Social Education, 35*(2), 196–230.

Schweber, S. A. (2003). Simulating survival. *Curriculum Inquiry, 33*(2), 139–188. DOI:10.1111/1467-873X.00255

Shavelson, R. J., Phillips, D. C., Towne, L., & Feuer, M. J. (2003). On the science of education design studies. *Educational Researcher, 32*(1), 25–28.

Shemilt, D. (1983). The devil's locomotive. *History and Theory, 22*(4), 1–18.

Sloane, F. C., & Gorard, S. (2003). Exploring modeling aspects of design experiments. *Educational Researcher, 32*(1), 29–31.

Stahl, S. A., Hynd, C. R., Britton, B. K., McNish, M. M., & Bosquet, D. (1996). What happens when students read multiple source documents in history? *Reading Research Quarterly, 31*(4), 430–456.

Stearns, P. N., Seixas, P. C., & Wineburg, S. S. (Eds.). (2000). *Knowing, teaching, and learning history: National and international perspectives.* New York, NY: New York University Press.

Stevens, R., Wineburg, S., Herrenkohl, L. R., & Bell, P. (2005). Comparative understanding of school subjects: Past, present, and future. *Review of Educational Research, 75*(2), 125–157.

Thornton, S. J. (2005). *Teaching social studies that matters: Curriculum for active learning.* New York, NY: Teachers College Press.

VanSledright, B. A. (2002a). Confronting history's interpretive paradox while teaching fifth graders to investigate the past. *American Educational Research Journal, 39*(4), 1089–1115.

VanSledright, B. A. (2002b). Fifth graders investigating history in the classroom: Results from a researcher-practitioner design experiment. *Elementary School Journal, 103*(2), 131–160.

VanSledright, B. A. (2002c). *In search of America's past: Learning to read history in elementary school.* New York, NY: Teachers College Press.

Wineburg, S. S. (1991). Historical problem solving: A study of the cognitive processes used in the evaluation of documentary and pictoral evidence. *Journal of Educational Psychology, 83*(1), 73–87.

Wineburg, S. S. (2001). *Historical thinking and other unnatural acts: Charting the future of teaching the past.* Philadelphia, PA: Temple University Press.

Wineburg, S. S., & Wilson, S. M. (1988). Models of wisdom in the teaching of history. *Phi Delta Kappan, 70,* 50–58.

Wissinger, D. R., & De La Paz, S. (2016). Effects of critical discussions on middle school students' written historical arguments. *Journal of Educational Psychology, 108*(1), 43–59. DOI:10.1037/edu0000043

PART I

Improving Practice through Iterative Design

2

FROM FORM TO FUNCTION

Learning with Practitioners to Support Diverse Middle School Students' Disciplinary Reasoning and Writing

Chauncey Monte-Sano, Ryan E. Hughes, and Sarah Thomson

Four years ago, a local middle school invited us to work with them to integrate literacy and social studies inquiry practices into their history courses in grades 6–8. Our middle school partners explained that they wanted to improve students' analytical thinking and writing in social studies, as well as develop curriculum to meet current standards initiatives. They particularly hoped to better support the learning and achievement of their African American, English learner, and low-income student populations, whose scores lagged significantly behind their White, non-English learner, and higher-income peers. After collaboratively developing, testing, and refining a series of curriculum units, we have seen students make statistically significant gains in their ability to: (a) exhibit disciplinary thinking in their writing, (b) craft a claim supported with evidence and reasoning, and (c) write with coherence and style. These gains were strongest for students who read at or below grade level. In this chapter, we share two examples of curriculum design work that highlight the importance of collaborating with practitioners, conducting multiple iterations, and using multiple sources of data in design-based research. Then, we share findings documenting students' growth in writing during the third project year, after this period of design work with our practitioner partners.

Study Context

Our project is grounded in a strong university–school relationship with shared goals. Starling Middle School has a formal partnership with the local university, cultivated by a faculty lead at the university who coordinates with the leadership team of the school. Together, we maintain focus on the school's priorities and needs as we determine whether potential collaborations align with our shared goals and should move forward.

After a school leader initially approached the first author (Monte-Sano) about collaborating, the first and third authors (Monte-Sano and Thomson) started meeting periodically with teachers at Starling Middle School in 2014–2015 to learn more about their school context and students, priorities and goals, and norms for social studies instruction. We learned that educators at Starling were concerned about the achievement gaps they observed in writing and social studies between students identified as Black, English learners, or economically disadvantaged and those students identified as White or economically advantaged. Educators there wanted to rethink the opportunities to learn that they provided and to develop their expertise in supporting the success of all their students. They were also interested in addressing the *C3 Framework for Social Studies State Standards* and the *Common Core State Standards for Literacy* in their instruction (NCSS, 2013; NGO & CCSSO, 2010). We shared with them examples of lessons that framed social studies as inquiry, sources that could be used to support it, and ways of thinking, reading, and writing central to history and social science— all stated interests of the teachers and school. We knew from prior research that these types of lessons can support all learners, including those who struggle with reading and writing (De La Paz et al., 2017; Reisman, 2012). In project year one (2014–2015), we worked with teachers to identify topics for inquiry units and developed and tested a few in a handful of classrooms.

During the following school year (2015 2016), we developed and piloted four investigations per grade level (sixth, seventh, and eighth), observed in classrooms, interviewed a subsample of sixth-grade students, and talked with teachers about the materials during professional development time. Then in our third year (2016–2017) we iteratively refined the curriculum, continuing to pilot and test as we had the year before, and interviewed the same students who were then in seventh grade. (We went through the same process in year four [2017–2018], with particular focus on the eighth-grade curriculum, but that is beyond the scope of this chapter.)

Over the course of our collaboration, we have worked with seven social studies teachers at Starling Middle School. In this chapter, we focus on two teachers as we illustrate our iterative design process: Mr. Kerr and Mr. Smith. Both middle-aged White men, each had taught abroad before returning to the U.S. to teach middle-school social studies. Mr. Kerr majored in history as an undergraduate, taught abroad for 15 years in an alternative setting, and completed a post-baccalaureate program in Secondary Social Studies Education. When we started working together, he had been teaching in mainstream middle-school social studies classrooms for two years. Mr. Smith majored in Geography and English Education, taught out-of-state for four years, did other jobs, and taught abroad for two years. He had been working as a middle school social studies teacher for two years when we started to work together. We focus on these two teachers because they illustrate contrasting ways the curriculum was taken up and implemented.

Starling Middle School has a diverse student population, with 52% categorized by the state as economically disadvantaged (qualifying them for Free and Reduced Meals), 13% categorized as English learners with a wide range of languages spoken, and many more multi-lingual students. About one third of the student population identifies as White (which includes a sizeable Middle Eastern or Arabic-speaking population), one third identifies as Black, and the remaining third identifies either as Latinx, Asian American, bi-, or multi-racial. Based on county-wide data, we could see that in the region about 60% of Black and economically disadvantaged students scored below grade level on state assessments of writing, and about 80% scored below grade level in social studies. Starling Middle School recognized these inequities and wanted to better support their students.

In addition to inviting all students across sixth and seventh grade social studies to participate in the study, we invited a subsample of ten sixth graders to be interviewed during each investigation in year two, so that we could learn more about how they interacted with and made sense of the curriculum materials. We invited this same group of students in year three; six of the ten returned and four more joined to maintain a total of ten interviewees. Across both years, the subsample included English learners, African Americans, and students who scored below or at grade level on state reading assessments with a couple of above-grade-level readers, White students, and non-English learners included for comparison.

Study Design

This project utilized design-based research (DBR) methodology, which seeks to create innovative learning environments, study those innovations in real-world contexts, develop theory, and inform practice (Brown, 1992; Cobb et al., 2003; Collins et al., 2004; diSessa & Cobb, 2004). In this case, we studied the curricular and classroom-level conditions that support students' learning of disciplinary thinking and writing at Starling Middle School. Year one (2014–2015) focused on learning more about the school and classroom contexts where the designed curriculum would be implemented, identifying research-based design principles to guide instruction, and initial testing with small groups of students to understand their experience with a few pieces of curriculum. In the two years following, we iteratively refined the curriculum through repeated cycles of inquiry. We studied the experiences of teachers and students as they used it, as well as what students were learning (as detected through oral participation, written work, and interviews). We paid particular attention to the experiences and learning of both high- and low-achieving students. This design-based approach is well suited to examining what aspects of the curriculum are or are not working, for whom, and why (Barone, 2011).

We integrated qualitative and quantitative analyses to understand students' experiences and learning with the designed curriculum. We used grounded theory (Glaser & Strauss, 1967) to examine student interviews, classroom observations, and students' written work during each curriculum unit (four each year). These qualitative analyses helped us understand how students experienced, made sense of, and learned about disciplinary thinking and argument writing. On this basis, we identified ways the curriculum could better support students, revised the curriculum accordingly, and then tested it in the next cycle of inquiry (that is, the next time a curricular unit was implemented). In year three, we analyzed sixth and seventh graders' written work on a pre- and post-assessment to ascertain growth from the beginning to the end of the year. In other reports of this research, we share qualitative analyses of students' disciplinary and linguistic work in their writing and classroom discourse (e.g., Monte-Sano, Schleppegrell, Hughes, & Thomson, 2018).

Two student learning goals drove our collaborative work with school partners: (a) developing students' disciplinary thinking through inquiry and (b) improving students' written arguments. The first goal refers to students' ability to read and reason in ways consistent with a given social studies discipline as they participate in inquiry. The second relates to students' capability to develop and produce argument writing, the genre most commonly associated with the work of historians and social scientists. This involves the complex work of generating a claim and supporting it with evidence and reasoning.

To ensure the disciplinary authenticity of the curriculum, we first interviewed historians about their approaches to historical writing (see Monte-Sano, 2017). We found that historians wrote many forms of arguments with different audiences and purposes, ranging from policy briefs to film reviews. Yet common features of writing dominated our findings regardless of form or audience—specifically, historians' engagement with sources and questions to construct evidence-based arguments or critique those of others. As we developed middle-school social studies curriculum to represent this disciplinary work, we again consulted with historians about the authenticity and accuracy of the content and adjusted the curriculum as needed.

Previous research (De La Paz et al., 2017; Monte-Sano, De La Paz, & Felton, 2014) worked toward similar student learning goals (argument writing and historical thinking), but the current study differed in several ways. First and foremost, this study is more consistent with DBR in its attention to context. For example, we got to know the teachers, their instruction, and their school setting first and used that knowledge to design the curriculum (see McKenney and Reeves, 2012). In addition, based on our research with historians (Monte-Sano, 2017), we designed a range of writing tasks with authentic purposes and audiences, provided support for the transition from reading to writing, and used more open-ended (as opposed to dichotomous) questions to guide the investigations. In the current study, we also included a greater range of sources and longer investigations to allow students to explore the topics in greater depth, and we worked across sixth, seventh, and eighth grade so that students could build their literacy and disciplinary practices over an extended period of time. Last, the current study focuses more directly on English learners. Over time we have modified our reading tool to increase support for reading comprehension alongside disciplinary thinking.

Design of the Curriculum

Drawing from our prior work, our interviews with historians, and other research literature, we identified several design principles as guidelines to ensure that our curriculum development work supported students' disciplinary thinking and literacy practices. We outline our eight design principles alongside the curriculum features we established to represent those principles.

Framing History as Evidence-Based Interpretation

Research across multiple grade levels and classroom contexts shows that when teachers approach history as interpretation—rather than as a fixed narrative of names, dates, and events—there are increased opportunities for students to engage in disciplinary thinking and to build a wide range of literacy practices (Bain, 2006; De La Paz, 2005; Freedman, 2015; Monte-Sano, 2008, 2011; Reisman, 2012). Using central, compelling questions open to multiple interpretations as well as a set of sources with different perspectives to drive the investigations helped us enact this principle in the curriculum.

Helping Students Connect the Topic or Issue under Study to their Lives

The knowledge, resources, interests, and experiences that students bring with them to the classroom are crucial assets to build on in instruction (Ball & Ellis, 2010; Bricker & Bell, 2013; Epstein, 2000; Goldberg, Schwarz, & Porat, 2008; Gutiérrez, 2008; Lee, 2007). The first day of each investigation offers the opportunity to make connections between the topic or theme under consideration and the students' lives. When reading sources, teachers can offer students choice in which sources they spend time with, and students can determine the arguments they will make.

Extending Background Knowledge of the Topic or Concept

When students read complex sources, they use background knowledge about the topic, the people involved, and the place and time where the issue is embedded to make sense of the source and think about the larger issue under investigation (Chambliss & Murphy, 2002; Reisman, 2012; Shanahan, 2015). As such, before having students read complex sources, each investigation includes a day of learning about the topic itself that can involve watching a video, listening to a mini-lecture, or looking at maps and timelines.

Scaffolding Tools Support Reading Comprehension and Disciplinary Analysis of Complex, Grade-Level Texts

Students with diverse academic skills benefit from a range of supports that can provide access to the meaning of texts and open the door to critical thinking in the disciplines (De La Paz, 2005; Monte-Sano, 2008, 2011; Reisman, 2012; Shanahan, 2015; Wineburg & Martin, 2009). We drew on this principle by adapting texts to students' grade levels and creating a tool ("The Bookmark") to guide students in comprehending what texts say and what they mean. As inquiry poses high literacy demands, adolescents benefit from supports that enable them to access complex texts and develop their literacy practices.

Explicit Strategy Instruction in Reading, Historical Thinking, and Argument Writing

Beyond providing students with tools, teachers must also explicitly model disciplinary and literacy practices, or co-construct models with the class (De La Paz et al., 2017; Monte Sano, 2008; Monte-Sano, De La Paz, & Felton, 2014; Nokes, Dole, & Hacker, 2007). Modeling involves demonstrating and implementing the targeted literacy practice, as well as thinking aloud and high-lighting "moves" made as the practice is implemented. We translated these ideas by creating videos of us reading and thinking aloud about texts for use in the classroom. We also created tools to make the expectations for writing explicit, including mentor texts, a planning graphic organizer that builds on De La Paz's work (2005, 2017), and reflection guides that build on Monte-Sano's prior work with De La Paz and Felton (2014). These forms of modeling make visible the ways in which readers make sense of texts, and writers construct and communicate arguments.

Classroom Discussion of Debatable Questions

As students work with sources and central questions, they benefit from opportunities to share and discuss their emerging interpretations (Applebee, Langer, Nystrand, & Gamoran, 2003; Monte-Sano, 2011; Nystrand et al., 1998; Reisman, 2015). Regular opportunities for talk about substantive content are also important to English learners' growth (Téllez & Waxman, 2006). Yet as some students talk more than others in whole-class discussion, we built in frequent opportunities for partner and small-group dialogue, followed by whole-class discussion, to allow a greater range of students to engage in classroom discourse that develops their thinking and prepares them for writing.

Approaching Writing as a Process

Writing is an iterative process that involves reading, questioning, and analysis, as well as planning, composing, reflection, and revision (De La Paz et al., 2017; Flower & Hayes, 1981; Graham & Harris, 2003; Graham & Perin, 2007a; Monte-Sano, 2017; Troia, 2013). Asking students to sit and write without situating their writing in a larger process does not position them for success. Therefore, in addition to supporting reading and analysis, the investigations we designed included time for planning, composing, reflection, and revision.

Writing with a Real Audience and Purpose

Writing five-paragraph essays for the teacher frames writing around doing school, and misses opportunities to connect students' work to the world around them or to align it with authentic work in the discipline. Instead, having an audience and purpose can motivate students by giving them a more compelling reason to engage in the work and a more specific audience to address (Duke et al., 2012; Graham & Perin, 2007b; Monte-Sano, 2017; Monte-Sano & De La Paz, 2012; Troia, 2013). We developed writing tasks that connected each investigation to a contemporary issue and provided an authentic audience to drive the writing.

Together, these design principles provided us with a research-based framework for making decisions in support of the student learning goals we collaboratively established with the teachers at Starling Middle School. Drawing on these principles, we created, piloted, and refined *Read.Inquire.Write.*, a curriculum that aims to extend the social studies argument writing and disciplinary thinking of all students—including English learners and those below grade level in reading (see readinquirewrite.umich.edu). We developed four, one-week investigations of historical and social issues for sixth grade, four investigations for seventh grade, and four for eighth grade. The investigations increase in complexity from the beginning of sixth grade through the end of eighth grade. Each is driven by

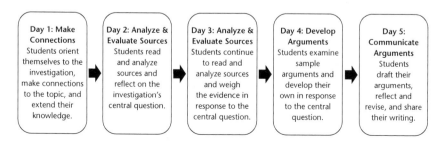

FIGURE 2.1   *Read.Inquire.Write.* Five-day Investigation Sequence.

a central (or compelling) question, a set of sources representing multiple perspectives on the issue, and a writing assignment with an authentic audience and form. Investigations last approximately five days, as more than that seemed challenging for teachers to implement given the myriad topics they were required to teach, but less than that limited students' understanding and writing. Each inquiry follows a similar pattern, as shown in Figure 2.1. Day one focuses on the central question, making connections to the topic, and extending students' background knowledge; days two and three focus on reading, analysis, and discussion of sources; day four focuses on understanding the assignment, analyzing mentor texts, and planning for writing; and day five focuses on composing, reflection, and revision. For each investigation, the curriculum includes a set of disciplinary literacy tools to support students' reading, thinking, and writing with sources. In the remainder of this chapter, we detail the iterative process of testing and refining this curriculum—a hallmark of design-based research—to better support students' social studies argument writing and disciplinary thinking.

Data Sources and Analysis

We collected and analyzed a range of data that shaped how we understood who the curriculum was working for and how well it was working. All iterations of the curriculum were grounded in our analyses of these data.

Qualitative Data

Field notes and video recordings of classroom observations. We observed one class per teacher at each grade level in project years two and three to gain insight into how the curriculum was working for teachers and students, and we video-recorded those who were willing. Our observation protocol in year two organized notes by key features in the curriculum derived from our design principles (e.g., central question, sources/texts, tools to support reading/analysis of sources). This allowed us to focus our initial attention on our design principles. In year three, our observation protocol involved detailed notetaking of everything happening, which allowed us to step back and look holistically at the class setting to see how and for whom the curriculum was functioning. In both years, the protocol included separate columns to capture what the students and teachers were doing or saying.

Students' written work from investigations. During years two and three, we collected students' written work from each investigation in sixth and seventh grade, including worksheets to guide review of background knowledge, sources with annotations, charts and planning sheets to organize thinking, annotated mentor texts or assignments, and draft and final essays with reflection.

Student and teacher informal commentary, feedback forms, and video-recorded interviews. As we observed classes, we noted moments when students or teachers commented on the investigations to each other or us. We also asked both groups to complete a feedback form to rate their interest in the investigation, including parts they found enjoyable or challenging, and the usefulness of the materials in helping them learn. Last, we interviewed a subsample of ten sixth-grade students in year two and ten seventh-grade students in year three to understand how they made sense of the curriculum. During one-on-one interviews, we asked them to think aloud while reading sources, share their thinking about the central questions, give feedback on the disciplinary literacy tools they found helpful or unhelpful, analyze their writing and the writing of others, and identify challenges when reading or writing. These interviews gave us greater insight into how students were making sense of the curriculum and why they might have completed written work in the way that they did.

Analysis of Qualitative Data

We initially took a grounded theory approach to data analysis, relying primarily on the constant comparative method (Glaser & Strauss, 1967) and open coding (Strauss & Corbin, 1990). In working with classroom observations and student and teacher feedback/interviews, we looked to see how students and teachers worked with key features of the curriculum that represented our design principles. We looked for patterns in how students and teachers responded to each feature of the curriculum and identified whether those features were being taken up in ways that supported students' argument writing and disciplinary thinking. We compared various students' work on each investigation and also tracked individual students across time to see how their writing progressed.

In subsequent analyses, we used a deductive approach by comparing our findings to a framework for argument writing that attends to claim, evidence, reasoning, and evaluation of evidence (Monte-Sano, 2010; Toulmin, 1958). We also compared our findings to standards for historical thinking that attend to concepts such as perspective taking, accounts, evidence, causation, and change (Bain, 2006; Lee, 2005; Seixas, 2009; Shemilt, 1983) and to heuristics like sourcing, contextualization, and corroboration (Wineburg, 1991). Lastly, we compared findings across demographic and achievement groups.

Pre- and Post-Assessment Data

We administered a pre- and post-assessment of the argument writing and disciplinary thinking of all sixth- and seventh-grade students in year three. Both tasks provided students with a claim an imaginary historian wrote about a historical topic, along with sources of evidence the historian might use to support the claim. The tasks asked students to write an email to the historian making an argument about which sources better support the claim and which support it poorly. For example, the sixth-grade assessment task provided students with a claim about the plague ("The Black Death destroyed people's way of life in Florence, Italy, in the 1300s") and two sources the historian might use as evidence. The first source, an excerpt from *The Decameron* (1353) that describes how the plague spread, was a fictional account by an author not in Florence at the time of the Black Death. By contrast, the second source, an excerpt from *The Florence Chronicle* (1370–1380) that speaks directly to the ways the Black Death impacted people's lives, was an eyewitness account by an author who lived in Florence. In this way, the task provided students an opportunity to engage in disciplinary thinking about the sources' value as evidence (e.g., by considering the purpose of creation, authorship, and date of publication) and to construct an argument in the email for or against the use of certain sources as evidence. We used the same post-assessment, as research indicates that when the learning material is complex and the assessments are far apart (8.5 months in this case), practice effects tend to disappear or become negligible (van Gog & Sweller, 2015). In both grade levels, we administered the pre- and post-assessment before and after students participated in our inquiry investigations, during a regular, 50-minute class period without any of the supports provided by the curriculum.

Analysis of Pre- and Post-Assessment Data

We created a four-point rubric (Appendix 2.D) for each assessment task that included three separate criteria: (a) *disciplinary thinking*, to assess students' understanding of what makes good evidence in a historical argument; (b) *claim-evidence-reasoning*, to assess students' use of these elements in their argument; and (c) *coherence and style*, to evaluate the organization and logical structure of the argument overall (see De La Paz et al., 2017; Monte-Sano, 2010).

Two undergraduates scored the full sample of essays independently after training on the sixth- and seventh-grade rubrics. Inter-rater agreement (Pearson correlation coefficient) on the sixth-grade assessments was .96 for Disciplinary Thinking, .95 for Claim-Evidence-Reasoning, and .70 for Coherence and Style. On the seventh-grade assessments, inter-rater agreement was .95 for Disciplinary Thinking, .87 for Claim-Evidence-Reasoning, and .85 for Coherence and Style. Throughout all training and scoring, scorers were scored blind to time of the assessment (i.e., pre versus post).

Refining the Curriculum Through Design-Based Research

The DBR process allowed us to refine the curriculum to better support all students' argument writing and disciplinary thinking. As we analyzed our classroom data during year two, we identified ways in which the curriculum was not working as we had hoped. Here we present two "design challenges" we encountered during that school year and share the ways we used our findings to iteratively refine the curriculum for year three.

Design Challenge One: Sixth-Grade Museum Wall Card Writing Task

The first design challenge relates to the form of writing called for by the tasks we piloted in year two. As we worked with our school partners, we used the findings from our interviews with historians to ground the design of writing tasks and supports. Given the great variety in historians' writing, we created tasks that called for several different forms of argument writing, including museum wall texts, brief emails, formal letters, Op-Eds, and blog posts. We selected museum wall text—the writing on the walls and placards in a museum exhibit—to pilot with sixth-grade students because the writing is shorter, the audience and purpose are relatively straightforward, and the purpose fit well with ancient history topics the school worked on that year. However, through piloting, analyzing student writing, and interviewing students, we found that the museum wall card writing tasks limited and confused sixth graders.

In developing the task, we saw that museum wall texts tend to share a claim and explanation first and then point to the artifact on display, which essentially served as the evidence for the claim (see Serrell, 1996). We tried to represent this authentically by creating numbered spaces for a claim, then explanation, and then evidence. Yet, in our effort to be authentic to the disciplinary work and abide by our design principles, we created something overly complicated and constraining.

The DBR process unearthed this problem during the first investigation in year two. For sixth grade, that investigation asked, "Why do people make rules?" and involved examination of Hammurabi's Code. We observed teachers encounter challenges when explaining the wall card assignment, and our interviews with students revealed difficulty understanding it. For example, Melissa shared her confusion about how to complete the museum wall card when the interviewer (Hughes) asked her to explain the elements of the task:

Interviewer: Yeah, so just tell me in your own words, what are they asking you to do there in the section-three explanation?

Melissa: Um . . . telling them in a few sentences . . . mm . . . um . . . I don't know . . . I don't know how to do this . . . um, I'm not quite sure 'cause it confuses me.

This confusion was also reflected in her written work, as her wall card was incomplete (see Appendix 2.A). Melissa wrote a clear claim and referenced Hammurabi's Code but did not include evidence in support. Although she did explain how the artifact relates to her claim ("This artifact tells me. . ."), she included this statement in the wall section labeled "evidence" and was unable to articulate what the prompt meant by an explanation.

Like Melissa, Joshua also explained during an interview that he did not understand what to put where on the wall card assignment for Hammurabi's Code. Given students' feedback in interviews, we modified the claim-evidence-reasoning prompts explaining what to write in different places for the second sixth-grade investigation in year two about the Middle East. When we interviewed Joshua about the wall card template that accompanied the Middle East assignment, Joshua expressed that some elements of the template were helpful ("[the wall card boxes] help me see more of what I've got to work on"), but also continued to express confusion: "I kept on forgetting what to do with these boxes." Multiple students expressed similar confusion over the wall card assignment during our interviews.

Our classroom observations while teachers and students worked on creating wall cards also helped us see the need for change. In our field notes from three different days during the first investigation of Hammurabi's Code, Monte-Sano wrote the following: "Template is too detailed—hard to fill in with quotes, and how to support claim—spaces where [students] need to fill in are tough to see and too many questions [for students to address]"; "Ways to make our [wall card] template more kid-friendly?"; and "I wonder if museum wall card text is even the right form for sixth grade." These comments stemmed from watching students express frustration with the assignment, ask repeated questions about what to do or how to respond to the prompts, and confuse what part of their argument should go where.

Other students expressed competence in completing the museum wall card assignment, but were limited by it. For example, Matt easily explained the features of the wall card in an interview, but mentioned a constraint when he said, "Everything here was easy, interesting for me. Maybe make the bottom part a little bigger?" Looking at Matt's wall card (Appendix 2.B) reveals that he took up the assignment as it was intended, but ran out of room to explain his thinking. In this sense the wall card assignment limited what he could do. Matt was not alone; other strong readers had similar experiences. We had not been aware of this challenge until interviewing these students one-on-one.

Given the problems with the wall card assignment, we tested a new sixth-grade writing task for the subsequent investigations in year two. In particular, we focused more on the specific learning goals the task was intended to target, highlighting the type of argument for students over the form it was supposed to take. We identified a single-sided argument as the central goal—an argument that includes a claim, evidence to support it, and reasoning that links evidence to claim and that assesses the reliability of evidence. As this type of argument does not acknowledge other perspectives or arguments on the issue, we considered it a good starting point for students just beginning to grasp the elements of argumentation. We referred to this type of argument as "interpretation." To establish an authentic audience and purpose for the sixth-grade assignment, we selected email as the form. This genre is not as highly specialized or intricate as museum wall text. We reasoned that using an email as the form of argument writing would reduce students' confusion, highlight the purpose of the assignment, and allow them to write as much as they wanted.

We implemented the email writing task beginning with the third investigation in year two, which focused on the Inca Empire. We saw marked improvement in students' writing and analytical thinking as a result of our modifications. During interviews, for example, we asked students: "What did you think about writing this email [about the Inca] as compared to writing the wall cards as you did for the last two investigations?" Melissa reported, "This seems more, like it makes more sense. 'Cause the wall cards—I'm not good with organizers and stuff." Joshua immediately said the email was "easier." When asked why, he replied, "Because it tells you what they specifically want you to do. There's less, there's less things you have to write about. It's to the point. And it's just not complicated." Even Matt, who did not report difficulty with the wall card writing task, said he preferred the email task: "I think this is easier because museum wall cards, I didn't really understand it. But like with this one, you're basically writing a paragraph, which is very easy to write." In this sense, student feedback clearly favored the email task. We also observed that teachers had much greater ease in explaining the task during instructional time, and that students' writing was stronger after switching tasks. In sum, our analysis of qualitative data helped us create a task that supported sixth graders in achieving the function of disciplinary writing without getting lost in the task's form. Given the success of the email writing task, we used this same task in all of the sixth grade investigations in year three, when we administered the pre- and post-assessments.

Design Challenge Two: Preparing Seventh Graders to Write Critiques

In contrast to our initial effort to try out different forms of writing in sixth grade, we consistently asked seventh-grade students to write letters in year two. At the same time, we asked them to focus their letter-writing on a particular type of argument, what we call a "critique," with the purpose of arguing *against* an interpretation put forward by someone else.

Through our interviews with historians, we identified critiquing other people's arguments as a prevalent disciplinary practice. The *C3 Framework for Social Studies State Standards* states that students in grades 6-8 should "Critique arguments for credibility" and "Critique the structure of explanations" (NCSS, 2013; D4.4.6-8, D4.5.6-8), and the *Common Core* (NGA/CCSSO, 2010) specifies that by ninth and tenth grade, students should address counterclaims in their arguments. Based on prior research (De La Paz et al., 2017), we also knew that eighth grade students could achieve these goals with instructional scaffolding.

Therefore, we specified "counterargument" as the form that eighth grade students would work on in our curriculum, and focused seventh graders on writing "critiques" as preparation. In a critique, students are asked to find problems in an argument made by another person. That argument could appear in a museum exhibit, news story, political speech, etc. We reasoned that this progression would set up eighth graders to make their own arguments and rebut others, thereby addressing counterclaims.

Through piloting the assignment, observing classroom instruction, and gathering teacher feedback in year two, we identified the complexities of our initial seventh-grade critique-writing task and the challenges of teaching it. Specifically, writing a critique means that students do not write a response to the central, compelling question; instead, they critique someone else's response to it. Yet, the central question had been the organizing framework and focus for our investigations. So, for the bulk of an investigation students used the central question as a guide while they read, analyzed, and discussed sources, working toward an argument in response to that question. In a critique investigation with that same structure, students would have to work toward their own response to the central question for most of the investigation, but then switch to critiquing someone else's response when they wrote. As such, the investigation would not directly build toward the final writing assignment, because the focus of the writing was different than the focus of the investigation leading up to it.

Our observations and teachers' feedback from the first year of trying the critique task in year two highlighted these challenges. For example, as Monte-Sano sat in on the first investigation for seventh grade students focused on critique writing, she observed a student ask, "What am I rejecting?" Monte-Sano wondered, "How can they go from what they think to figuring out what to reject?" At the end of that investigation, Mr. Kerr gave similar feedback. When asked what materials from that day's investigation were difficult to teach with, Mr. Kerr wrote, "Transitioning from defending a claim to rejecting a claim." Mr. Smith reported similar difficulties in teaching critique as part of an investigation about the Silk Road.

We learned how to improve the curriculum to support students' critique writing from observing the teachers experiment across investigations. However, the teachers themselves showed different levels of comfort in experimenting with this type of writing. As we continued to observe, we saw Mr. Kerr begin to make adaptations to support students. For example, in the second seventh-grade investigation, Mr. Kerr added a partner discussion that gave students a chance to think about the different interpretations together and decide which to critique. He also added a partner discussion to reflect on their writing in progress and to support revision. Our field notes from the second critique investigation in Mr. Kerr's classroom reported, "By the end of the investigation, students seemed to have a clear idea of how to write a rejection letter." We noted that one student explained the critique by saying, "You write a letter about all of the things you disagree about." Mr. Kerr also reported to us after class that "this went much more smoothly than the Silk Road rejection letter." Mr. Smith, who did not experiment in these ways, reported at the end of the same investigation that his seventh graders had "trouble switching from making an argument to rejecting a photo representing someone's argument." We did not change the writing task after the second investigation (as we had in sixth grade) because analysis of students' writing showed us that students were having some success with the critique tasks already. Yet, based on observations and feedback, we knew the tasks could be improved.

During the third seventh-grade investigation of that year, Mr. Kerr extended his scaffolding to support students' transition from reading and analyzing sources to writing a critique. He now asked students to pick apart each interpretation up for critique by discussing its claims, identifying weaknesses, and comparing it to evidence in the sources that challenged it. As students raised their concerns during discussions, the teacher projected the interpretation up for critique on the board, underlined the segments students identified as problematic, and wrote marginal notes to record the weaknesses students found. Mr. Kerr realized before we did that the critique investigations needed additional time for discussion and processing if we expected students to discuss how they would respond to the central question *and* how they would critique someone else's response. He also identified the importance of tracking students' thinking in discussions visibly on the board to support their writing later—something a colleague started doing at the eighth-grade level and shared with everyone. Mr. Kerr's adaptations helped us see that students needed time to process the arguments they were to critique in order to develop their disciplinary thinking. By contrast, Mr. Smith focused on the form of the writing task and scaffolding students' understanding of how to format a letter by teaching them how to include a proper salutation.

Observing each teacher's adaptations allowed us to then compare the instructional innovations to students' written work products and identify more and less productive adaptations. Whereas Mr. Kerr's students wrote an actual critique of a news article as we had envisioned, most of Mr. Smith's students wrote a response to the central question and did not critique the article. In Appendix 2.C, we see Mr. Kerr's student clarify that she disagrees with the news article's claims and share evidence from two sources to challenge the claim. Next to that, we see Mr. Smith's student make an argument against child labor and reference one source (Vijay), as well as everyday examples to support her claim. This student does not critique the news snapshot as the task asks, and instead shares her opinion about the problems with child labor. By contrast, Mr. Kerr's adaptations enabled students to do the complex work of critiquing arguments. (Mr. Smith's student had a slightly higher Lexile score, but both students were comparable in reading test scores.)

Our analysis of classroom observations, teacher feedback, and student writing led us to revise the seventh-grade task and the supports teachers could offer

What can you critique?	Discuss: What can you critique?	Reflect and Discuss
Critique the **claim** if. . . • there is no or not enough evidence to support it. • there is evidence that challenges the claim. • the evidence provided does not support it or supports a different claim. Critique the **evidence** if. . . • it is not relevant or does not match with the claim. • it is not accurate. • it has been misunderstood or misinterpreted. • it is unreliable for the issue that is the focus. Critique the **reasoning** if. . . • the writer misinterprets or misunderstands evidence or key issues. • the writer doesn't explain how the evidence supports the claim. • the writer doesn't assess the reliability of the sources or gives bad reasons to trust the sources of evidence. • the writer doesn't make sense.	What problems do you see with the **claim**? • <u>Consider:</u> Can it be supported? Is there evidence that challenges the claim? What problems do you see with the **evidence**? • <u>Consider:</u> Is the evidence relevant to the claim? Is it accurate? Has it been misunderstood or misinterpreted? Is it reliable for the issue? What problems do you see with the **reasoning**? • <u>Consider:</u> Does the writer misinterpret or misunderstand the evidence or key issues? Does the writer explain how the evidence supports the claim clearly? Does the writer assess the reliability of the sources or give good reasons to trust the sources of evidence? Does the writer make sense?	• Which politician offers the <u>weakest</u> argument about whether South Africa is living up to its promises? Why is it a weak argument? • What **claim** will you make in your letter to the New York Times about which politician's speech offers a weaker argument about whether South Africa is living up to its promises? Why? • What **evidence** will support your claim?

FIGURE 2.2   Supports for Discussing Critiques in Preparation for Writing, from the South Africa Investigation in Year Three.

students in year three. In the new format, we introduced the critique task on the first day so that students could view it as their driving goal. To support discussions of the central question and sources, we added a "Weigh the Evidence" chart for tracking ideas visibly with the entire class, as Ms. Henry had developed to support eighth-grade writing down the hall. We also included a discussion of the interpretations up for critique with an explicit set of guidelines for thinking about how to critique other people's arguments, prompts to support discussion and critique of arguments, and cues to reflect on the weaknesses in different arguments in preparation for writing (see Figure 2.2). These supports were in place for students by year three, when the pre- and post-assessments were administered.

Students' Growth in Writing During Year 3

After two iteration cycles like this, we took a more careful look at students' disciplinary writing and thinking at the beginning and end of the year. We use paired sample *t*-tests for comparisons between students' pre-assessments and post-assessments in year three. The sample included sixth graders ($n=77$) and seventh graders ($n=79$), which we combined for a total sample of 156. During that school year, both grade levels completed four social studies inquiry

TABLE 2.1 Paired T-Test Comparisons of Pre- and Post-Assessments for 6th and 7th Graders in 2016-2017

	n	Pre-assessment M (SD)	Post-assessment M (SD)	Change (post − pre) M (SD)
Disciplinary Thinking	156	2.29 (1.23)	2.61 (1.25)	0.31 (1.38)*
Claim, Evidence, Reasoning	156	2.84 (0.93)	3.32 (0.77)	0.49 (0.97)**
Coherence and Style	156	2.45 (0.74)	2.73 (0.71)	0.28 (0.82)**

Note. *$p < .01$; **$p < .001$.

investigations, or roughly 20 days of instruction. Our analyses of the pre- and post-assessments showed that students' scores were significantly higher on the post-assessment than on the pre-assessment for all three criteria, as shown in Table 2.1. Subsequent analysis showed that below and on-grade level readers made the most significant gains.

We found that students achieved statistically significant growth in *disciplinary thinking*, as their average scores on that criterion moved closer to a score of "3" on the post-assessment, meaning that they developed greater proficiency in evaluating evidence using a disciplinary lens. Recall that the sixth-grade task asked students to evaluate two pieces of historical evidence and to recommend one of them to a historian making a claim about the Black Death. At the beginning of sixth grade, students were more likely, on average, to recommend the fictional source (*The Decameron*) to the historian, or to select the more relevant source (*The Florentine Chronicle*) but fail to articulate the reasons that make it good evidence for the historian's claim. For example, one African-American sixth grader, who read below grade level and received special education services, selected *The Florentine Chronicle* on her pre-assessment, but offered this explanation for doing so:

> I picked source B [*The Florentine Chronicle*] because it gave more details and it was like a poem. And it made me feel more interested in this source and want to read more . . . The other source was more bland to me, it diden't [sic] want me to read more.

Here, the student shares her criteria for selecting a source as evidence—level of detail, poetic prose, engaging—but these criteria do not express understanding of what makes good evidence from a disciplinary perspective. Therefore, this student received a score of "2" for her disciplinary thinking on her pre-assessment response (see Appendix 2.D for the full rubric).

By the end of sixth grade, however, the students were more likely, on average, to offer disciplinary reasoning for the source they selected. For example, the student above noted in her post-assessment that *The Florentine Chronicle* was a better source of evidence because it was a first-hand account produced in Florence during the time period of interest. She wrote:

> Source B [*The Florentine Chronicle*] supports your claim because we can trust Marchionne di Coppo di Stefano Buonaiuti because in the evidence it says "Marchionne di Coppo di Stefano Buonaiuti was born their [sic] and lived their and wrote [the] article in late 1370s and early 1380s."

This student showed attention to aspects of the source that are critical to its historical value, such as the time, place, and author's perspective. In addition, she argued that the specific information in *The Florentine Chronicle* provided a better match for the historian's claim: "Plus it told us how father to husband and etc. Black Death destroyed people's way of life in Florence, Italy in the 1300s." The student's attention to the source's origin and the usefulness of its content to the historian warranted a score of "4" for disciplinary thinking. We were more likely to see this level of disciplinary thinking at post-test than at pre-test.

In addition to growth in disciplinary thinking, the *t*-test results demonstrated that students made statistically significant gains in their ability to write an argument with a *claim, evidence, and reasoning*. On their pre-assessments, students were less likely, on average, to include at least two of these three elements, with most students including just one. Some students presented none of these features in their pre-assessment response, such as this student, an African American boy who read below grade-level:

> The black death was harmful because it killed people and it spread like a peanut butter sandwich wich [sic] is fast and people got rid of there [sic] stuff because they thought it wouldn't kill them to [sic] but they where [sic] wrong it killed them.

Although the student is able to share his ideas about the Black Death, and his writing shows some understanding of the sources, he does not make an argument about which source makes for better evidence to the historian. Therefore, he received a score of "1" on his pre-assessment for claim, evidence, and reasoning.

On post-assessments, the sixth- and seventh-grade students were more likely, on average, to receive a score of "3" for claim, evidence, and reasoning, meaning that they included two out of three of these features. For example, the student above moved from a score of "1" to "3" on his post-test, since he wrote an argument that provided a claim and evidence:

> I think source A [*The Decameron*] is the best source because it geos [sic] into details on how it was a really bad illness. [In] source A you quoted that 2 pigs droped [sic] dead just by putting their snots [sic] to it and saying it's why they drank poison. I think Source B [*The Florentine Chronicle*] was the bad source because it was just talking about people abandoning their houses and stuff.

Here, we see that he wrote a claim in response to the prompt in the first sentence and supported the claim with specific reference to evidence in the second sentence. This ability to produce an argument using some features of claim, evidence, and reasoning was more common of students on their post-assessments.

It is important to point out that although this particular student improved in his ability to write using the features of argument, he argued that the historian should select the less useful source, thereby making no gains in disciplinary thinking from pre to post. This fact highlights the complex relationship between achieving the learning goals of disciplinary thinking and argument writing: Students did not demonstrate learning of these goals in tandem or in linear paths, even if the overarching arc of their trajectory shows improvement over time.

Lastly, we found that students achieved statistically significant growth in their ability to write arguments with *coherence and style*. This portion of the rubric evaluated students' ability to write with clear organization and logical structure, appropriate word choice, and sentence variety, and to observe the conventions of written English. On average, students scored closer to a "2" on their pre-assessments, which means their arguments at the start of the school year were more likely to have unclear organization, inaccurate word choice, little sentence variety, and problems with the conventions of written English. For example, this student, a boy who received special education services and read below grade level, received a score of "2" on his pre-test for coherence and style: "You should use source 1 [*The Decameron*] to get the most information about the Black Death. I think I'm right because I think I am." His response is simple in its overall construction, and his word choice is both vague ("to get the most information") and casual ("I think I'm right. . .").

By contrast, on their post-assessments students were more likely to write with greater coherence and style, with the overall average score moving closer to a score of "3." For example, the student above improved his coherence, organization, sentence variety, and word choice on his post-assessment response:

> Your claim that the Black Death destroyed people's lives is wrong I have a way better source that explains more about the Black Death It's called Florence chronicle. The reason why I picked this source is because it explains more about the Black Death for example It said that child abandoned the father husband the wife wife the husband one brother the other one sister the other. That is why I chose this source.

This response received a "3" for coherence and style. The overall coherence and organization are clear, with the first sentence arguing for a source and the next sentence providing a direct quotation from the source ("Child abandoned the father, husband the wife, wife the husband, one brother the other, one sister the other"). Although the response showed problems with punctuation that made it difficult to distinguish the quotation and individual sentences, the student varied his sentences by using phrases such as "The reason why. . ." and "For example. . ." He also used more precise word choice than at pre-test, such as naming the source ("Florence Chronicle").

Overall, these assessment results indicated that the curriculum supported students' growth; however, we continued to observe that teaching the critique was more challenging for some teachers than for others, and it was cumbersome, taking more time than other types of investigations. As mentioned earlier, for year three we added a "Weigh the Evidence" chart to support discussions of the central question and sources and to track ideas visibly. However, this tool remained focused on responding to the central question of the investigation and did not directly support students in devising their critique. Not only did this take more time (teachers had to lead a "Weigh the Evidence" discussion of the central question and then a discussion of the arguments to be critiqued), but it also was challenging to shift focus mid-way through the investigation. Therefore, in year four we continued to revise the sequencing and scaffolds associated with the critique investigations to better support both teachers and students.

Conclusions

Throughout this work, the design-based research we conducted in partnership with practitioners allowed us to understand student learning and iterate productively to generate a more effective curriculum. Moving forward, our work has both pedagogical and methodological implications.

Pedagogically, we found that selecting a complicated form of writing (museum wall text) and focusing on its elements with middle schoolers prevented them from engaging in the very disciplinary work we aimed to cultivate. Over multiple iterations, we realized the importance of providing learning opportunities that have a clear purpose and function, and then allowing students the space to work with the task. Such an approach enables students to spend their energy working on the targeted outcomes rather than trying to figure out what they should be doing. In our case, seeing students' confusion prompted us to highlight the function of the writing tasks at each grade level, simplify their form, and give students improved opportunities to do disciplinary work. Like Duhaylongsod et al. (2015), we found that even if students engaged in a so-called "lighter" version of the work of professional historians (p. 604), the curriculum nonetheless positioned students to construct and critique knowledge (see also Learned, 2018).

Methodologically, our experience highlights the central role of teachers and students in curriculum design and research. Watching teachers adapt the curriculum allowed us to build on their innovations that improved students' learning experiences and make revisions where teachers visibly struggled with using the curriculum or openly critiqued it. Students shared insights regularly via interviews, comments during class, and written work. Taking teachers' expertise and students' voices seriously helped us understand what was working, for whom, and under what conditions, in ways that a pre- and post-test design alone would not have allowed. As a consequence, we have been able to improve the curriculum over time and develop a deeper understanding of student learning and teacher practice.

In light of these implications, we find that our design principles create a useful framework for developing curriculum focused on disciplinary thinking and writing in social studies. However, we suggest adding one more principle to make a core part of the DBR approach explicit: *Learn from teachers and students in an iterative process that responds to their successes, expertise, and challenges.* Adaptation through iteration is foundational to DBR; data gathered from teachers and students should be paramount in making such revisions.

As social studies educators continue to explore how to achieve the ambitious standards of the *Common Core* and *C3 Framework*, we have found that design-based research holds great potential for developing powerful interventions and a deeper understanding of how and why these interventions work for a range of students in actual classrooms. Like other researchers designing disciplinary social studies curriculum for middle-school students (e.g., Duhaylongsod et al., 2015), we found that the diverse youth in our study could participate in sophisticated disciplinary work when the curriculum was adapted to their needs. Although our initial writing tasks were informed by our interviews with historians, we needed a methodology that best positioned us to learn with teachers about using these tasks with adolescents. DBR positioned us to bridge the authentic disciplinary work of historians and the perspectives of diverse middle schoolers in real-world classroom contexts.

Note

The work reported here was supported by grants from the Braitmayer Foundation, the Library of Congress Teaching with Primary Sources program, and the Spencer Foundation. The views expressed herein are those of the authors.

References

Applebee, A., Langer, J., Nystrand, M., & Gamoran, A. (2003). Discussion-based approaches to developing understanding: Classroom instruction and student performance in middle and high school English. *American Educational Research Journal*, *40*(3), 685–730.

Bain, R. (2006). Rounding up unusual suspects: Facing the authority hidden in the history classroom. *Teachers College Record*, *108*(10), 2080–2114.

Ball, A. & Ellis, P. (2010). Identity and the writing of culturally and linguistically diverse students. In C. Bazerman (Ed.), *Handbook of Research on Writing* (pp. 499–514). Mahwah, NJ: Lawrence Erlbaum.

Barone, D. (2011). Case study research. In N. Duke & M. Mallette (Eds.), *Literacy Research Methodologies, second edition* (pp. 7–27). New York, NY: Guilford Press.

Bricker, L. & Bell, P. (2013). "What comes to mind when you think of science? The perfumery!": Documenting science-related cultural learning pathways across context and timescales. *Journal of Research in Science Teaching, 51*(3), 260–285.

Brown, A. L. (1992). Design experiments: Theoretical and methodological challenges in creating complex interventions in classroom settings. *The Journal of the Learning Sciences, 2*(2), 141–178.

Chambliss, M. J. & Murphy, K. (2002). Fourth and fifth graders representing the argument structure in written texts. *Discourse Processes, 34*(1), 91–115.

Cobb, P., Confrey, J., diSessa, A., Lehrer, R., & Schauble, L. (2003). Design experiments in educational research. *Educational Researcher, 32*(1), 9–13.

Collins, A., Joseph, D., & Bielaczyc, K. (2004). Design research: Theoretical and methodological issues. *Journal of the Learning Sciences, 13*(1), 15–42.

De La Paz, S. (2005). Effects of historical reasoning instruction and writing strategy mastery in culturally and academically diverse middle school classrooms. *Journal of Educational Psychology, 97*(2), 139–156.

De La Paz, S., Monte-Sano, C., Felton, M., Croninger, R., Jackson, C., & Piantedosi, K. W. (2017). A historical writing apprenticeship for adolescents: Integrating disciplinary learning with cognitive strategies. *Reading Research Quarterly, 52*(1), 31–52.

diSessa, A. A., & Cobb, P. (2004). Ontological innovation and the role of theory in design experiments. *Journal of the Learning Sciences, 13*(1), 77–103.

Duhaylongsod, L., Snow, C. E., Selman, R. L., & Donovan, M. S. (2015). Toward disciplinary literacy: Dilemmas and challenges in designing history curriculum to support middle school students. *Harvard Educational Review, 85*(4), 587–608.

Duke, N., Caughlan, S., Juzwik, M., & Martin, N. (2012). *Reading and writing: Genre with purpose in K-8 classrooms.* Portsmouth, NH: Heineman.

Epstein, T. (2000). Adolescents' perspectives on racial diversity in U.S. history: Case studies from an urban classroom. *American Educational Research Journal, 37*(1), 185–214.

Flower, L., & Hayes, J. (1981). A cognitive process theory of writing. *College Composition and Communication, 32*(4), 365–387.

Freedman, E. B. (2015). "What happened needs to be told": Fostering critical historical reasoning in the classroom. *Cognition and Instruction, 33*(4), 357–398. DOI:10.1080/0 7370008.2015.1101465

Glaser, B. & Strauss, A. (1967). *The discovery of grounded theory: Strategies for qualitative research.* Chicago: Aldine.

van Gog, T. & Sweller, J. (2015). Not new, but nearly forgotten: The testing effect decreases or even disappears as the complexity of learning materials increases. *Educational Psychology Review, 27*(2), 247–264.

Goldberg, T., Schwarz, B. B., & Porat, D. A. (2008). Living and dormant collective memories as contexts of history learning. *Learning and Instruction, 18*(3), 223–237.

Graham, S. & Harris, K. R. (2003). Students with learning disabilities and the process of writing: A meta-analysis of SRSD studies. In H.L. Swanson, K.R. Harris, & S. Graham (Eds.), *Handbook of Learning Disabilities* (pp. 323–344). New York, NY: Guilford Press.

Graham, S., & Perin, D. (2007a). A meta-analysis of writing instruction for adolescent students. *Journal of Educational Psychology, 99*(3), 445.

Graham, S., & Perin, D. (2007b). *Writing next-effective strategies to improve writing of adolescents in middle and high schools.* New York: Carnegie Corporation of New York. Retrieved from https://www.carnegie.org/media/filer_public/3c/f5/3cf58727-34f4-4140-a014-723a00ac56f7/ccny_report_2007_writing.pdf

Gutiérrez, K. (2008). Developing a sociocritical literacy in the third space. *Reading Research Quarterly, 43*(2), 148–164.

Learned, J. (2018). Doing history: A study of disciplinary literacy and readers labeled as struggling. *Journal of Literacy Research, 50*(2), 190–216.

Lee, C. (2007). *Culture, literacy, and learning: Taking bloom in the midst of the whirlwind.* New York, NY: Teachers College Press.

Lee, P. (2005). Putting principles into practice: Understanding history. In M.S. Donovan and J.D. Bransford (Eds.), *How students learn: History in the classroom* (pp. 31–76). Washington, DC: National Academies Press.

McKenney, S. E., & Reeves, T. C. (2012). *Conducting educational design research.* New York, NY: Routledge.

Monte-Sano, C. (2008). Qualities of historical writing instruction: A comparative case study of two teachers' practices. *American Educational Research Journal, 45*(4), 1045–1079.

Monte-Sano, C. (2010). Disciplinary literacy in history: An exploration of the historical nature of adolescents' writing. *Journal of the Learning Sciences, 19*(4), 539–568.

Monte-Sano, C. (2011). Beyond reading comprehension and summary: Learning to read and write in history by focusing on evidence, perspective, and interpretation. *Curriculum Inquiry, 41*(2), 212–249.

Monte-Sano, C. (2017). Bridging reading and writing: Using historians' writing processes as clues to support students. In G. Andrews and Y. Wangdi (Eds.), *The role of agency and memory in historical understanding: Revolution, reform, and rebellion* (pp. 247–265). Cambridge, UK: Cambridge Scholars Publishing.

Monte-Sano, C. & De La Paz, S. (2012). Using writing tasks to elicit adolescents' historical reasoning. *Journal of Literacy Research, 44*(3), 273–299.

Monte-Sano, C., De La Paz, S., & Felton, M. (2014). *Reading, thinking, and writing about history: Teaching argument writing to diverse learners in the Common Core classroom, Grades 6–12.* New York: Teachers College Press.

Monte-Sano, C., Schleppegrell, M., Hughes, R., & Thomson, S. (2018, April). Disciplinary and linguistic approaches to analysis of middle school students' writing in history. Presentation at the annual meeting of the American Educational Research Association, New York City, NY.

National Council for the Social Studies (NCSS). (2013). *College, career & civic life (C3) framework for social studies state standards: Guidance for enhancing the rigor of K-12 civics, economics, geography, and history.* Silver Spring, MD: Author.

National Governors Association Center for Best Practices & Council of Chief State School Officers (NGA & CCSSO). (2010). *Common core state standards for English language arts.* Washington, DC: Author.

Nokes, J., Dole, J., & Hacker, D. (2007). Teaching high school students to use heuristics while reading historical texts. *Journal of Educational Psychology, 99*(3), 492–504.

Nystrand, M., Gamoran, A., & Carbonaro, W. (1998). *Towards an ecology of learning: The case of classroom discourse and its effects on writing in high school English and social studies* (CELA Research Report Number 11001). Albany, NY: National Research Center on English Learning & Achievement, State University of NY at Albany.

Reisman, A. (2012). *Reading Like a Historian*: A document-based history curriculum intervention in urban high schools. *Cognition and Instruction,, 30*, 86–112.

Reisman, A. (2015). Entering the historical problem space: Whole-class, text-based discussion in history class. *Teachers College Record, 117*(2), 1–44.

Téllez, K., & Waxman, H. C. (2006). A meta-synthesis of qualitative research on effective teaching practices for English Language Learners. In J. M. Norris & L. Ortega (Eds.), *Synthesizing research on language learning and teaching* (pp. 245–277). Amsterdam: John Benjamins.

Toulmin, S. (1958). *The uses of argument.* Cambridge [Eng.]: Cambridge University Press.

Troia, G. (2013). Effective writing instruction in the 21st century. In B. Taylor & N. Duke (Eds.), *Handbook of Effective Literacy Instruction* (pp. 298–245). New York, NY: Guilford.

Seixas, P. (2009). A modest proposal for change in Canadian history education. *Teaching History,* (137), 26–30. Retrieved from http://proxy.lib.umich.edu/login?url=https://search.proquest.com/docview/822068930?accountid=14667

Serrell, B. (1996). *Exhibit labels: An interpretive approach.* New York: Rowman & Littlefield.

Shanahan, T. (2015, March 2). Raising achievement for all with complex text. Talk presented to the Annual Conference of the *International Reading Association.*

Shemilt, D. (1983). The devil's locomotive. *History and Theory, 22*(4), 1–18.

Strauss, A. & Corbin, J. (1990). *Basics of qualitative research: Grounded theory procedures and techniques.* Newbury Park, CA: Sage.

Wineburg, S. S. (1991). Historical problem solving: A study of the cognitive processes used in the evaluation of documentary and pictorial evidence. *Journal of Educational Psychology, 83*(1), 73–87.

Wineburg, S. & Martin, D. (2009). Tampering with history: Adapting primary sources for struggling readers. *Social Education, 73*(5), 212–216.

Appendix 2.A Melissa's Museum Wall Text for Hammurabi's Code in Year Two

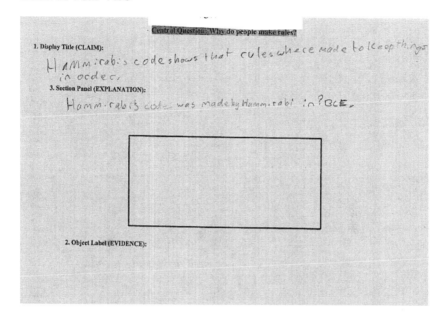

Central Question: Why do people make rules?

1. Display Title (CLAIM):

HAMMirabis code shows that rules where made to keep things in order,

3. Section Panel (EXPLANATION):

Hammirabis code was made by Hammirabi in ?BCE,

2. Object Label (EVIDENCE):

Appendix 2.B Matt's Museum Wall Text for the Middle East as a Region in Year Two

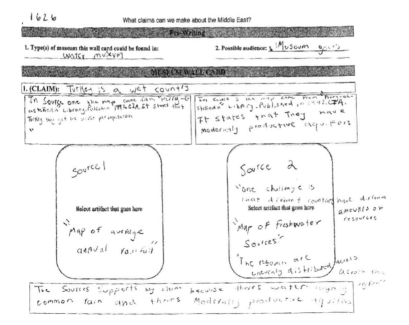

1626

What claims can we make about the Middle East?

Pre-Writing

1. Type(s) of museum this wall card could be found in: Water museum

2. Possible audience: Museum goers

MUSEUM WALL CARD

1. (CLAIM): Turkey is a wet country

In Source one the map came from "Perry-G as Menical Library.Published in MzCIA. It states that Turkey they get the most precipitation

In source 2 the map came from "Perry-ak stefieda" Library.Published in 1943.CIA. It states that Trey have moderatly productive aquifers

Source 1

Select artifact that goes here

Map of average annual rainfull

Source 2

"one challenge is that different countries have different amounts of resources

Select artifact that goes here

Map of freshwater Sources"

"The resourin are unevenly distributed across the region"

The Sources supports my clam because theres water highly common rain and theres Moderatly productive aquifers

Appendix 2.C Critique Writing from Students Who Read Below Grade Level in Mr. Kerr's Class (left) and Mr. Smith's Class (right) in the Third Investigation in Year Two

Dear Claim 2

Thank you for submitting your Snapshot. I did not select your News Snapshot because I disagree with your news snapshot about why does hazardous Child labor exist in Nepal.

I disagree with your claim that kids like child labor Because in Source 4 it Claims that "Parents then tell the children to stop working, but the moment the supervisor turns his back the children start working agian." It saying that kids don't like working.

There is other, stronger evidence that will suppor why kids don't want to work. This evidence is stronger because in source 1 Komar saip "He don't like working but his family is poor so I have to".

Thank you again for submitting your Snap-shot.

MY REJECTION LETTER

Dear Vijay and the people of the U.S.

Child labor in any kind of place including Nepal should not be happening. It's one thing to earn money for doing something that is not that hard, but it is another thing when you wake 5 year olds up in the middle of the night and tell them to pick up bricks and pile them. Child labor happens even in Michigan and they should make a law in every country, continet and state. I feel like Vijay was probably forced to say what he said. It's highley likely no child would like to wake up very early like 3:00 in the morning and work with the bricks or do a hard job and not even eat breakfast. Where are their parents? What are they doing? Why? These are the type of questions us kids who do have a better life ask. These children are bassically slaves. They work for food and shelter. Thats what they did in the old days. This is something that should not be happening at all. I feel like Vijay was maybe paid to say what he had said. But there are some places in Nepal like the city where there is enough shelter food and things that can help to make your lives better.

Appendix 2.D Sixth-Grade Rubric

CRITERIA		SCORE			
		4 – Advanced	**3 – Proficient**	**2 – Developing**	**1 – Beginning**
	Disciplinary Thinking	Student selects *The Florence Chronicle* and points out two specific reasons why it is good evidence for authors' claim or two specific reasons why *The Decameron* is not good evidence, or one reason for *The Florence Chronicle* and one reason against *The Decameron*.	Student selects *The Florence Chronicle* and points out one specific reason why it is good evidence for author's claim, or one specific reason why *The Decameron* is not good evidence. May also include a second reason that is vague or unclear.	Student selects *The Florence Chronicle* but may not point to specific reasons, or may show incomplete understanding of the sources. May share more than one reason, but the reasons are vague or unclear.	*The Decameron* as best source to support the claim, or no source, or vague references to sources.
	Claim – Evidence – Reasoning	Student demonstrates understanding of claim, evidence, *and* reasoning—either through evaluating the author's; sharing	Student demonstrates understanding of either claim, evidence, or reasoning (two of these only)—either through	Student demonstrates understanding of either claim, evidence, or reasoning (one of these only)—either through	No attention to components of argument; or may just tell a story or share their personal opinion about the topic without reference to the

		explanations of claim, evidence, and reasoning; or providing an explicit claim, evidence, and reasoning.	evaluating the author's; sharing explanations of claim, evidence, or reasoning; or providing an explicit claim, evidence, or reasoning.	evaluating the author's; sharing explanations of claim, evidence, or reasoning; or providing an explicit claim, evidence, or reasoning.	author's argument; or may mimic or retell a source; or no clear indication that the student understands those terms/concepts.
	Coherence & Style	Coherent and fluent, with more complex style than a 3. – Clear organization and logical structure. – Word choice is precise and sophisticated at times. – Sentence structure is varied and effective. – Writer observes the conventions of written English	Coherent and fluent as indicated by some of the following qualities: – Clear organization and logical structure. – Word choice is appropriate. – Sentence structure has some variety. – Few problems with conventions of written English.	Paper may show weaknesses in one or more of the following ways: – Heavy borrowing of language from sources. – Unclear organization and logical structure, or lacks flow. – Simplistic or inaccurate word choice. – Little sentence variety, sentence fragments, choppy. – Pervasive problems with the conventions of written English	Incoherent or unclear; difficult to follow; or no attempt to write a letter.

3

USING ITERATIVE DESIGN TO IMPROVE STUDENT ACCESS AND ENGAGEMENT IN AN ONLINE POLITICAL COMMUNICATIONS SIMULATION[1]

Jeremy D. Stoddard and Kimberly S. Rodriguez

The use of role-plays and simulations in civics classes is far from new. Opportunities to participate in high-quality simulations, however, are often limited to student populations in affluent schools or in upper-level or Advanced Placement Government courses (e.g., Parker et al., 2013). Students from low-income or marginalized communities also have less access to quality *digital* simulations, as schools tend to place greater emphasis on credit-recovery programs or other forms of technology-rich but intellectually thin curriculum (Margolis, 2008). Further, simulations often model official roles within the government hierarchy, rather than the dynamic nature of how government processes actually occur, which may be more relevant for students from marginalized backgrounds (Raphael, Bachen, Lynn, Baldwin-Philippi, & McKee, 2010; Stoddard, Banks, Nemacheck, & Wenska, 2016)—nor do many simulations model the media-rich world that today's citizens inhabit (Stoddard, 2014).

This chapter describes our attempts to increase student access and engagement during a design-based research (DBR) study of PurpleState Solutions. PurpleState is a Virtual Internship simulation that aims to develop the skills and knowledge needed to engage as democratic citizens in the current media-driven U.S. political environment (Gould, 2011; Hess & McAvoy 2014; Stoddard, 2014). Through PurpleState, we address some of the issues identified above by creating a simulation accessible to a wide range of students, focusing on a relevant state-level policy issue, and modeling the dynamic and authentic context of politics and media. However, as with any design, the first version needed revisions to allow students to engage fully and deeply in the simulation. Over three iterations, we collected and analyzed data to inform our revisions, with the goal of maximizing student engagement (behavioral, emotional, and cognitive) and learning of core skills and concepts in civic and media education. These changes centered around adjusting the reading level and clarity of simulation resources, removing unnecessarily frustrating tasks, and improving supports and interactions between student participants, classroom teachers, and our online mentors.

PurpleState utilizes an online platform and computer-supported collaborative learning (CSCL) design (Stahl, Koschmann, & Suthers, 2006). Such virtual environments are no guarantee of authentic intellectual engagement, despite the vast funding dedicated to the purchase of computers and Internet access in schools (e.g., Cuban, 1986, 2001; Margolis, 2008). However, some studies have demonstrated the potential of online learning environments to achieve that aim. For example, Saye and Brush (2007) found that problem-based historical inquiry using digitized primary sources led to significant learning gains for both students and teachers. They identified the need, however, for both hard forms of scaffolding, such as embedded links with word definitions, and soft scaffolding, such as the support teachers provide based on their knowledge of students and context (see also Barron et al., 1998).

We chose an online platform for PurpleState because of three affordances: (a) the platform facilitates collaborative, peer-to-peer activities and connects students with an online mentor who facilitates their work from a distance; (b) the platform affords access to curricular material, tasks, assessments, and both hard and soft scaffolding; and (c) the platform allows researchers to collect a broader array of data than they could in a classroom-based simulation. In the rest of this chapter, we focus on the development of the PurpleState simulation over three iterations.

Democratic and Media Education in PurpleState

The Guardians of Democracy report (Gould, 2011) identified a number of best practices for civic education, including engaging with controversial issues, understanding the structures and processes of government, and participating in interactive simulations. Levine and Kawashima-Ginsberg (2017) add that many state curricula do not address contemporary issues or authentic political processes, and instead present textbook versions of these processes that do not reflect political realities (see also, Kahne, Hodgin, and Eidman-Aadahl, 2016). Understanding how government actually functions is vital for contributing effectively in contemporary civic life. PurpleState is designed around several of these recommended best practices, while also addressing the need to help young people understand the role of media in current politics, develop the skills needed to analyze these media, and take action through media on issues they care about.

In particular, the simulation places students in the role of political communication consultants, a group that plays a central role in politics today. Our goal is not to encourage students to become political consultants after graduation, but to help them understand the strategies consultants use to sway public opinion. Participants also learn about the role of special-interest groups, the news media, and data (e.g., polling) in the political system. Beyond acquiring basic skills in analyzing political advertising, we want participants to begin to reflect on their own role in the larger political media ecosystem. For example, we want them to understand how media and persuasive messages are used to target specific populations, and how those targeted may be contributing to this system through the news feeds they follow or their habits of sharing stories through social media. The simulation is set in an authentic state-level context, so that students could apply the skills and understandings they develop when acting on issues outside of school. In this way, PurpleState is designed to help students develop the understandings and skills necessary to engage in contemporary politics, in addition to those needed for college and career readiness.

Virtual Internship Design

PurpleState was designed using Shaffer's (2006a, 2006b) Virtual Internship model that employs epistemic frames and communities of practice from professions as a model for learning (see Lave & Wenger, 1991). An epistemic frame comprises the skills, knowledge, values, and identity of a particular professional practice and goes beyond cognitive modeling to also consider the values and identity of those individuals (Shaffer, 2006a, 2006b). Shaffer and the Epistemic Analytics Lab at the Wisconsin Center for Education Research have developed Virtual Internships modeled on the work of engineers, journalists, and urban planners. William & Mary researchers partnered with the Epistemic Analytics Lab and professionals in the field to develop PurpleState, which sought to model the epistemic practices of political communication consultants (see Stoddard, Swiecki, & Shaffer, 2018).

As we introduced above, students in PurpleState act as interns at a communications firm that specializes in designing media campaigns on highly contested public-policy issues. The student interns collaborate within the simulation to research a controversial public issue (e.g., fracking) and then develop a media campaign to help persuade voters to adopt the view of their assigned client (one of two opposing special-interest groups). The organizational structure and many of the tasks are based on those of interns at the actual strategic-communications firm where one of our design team members had worked (Figure 3.1).

Tasks in PurpleState emphasize the application of political-communications concepts, such as the persuasive techniques used in political media (e.g., card-stacking) and the ways different media channels (e.g., television, social media) are used to reach different regional and demographic groups. Students learn about rarely taught but prescient topics, such as "earned media," or the free coverage of a candidate's views among legitimate journalism outlets. They also research a controversial public-policy issue, in this case a potential ban on fracking, through examining technical reports and other sources arguing for and against the use of fracking.

The Virtual Internship takes place over ten "days," or tasks, comprising roughly ten hours of class time (or out-of-class online work). The first set of tasks (four sessions) engages students in our Campaign Design Manual, which introduces concepts in political communications (e.g., media audit, polling data) and then asks them to apply this new knowledge in tasks such as analyzing and cataloging sample political media. The middle set of tasks (three sessions) asks collaborative

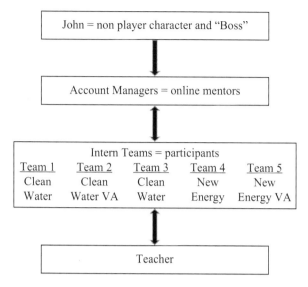

FIGURE 3.1   PurpleState Virtual Internship Organizational Structure.

teams to begin research on the issue for their assigned special-interest group. Each team receives a Request for Proposals (RFP) from either a petroleum trade association (New Energy Virginia) or an environmental organization (Clean Water Virginia), and the team explores the RFP and position of the special-interest group and researches the technical aspects of fracking and the controversy surrounding it. The team then distributes research tasks to prepare their media campaign proposal for their client. These tasks include a media audit, where they identify favorable publishing and news organizations, politicians, and celebrities who may be good surrogates or outlets for their campaign. They also use polling data to identify target populations and regions amenable to their position and determine the best media channels to reach them. The final set of tasks (three sessions) asks the teams to revise their media campaign proposal based on feedback and to prepare a final version, along with a presentation or "pitch" for their special-interest group. (See Appendix 3.A for an outline of all simulation tasks.)

All of these activities take place in WorkPro, an online productivity suite with email and chat functions, a notebook, and other tools and resources. Students use WorkPro to interact with other students in the simulation, as well as with their supervisor and online mentors (see Figure 3.2). For example, John the supervisor (a mentor-controlled non-player character) sends tasks to students and evaluates their work products. John's account managers (played by other mentors) answer questions, offer suggestions, guide reflective team meetings, facilitate team collaboration, and provide other types of support. The mentors were William & Mary students trained to facilitate the simulation. Mentor screens show each student's username, their notebook status, and all chat streams (see Figure 3.3). Mentors also can choose to see the screen from each student's perspective to better assist them.

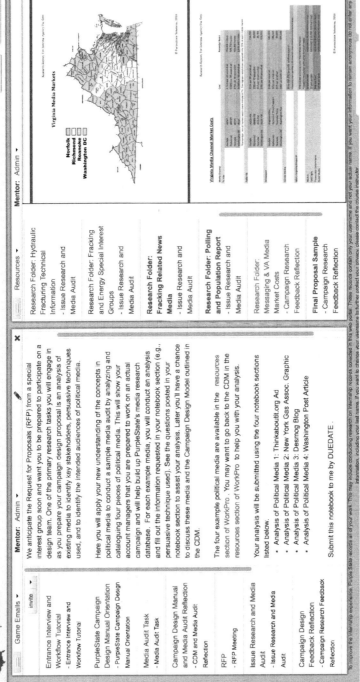

FIGURE 3.2 Sample Intern WorkPro View.

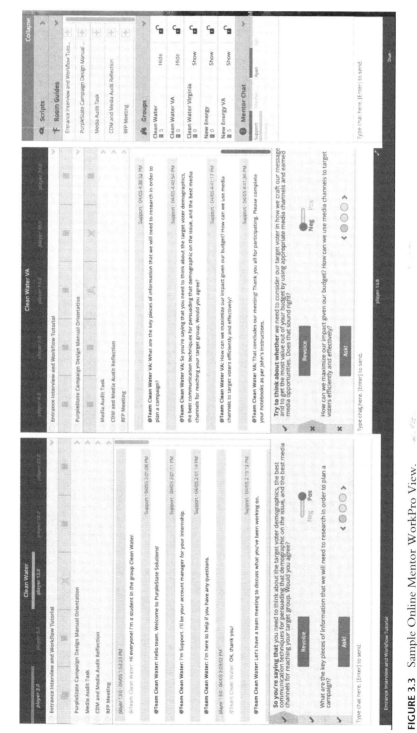

FIGURE 3.3 Sample Online Mentor WorkPro View.

Collaborating teachers in the physical classrooms serve as external simulation supervisors. The teachers' role evolved over the course of the project, but at the outset included primarily providing in-class student support, helping to "sell" the authenticity of the simulation, and communicating with mentors to identify issues or challenges students faced. In our third iteration, the teacher took a more active role both in the simulation and in collaborating with project staff, as described below.

WorkPro is a custom-designed platform modeled on project management systems used by most consulting firms. The platform can capture as data student chat sessions, the tasks they submit, and even the number of times they access a particular resource. Both the research team and the classroom teacher made use of this data to monitor student progress and to refine the simulation. The platform also allows for real-time communication between the classroom teacher, the online mentors, and other members of the design team. That team consisted of William & Mary faculty and students, our collaborating teachers, Epistemic Analytics Lab staff, and the real John, who works in a communications firm and helped us to model the work of interns based on his experiences designing political campaigns. In our third iteration, we focused in particular on how we could better utilize the platform's communicative functions to provide "soft scaffolding" in real-time for students identified as needing assistance.

Design-Based Research and Student Engagement

We selected a design-based research (DBR) methodology for our project, as our two primary goals were to design a virtual internship simulation that maximized student access and engagement, and to explore the internship's effects on participants' skills, knowledge, and beliefs on civic engagement. DBR is particularly suited to a project situated in a CSCL environment, where the goal is to refine a simulation over multiple iterations (Brown, 1992; Dede, 2004). As Amiel and Reves (2008) note:

> The ultimate goal of design-based research is to build a stronger connection between educational research and real-world problems. An emphasis is placed on an iterative research process that does not just evaluate an innovative product or intervention, but systematically attempts to refine the innovation while also producing design principles that can guide similar research and development endeavors.
>
> *(pp. 34–35)*

Throughout the project we worked closely with teacher collaborators, content and design experts, and professionals in media consulting. The DBR approach allowed for ongoing development of the simulation in response to the data collected in the WorkPro environment, and resulted in a more robust simulation and a broader array of rich data for measuring its effects.

As the rest of this chapter makes clear, we sought to use this iterative and collaborative design process to improve student access and engagement within PurpleState. "Access" in our case referred to the reading level of source materials, the clarity of instructions, and the logistical ease of finding and engaging with these resources. We consulted the data collected to identify areas where we could modify the instructions, reading level, and resource types (e.g., text, video) to better support English Learners in particular. Soft scaffolding provided by the classroom teacher also helped to improve access during the simulation for students who needed additional clarification (see Saye & Brush, 2007).

Access is only meaningful, of course, if the accessible resources are engaging for participants. Student engagement has been defined in numerous ways (Fredricks, Blumenfeld, & Paris, 2004). Here we use Henrie, Halverson, and Graham's (2015) conceptualization of engagement in a technology-mediated environment as including behavioral, cognitive, and emotional aspects. Behavioral engagement refers to observable participant actions, including completion of tasks, attendance, and participation in activities. Cognitive engagement refers to "the focused effort learners give to effectively understanding what is being taught" (p. 37). Finally, emotional engagement refers to expressions of interest and excitement (or conversely, frustration and boredom) with learning activities. Data collected using these categories of engagement informed our revisions to the simulation over three iterations.

Methods and Iterative Design Process

We implemented the simulation over three iterations from 2016 to 2017, with each iteration including a round of data collection, analysis, and revision. The first two iterations took place in twelfth-grade government courses in Virginia (one section each in spring and fall, 2016), while the third iteration took place in two ninth-grade classes in Wisconsin in spring, 2017 (one civic institutions course and one AP U.S. Government course). This third iteration allowed us to test the changes made so far with a younger group of students. It also represented a different context, as Virginia employs high-stakes testing in social studies, whereas Wisconsin does not.

With each iteration, we modified aspects of the simulation with the goal of increasing student access and engagement. To determine what to change, we examined data collected in the WorkPro online environment, including team chat data, task deliverables (assessments), and descriptive statistics on task completion. The teacher dashboard in WorkPro provided the breakdown of individual participation in team chats (by percentage of utterances) and showed how many students scored at the proficient or exceptional level on each submitted task, as well as how many times they revised each task. We also collected data from our mentors and our teacher collaborators, including observations and reflections captured in daily memos.

We used a combination of analysis techniques ranging from basic counting of task completion rates to identifying examples of group discussions where we saw a high versus a low rate of participation and compared the mentors' activity in each case. We used *in vivo* inductive coding to identify and count signs of frustration, interest, or disinterest in particular tasks. We conducted this latter analysis primarily on the chat data, tallying utterances such as "I don't get this," "this is stupid," or "that is too much reading."

We used this data to assess how well the simulation promoted students' behavioral, emotional, and cognitive engagement. To ascertain behavioral engagement, we utilized data on student participation in the team chat rooms, their attempts to complete and revise internship tasks, and their general movements within the simulation platform (e.g., accessing resources, time spent on tasks). For emotional engagement, we examined data generated from the team chats, as well as feedback from our classroom teacher, to identify sources of excitement, interest, or frustration. Finally, we measured cognitive engagement primarily in the facilitated team discussions and in their successfully and unsuccessfully completed tasks. We analyzed both the written tasks and team chats using an adaptation of Newmann, King, and Carmichael's (2007) Authentic Intellectual Work observation and task rubrics. For example, to count as a high-quality facilitated discussion, the discourse needed to include multiple intern–intern or intern–mentor interactions on the topics being discussed, with participants building on each other's statements or questioning each other. Our assessment of behavioral, emotional, and cognitive engagement influenced how we revised the simulation's "hard scaffolding" over the course of the three iterations.

In the final iteration, which occurred with ninth-grade rather than twelfth-grade students, we interacted more continuously with our collaborating teacher to identify students who seemed to be disengaged, frustrated, or struggling, so that we could collaborate to support their successful participation in the simulation. These teacher and mentor supports counted as "soft scaffolding." As noted above, the final iteration also tested how well the changes we made after the first two iterations worked with a younger group of participants. That these ninth-grade classes also included English Learners and students with recognized disabilities provided part of the impetus for increasing the level of communication between the teacher and the PurpleState team.

Iterations, Results, and Revisions

Utilizing the data generated in WorkPro, we identified areas for revision to increase access and engagement in each round of implementation. Our goal of the first iteration was to make sure that the platform functioned as designed and that the participants could complete simulation tasks in the manner we intended. To this end, we focused on participants' emotional and behavioral reactions, as these would best reflect how they were experiencing the simulation. As we moved into the second iteration, we focused on improving more nuanced aspects of the design, such as revising discussion prompts to encourage greater participation in group chats. Our analysis suggested that these changes did increase student access and engagement, but not uniformly across the class. Thus in the third iteration, we focused on collaborating more closely with the classroom teacher to support students with varying needs. Below we explore each round of revision in greater detail.

Iteration One

As we began the first implementation, we were wary of asking students to participate in a very different school routine than they were used to. We also anticipated that simulation elements borrowed from other Epistemic Analytics Lab simulations that modeled engineering and scientific practices might not translate well to a simulation focused on political communication. We therefore used Iteration One to identify major structural problems in simulation tasks, instructions, and resources.

To this end, we focused on students' emotional and behavioral engagement. We sought to identify what excited the participants about the simulation, how to limit "bad" frustration (e.g., over unnecessary components), and how to scaffold areas of "good" frustration (e.g., over intellectually challenging tasks). We wanted to ensure that all students could succeed and that none would give up. To identify variation in emotional and behavioral engagement, we relied heavily on the chat data that captured student interactions with each other and the online mentors, on the notes collected from the teacher and mentors, and on the completion and success rates on various tasks. We identified areas where students expressed confusion or frustration and coded the latter as either "good" or "bad." We then identified the most frequent sources of "bad" frustration, and examined the design to see what, if anything, we could change to minimize it. In some cases, students expressed frustration over factors beyond our control, such as the school schedule or the network crashing. In other cases, however, we realized that the task instructions were unclear, or that less-significant tasks provoked unnecessary angst.

For example, in the exchange below from a team chat session, several students and their mentor attempt to complete an initial task asking them to read through a tutorial on the WorkPro platform and write a summary to show they understood it. Yet some students struggle to follow the instructions or grow frustrated by the task.

Mentor: Have you submitted your notebook tasks?

Student 1:   I finished the survey and it said it was sent[,] is that all?

Student 1:   notebook tasks?

Mentor: In your notebook you need to record the date and time you completed the interview, and write up the workflow process. When you're done with your notebook entry, sign and submit it. Remember to use a professional tone in your notebook entries. John reads these and uses them to monitor your progress and improve the internship experience.

Student 1:	Where do you go to the notebook entry?
Student 1:	How do you get to it?
Student 2:	how?
Mentor:	You can access your notebook from your dropdown menu
Mentor:	Also, you can exclude the date and time, we've modified our notebook submission system.
Student 1:	FFFOUND IT!
Mentor:	Great!
Student 2:	I did it but is there anything I suppose to put in those boxes in particular?
Student 1:	What is the entrance interview record?
Student 1:	It also won't let me put the date in.
Student 3:	this is confusing. . .
Mentor:	Did you all read the workflow document, or simply complete the survey?
Student 2:	yes I did the survey and read the email sent to me
Student 1:	We told you that was too much to read [mentor name]
Student 3:	I've read most of it but it's still not clicking at all.

While overall, the simulation worked toward the goals we had set and functioned as designed, we saw numerous instances like this where participants were unnecessarily frustrated, confused, or disengaged. In some cases, as the chat above highlights, this may have resulted from participants not taking the time to read instructions carefully or not wanting to do the work. Still, we wanted to make sure that the simulation materials were as accessible and engaging as they could be, particularly for students who may not normally engage in regular classroom activities.

Revisions for Iteration Two

After analyzing the data from our first implementation, we adjusted a number of simulation elements. We reworded emails and task descriptions to improve clarity and better identify student roles and expectations. This included adding language to emphasize chronological order where appropriate (e.g., first, second. . .). We also revised the task rubrics to focus more explicitly on elements we felt were most important from an intellectual standpoint, such as the use of evidence. Further, we developed additional instructions and scaffolding for mentors to aid them in providing students specific feedback. We also revised the discussion questions and prompt scripts provided to mentors to help them better encourage student participation. Finally, we eliminated tasks peripheral to the intellectual work. (Most were holdovers from other simulations developed by the Epistemic Games group that seemed unnecessary for PurpleState.)

We did not focus on cognitive engagement in this first round of revisions, as we were more concerned with student access and participation. However, we did notice one issue arise in several teams' final projects: Instead of targeting regions with high percentages of undecided yet persuadable voters, they were targeting regions with high percentages of voters holding the opposing view, assuming that they could change these people's minds. We revised a section of the Campaign Design Manual on polling to make this strategic decision more explicit, and also made the mentors aware of the issue for when they facilitated discussions of campaign strategy. Our discovery of this misconception marks a good example of how DBR can help educators identify and address weaknesses in instructional designs that might otherwise go unnoticed. See Table 3.1 for a full summary of data, analysis, and revisions after the first iteration.

In terms of student access—or their ability to engage with the simulation as designed—we focused primarily on the reading level and clarity of resources. Figure 3.4 provides an example of how we revised one section of the Campaign Design Manual, used throughout the simulation to teach core concepts in political communications. The section outlines techniques commonly used in persuading target populations. For the version used in the second and third iterations, we simplified vocabulary, reduced the amount of text, and attempted to make the content easier to read onscreen (e.g., by adding boxes, etc.).

After implementing these revisions, we noticed increases in students' emotional and behavioral engagement—most notably, through a reduction in participant frustration and higher rates of successful completion of tasks. As Iteration Two

TABLE 3.1 Revisions Following Iteration One

Data collected/analyzed	Revisions
Behavioral engagement:	
• Imbalance in student participation (some students participated far more frequently than others).	• Increased classroom management support from classroom teacher. • Mentors encouraged to check in more frequently while students are working to offer assistance, and also to redirect off-task behaviors.
Emotional engagement:	
• Students demonstrate confusion on workflow and location of resources as evidenced by chat streams.	• Adjusted mentor scripts to guide student thinking. • Revised daily emails to outline tasks more clearly.
Cognitive engagement:	
• Students had difficulty completing deliverables, indicating misunderstanding of the task content and "too much reading." • Mentors gave limited feedback to students in key areas of tasks.	• Truncated reading amount (emails, task descriptions, etc.) while maintaining reading levels. • Eliminated tasks not core to intellectual work. • Mentors encouraged to engage with students frequently for lengthier and more complex tasks.

was conducted at a different high school (though with a similar population), we cannot attribute these outcomes definitively to the changes we made. However, we did observe that when mentors gave clearer instructions and more targeted constructive feedback on task deliverables, students submitted higher-quality work with fewer requested resubmissions. Improvements in the clarity of emails that explain the tasks also could have contributed to this outcome. Despite the reduced confusion and higher engagement in Iteration Two, however, we continued to notice inconsistencies in the level of mentor feedback, with some providing more direction than others. Students also continued to complain about the large amount of reading requested in the time allotted.

Revisions for Iteration Three

During and after the second implementation, we continued to examine the areas previously flagged for further revision. After the first iteration, most of our changes had involved clarifying wording, reducing the reading level, or simplifying vocabulary in instructional emails and simulation resources. During the second iteration, we looked more closely at the ways our most effective mentors were refining discussion questions and providing soft scaffolding, so as

Original Resource for Iteration 1

Purple **State Solutions**

CDM: Campaign Design Manual

1 Persuasive Techniques[1]

These are commonly used techniques for persuading potential voters or for framing or priming an issue in campaign media and advertising. The technique should align with the overall campaign message most likely to be effective for the clinet, issue, and target voter demographic.

1.1 Statistics/Card-Stacking: Using facts and/or numbers, often in the form of authoritative quotes or data/graphics to create a positive or negative image for a candidate or policy. The use of this data becomes "card-stacking" when certain facts are omitted in a misleading way.
- *Beneficial in situations where there is a large amount of data available to pick information from that presents the most positive image for the campaign.*

1.2 Testimonials: Using witness, usually more well-known people, to legitimize your claims and arguments.
- *Helpful if you have a significant public or popular figure to support your agenda.*

1.3 "Plain-Folks": Speaker tries to present his or herself as a "normal" person or an "average joe" in order to come across as more relatable and to show that he or she is "just like you." These advertisements generally involve personal stories, everyday language, and mainstream music.
- *This technique could be used to target any voter group, but often most successful when appealing to rural/suburban populations.*

1.4 Appeal to Emotions: Encourages audiences to be excited, fearful or patriotic through the use of powerful but often vague language (freedom, justice, hope) or iconic symbols (flag, beautiful landscape, environmental disaster) to get the viewer to associate the values of that language or symbol with that candidate or policy. This technique be used to evoke both positive and negative emotions.
- *This technique is best used when you are looking to appeal to people's emotions rather than their reason. How people feel about an issue can have a significant impact on how they think about it.*

1.5 Simple Solutions: Avoiding complexities by claiming to attack many issues with one solution.
- *If you feel that your issue/agenda is too complicated to explain in an advertisement, it might be impactful to simply tell your audience what the end result will be rather than providing background details.*

Revised Resource for Iterations 2 and 3

Purple **State** Solutions

CDM: Campaign Design Manual

1 Persuasive Techniques[1]

These are commonly used techniques for persuading potential voters or for framing an issue in campaign media and ads. The technique should fit with the overall campaign message most likely to work for the client, issue, and target voter group.

1.1 Statistics/Card-Stacking

Using facts and/or numbers to create a positive or negative image for a candidate or policy. The use of this data becomes "card-stacking" when certain facts are left out in a dishonest way.

- *Good for situations where there is lots of data available to pick information from that presents a positive image for the campaign.*

1.2 Testimonials

Using witnesses, usually well-known people, to support your arguments.

- *Helpful if you have a major public/popular figure to support your agenda.*

1.3 "Plain-Folks"

Speaker tries to present his or herself as a "normal" person in order to appear relatable and to show that he or she is "just like you." These advertisements generally involve personal stories, common language and mainstream music.

- *This technique could be used to target any voter group, but often works best for appealing to rural/suburban populations.*

1.4 Appeal to Emotions

Encourages audiences to be excited, fearful or patriotic by using powerful, simple language (freedom, justice, hope) or iconic symbols (flag, beautiful landscape, environmental disaster) to get the viewer to connect these ideas with the candidate or policy. This technique can be used to create both positive and negative emotions.

- *This technique works best when you are looking to appeal to people's emotions, not their reason. How people feel about an issue can have a serious impact on how they think about it.*

1.5 Simple Solutions

Avoiding complexities by claiming to attack many issues with one solution.

- *If you feel that your issue/agenda is too complicated to explain in an ad, it might be best to simply tell your audience what the end result will be instead of providing background details.*

FIGURE 3.4   Sample PurpleState Resource Revision.

to create training and scripts for other mentors in the future based on the effective models we observed. We also studied remaining sources of frustration or other emotional engagement issues and worked to further develop simulation materials to not only be accessible but also better align with the tasks.

We focused in particular on the quality of the structured reflection meetings. The purpose of these meetings was to help the teams come together at key points to make sure all members were on the same page or to help them plan for the next step. We analyzed the chat data from these meetings to identify reasons why some groups displayed higher participation or more sustained student interaction. As described above, we developed a rubric based on criteria from the "substantive conversation" standard in Newmann, King, and Carmichael's (2007) Authentic Intellectual Work (AIW) framework. Substantive conversation refers to interchanges among participants that build upon one another's statements to develop a shared understanding. Figure 3.5 depicts an exemplar that we used to refine our question sets and mentor preparation. In this case, the mentor went beyond the preset questions (see below) to probe at the key elements the team should consider

Mentor	What are the key pieces of information that we will need to research in order to plan a campaign?
Student 1	yes
Student 2	Well, you definitely want to research the target audience you are reaching out to
Student 1	You also need to know where that audience is located
Student 2	You would also want to know a lot of information about the campaign; such as their beliefs and political standpoints on certain issues
Student 3	You should also do research on the different ways that would be better to portray the information back to them
Student 1	you would need to figure out what issues people care about the most.
Mentor	These are all awesome answers,
Mentor	How important is it to understand the political landscape of the state or region we are targeting?
Student 2	Very important. You want to know how to appeal to them using trends and values that they accept.
Student 1	very important because in different areas there are different issues.
Mentor	How can we do that?
Student 1	social media
Student 1	polls
Student 2	Using polls and trends in social media. That's where there are specific offices that many advertising businesses use to study these trends
Mentor	Great answers-- how can we use polls to help us identify the target voters?
Student 3	Polls are the most effective way
Mentor	And more importantly, what are the limits of using polling data?
Student 2	By asking specific questions that get down to the issue at hand. If the questions are direct then they are easy to answer and decipher
Student 2	You will not always be able to get a complete and fair poll. Some people may not answer the questions and some may even answer them incorrectly
Mentor	Great responses Talitha, does anyone else have anything they want to contribute?
Student 3	The bell just rang and we have to get back to class
Student 1	sometimes the info just isnt there because you cant be that specific.
Mentor	If that's time on meeting today, try to think about your budgets and other media channels before tomorrow's meeting so you're ready to begin your proposals.

FIGURE 3.5 Example of a Structured Meeting Discussion Scored as Substantive.

as they planned their research. The mentor intended these utterances to encourage deeper discussion of the topic—in this case, identifying the research tasks that needed to happen before they designed their campaign. The mentor also gave positive feedback to encourage participation and invited others to contribute.

Based on our analysis of conversations like these, we modified the preset questions for these structured meetings to foster higher levels of cognitive engagement. In some cases, this meant being more explicit in our questioning; in others, it meant using a broad-to-specific sequence of questions to help guide students to the point needed to move to the next task. We also provided mentors additional guidance and examples of strategies for increasing the quality of discussion. Figure 3.6 presents an example of how we changed the preset structured meeting questions based on high-quality instances of discussion like the one in Figure 3.5. Here we condensed the question set for the meeting where students reflect on their learning from tasks surrounding the Campaign Design Manual. In this example, we reduced the total number of questions and

Initial Question Set for Iterations 1 and 2	Revised Question Set for Iteration 3
Using evidence and communication strategies to identify and reach persuadable voters:	**Using evidence and communication strategies to identify and reach persuadable voters:**
• What are the key pieces of information that we will need to research in order to plan a campaign?	• What are the key pieces of information that we will need to research in order to plan a campaign?
• How important is it to understand the political landscape of the state or region we are targeting?	• Why is it important to understand the political landscape of the state or region we are targeting?
• How can we do that?	• How can we use polling data to help us identify the target persuadable voter? What are the potential limits on using polling data?
• How can we use polling data to help us identify the target persuadable voter?	
• What are the potential limits on using polling data?	

FIGURE 3.6 Sample Question Set Revision.

reframed the second question from "how important" (which garnered responses such as "very") to "why is it important," which yielded evidence of students' degree of understanding and focused their attention more specifically on this discussion's main goal.

We also revised the discussion facilitation scripts that mentors could access during the reflective meetings. In the first two iterations, we had been providing mentors with a set of general scripts that they could cut and paste into the chat sessions to spark student engagement and interaction. The revised scripts were modeled after moves a teacher might make in a class discussion, such as asking "What do the rest of you think?" or "Does anyone disagree?" In line with existing scholarship (e.g., Hess, 2009; Parker 2003), we found that moves like these during the structured chat meetings had led to higher participation across the teams and to higher-quality conversation. While using high-quality examples of tasks, discussions, or interactions within teams as models for future changes was useful throughout this project, it was particularly so in our analysis of the chat discourse among team members, and between team members and their mentors. See Table 3.2 for a full summary of data, analysis, and revisions after the second iteration.

Ongoing and Future Revisions

As noted above, Iteration Two saw a dramatic reduction in the kinds of frustration we saw during Iteration One. We also saw improvements in cognitive engagement, perhaps a result of our changes to materials and tasks. However,

TABLE 3.2 Revisions Following Iteration Two

Data collected/analyzed	Revisions
Behavioral engagement:	
• Evaluated trends across individual/ student/mentor participation for each task. • Determined which questions/ tasks fostered highest levels of participation.	• Refined discussion questions to promote higher levels of participation for key content. • Mentors prompted students with the newly scripted follow-up questions.
Cognitive engagement:	
• Identified mentor actions that appeared to engage students in more in-depth discussions. • Identified levels of interaction (e.g., sharing, response to mentor, deliberation) using Authentic Intellectual Work rubric. • Continued to analyze mentor group chat to identify areas in need of more aggressive supports.	• Created a mentor training program (one hour duration) and created additional support and reference documentation for mentors. • Trained mentors to employ additional strategies during tasks to increase deliberation and promote sharing among students. • Mentors reworded questions to be more specific and included ad-hoc questions designed to ensure understanding.
Emotional engagement:	
• Identified instances from chat sessions where students were confused or were identifying issues with simulation processes or materials. • Analyzed occurrences of student difficulty with the flow of the WorkPro process or difficulty with content.	• Continued reducing reading amounts without compromising intellectual sophistication. • Created more accessible content to assist students at lower reading levels. • For complex tasks, planned for increased support and open communication between classroom teacher and mentors through more frequent mentor chat participation.

these improvements were uneven across teams and highly dependent on the level of support provided by mentors and the way they facilitated discussion. Unlike before, in Iteration Two we had poor communication overall from our collaborating teacher, who did not take as active a role in the simulation through supporting students and selling the simulation façade. These two elements—the role of mentors and the role of the collaborating teacher—became our focus during Iteration Three. Unlike with the changes to the structure, materials, or hard scaffolding of the simulation, however, we addressed these issues while the simulation was in operation, so that we could dynamically explore the evolving role of the mentors and collaborating teacher. Doing so was particularly vital in Iteration Three, as the ninth-grade students we worked with in that implementation were not only the youngest, but also the most diverse academically and linguistically.

To help the online mentors be more active during the sessions, we provided them daily tip sheets and strategies to better support students, based on needs identified by the collaborating teacher. We relied on examples of strong mentor support from earlier iterations to develop these forms of scaffolding, which we updated on an ongoing basis to align with their evolving expertise with the simulation and to address student needs that arose. Figures 3.7 and 3.8 show two examples of mentor resources that we developed in this way. Figure 3.7 is an excerpt of an outline we provided mentors to give them an overview of the tasks for the day, along with guidance on carrying out their role. The scripts in the mentor prompts refer to instructions, questions, and feedback pre-loaded into the simulation platform that mentors could insert into the chat window simply by selecting the appropriate script, instead of having to type everything into the chat window manually.

Figure 3.8 shows an excerpt of a second support we developed that outlines the tasks that teams will be working on each day, so that the mentors can easily pick up from where the team had left off the day before. We designed these mentor supports to be quickly accessible and as clear as possible. The mentor assigned to a given team could change over the course of the simulation (the participants did not know this), so mentors had to be able to step in and support

---

RFP Meeting
1. Send Start Meeting script
2. If teammates are confused about who is asking for the proposal, send the Questions about RFP script
3. After meeting has concluded, send Meeting Close script

Issue Research and Media Audit
1. Send general chat scripts plus your own feedback and guidance (most questions will be content-related)

Campaign Research Feedback Reflection
1. Ask teammates to review research feedback
2. Ask teammates to share notebooks and feedback
3. Send Start Meeting script
4. After meeting has concluded, send Meeting Close script

FIGURE 3.7   Mentor Instructions for Chat Prompts by Task (excerpt).

Days 2 & 3 – Campaign Design Manual Orientation
Teammates will provide:
1. **Synthesis of Key Strategies from Persuasive Communication Techniques**
2. **Synthesis of Steps for Conducting a Media Audit**
3. **Synthesis of Key Strategies from CDM: Using Political Polling Data to Target Voters**
4. **Media Channels for Targeting Voters**

Day 4 – Campaign Design Manual and Media Audit
Teammates will provide:
- **Campaign Design Summary (1 per team)**
- **Individual Reflections**

FIGURE 3.8   Mentor Daily Task Outline (excerpt).

the team where it had left off. Given the pace of work, some individual teams or team members could be a task or two behind if they had been absent. The mentor support shown in Figure 3.8 outlines the names and types of tasks to be submitted each day and who would be submitting them (e.g., individuals or the whole team). In addition to creating supports such as these, we also started asking mentors to review the content associated with particular tasks in advance, so they could better answer questions or provide support.

During the third iteration, these additions appeared to contribute to higher cognitive engagement among students due to more effective feedback and soft scaffolding. We also observed more consistency across mentors, as well as more effective use of the hard scaffolding we had built into the simulation platform for the second iteration, as described above. The types of tools and scaffolding developed for the mentors in Iteration Three will be particularly useful in any future uses of the simulation at a larger scale with larger numbers of mentors and class sections.

Another goal for this third iteration was a more prominent role for the classroom teacher, especially since his class was younger and included more students who had Individualized Education Programs (IEPs) or were English Language Learners. We had seen the lack of communication with the teacher in Iteration Two as a problem limiting success for all students. Our collaborating teacher in Iteration Three took a more active role in several ways. He helped us to form teams of students who could complement each other, provided us information at the outset on students who may need extra help, and provided us with day to-day updates on students who appeared frustrated and may need encouragement.[2]

The expanded role of the teacher evolved over the course of the third implementation. For example, the teacher identified early on that some of his students received ESL services. He indicated midway through the simulation that he was very impressed with the effort they had been putting in but was worried that they might fall behind, get overwhelmed, and stop trying. In response, our mentors made sure to check in regularly with these students through chat sessions and to ask their team members to check in if they finished tasks early. In this way, we provided soft scaffolding from three angles: teacher, online mentor, and teammates. These supports enabled English Learners to participate despite the challenge of a largely text-based simulation.[3]

At the teacher's request, we also tried to include him more fully in the instruction without breaking the façade of the simulation. For example, he identified the need for short review sessions to ensure that all students had a basic understanding of the core concepts and the tasks assigned. In addition, both he and the researchers wanted to get students to think about how the concepts they were learning applied to their own interactions with media. We saw some evidence of this in the chats and assignments but realized it was not built into the simulation explicitly enough. Therefore, we worked with the teacher to introduce what we called "autonomous moments" (see Parker & Lo, 2016) for students to interact with their classroom teacher outside of the online platform. These were short, in-class discussions at key moments in the simulation to help them reflect on their own media usage and role in political media culture. We plan to build these autonomous moments into future iterations of PurpleState.

Encouraging and developing this more active role for the teacher also greatly improved the coordination between online mentors, researchers, and students in the classroom. It helped the teacher to feel that he had a larger role in the simulation and to grow more invested in the project. Future iterations will include additional professional development for the collaborating teachers on the workings of the simulation and the political-communications concepts it covers. See Table 3.3 for a full summary of data, analysis, and planned revisions during and after Iteration Three. Since many of the modifications for this iteration did not require structural changes to the simulation, we could implement them on an ongoing basis.

Implications

This design-based project offers some clear lessons for the development of computer-supported collaborative learning (CSCL) environments in democratic education that aim for all students to succeed. We started this chapter by posing the problem that students in poorly funded or low-performing schools often lack access to high-quality opportunities for learning, such as simulations and other forms of CSCL. In this chapter we have shared examples of how we collected and analyzed data from our simulation, PurpleState Solutions, to systematically address such issues of student access and engagement.

Probably the most important implication of our work with PurpleState is that with any simulation or curriculum, constant development and reflection are needed to maximize the learning opportunities for all students. During the first iteration, we analyzed chat comments expressing frustration or confusion to determine which resources and instructions posed linguistic or other barriers to full participation.

TABLE 3.3 Revisions During and After Iteration Three

Data collected/analyzed	Revisions
Cognitive engagement:	
• Continued to analyze teacher–mentor collaboration in supporting students	• Increased communication between mentors and teacher during sessions to support students having difficulty.
	• Created a shared document for teacher/mentor debriefing after each session to address persistent issues.
	• Increased mentors' active engagement through use of tip sheets and conversation prompts.
• Determined key moments for student self-reflection on content and its real-life implications.	• Implemented reflective autonomous moments facilitated by classroom teacher.

In the second iteration, we analyzed the nature of students' online discussions to refine the facilitation scripts mentors received, in the hopes of enhancing students' cognitive engagement. In the third and final iteration, we made better use of the classroom teacher and online mentors to make sure all students received the support they needed to succeed in PurpleState. Of note is the shift from addressing issues of emotional and behavioral engagement in Iteration One and Two to focusing on cognitive engagement in Iteration Three. Perhaps similar to an early-career teacher, we first needed to establish clear ways of communicating expectations for project tasks before devising ways of involving students more deeply in collaborative problem solving. Too often, curricula are designed as "one size fits all" and lack ways of adapting them to particular contexts. Our analysis here shows the importance of the capacity to continue to develop and adapt.

Our work with PurpleState also reinforced our belief in the vital role of the teachers and mentors in computer-supported simulations. Too often, technology platforms are viewed as a replacement for classroom teaching (Cuban, 1986, 2001). Here, though, we harnessed the power of the online platform to assess student progress and to support their learning in a way that freed the teacher to spend more time with students who needed the most help. In-depth learning of sophisticated content will require both hard and soft scaffolding for all students to find success. This type of simulation may also serve as a crucial aid for teachers who are less experienced at engaging students in collaborative problem-solving tasks.

Despite these affordances of the simulation and WorkPro platform, we also encountered constraints that limited our ability to maximize access and engagement. The text-based nature of WorkPro posed a barrier to students with lower reading ability and to English Language Learners. However, we did find that these students were more successful when we better utilized all of our human soft-scaffolding resources, through communicating with the classroom teacher and encouraging the online mentors to provide additional supports. This was most apparent in Iteration Three, when we partnered with a teacher who wanted to take a more active role in the simulation itself. We cannot reiterate strongly enough that the simulation's success depended heavily on the support provided by the mentors and classroom teacher.

Still, we could have benefited even more from the DBR model if we had greater opportunities to collaborate with all members of our team. Many of the mentors made useful suggestions during their time on the project, but because of their schedules as college students, we did not engage with them consistently enough to gain as many insights from them as we could have. Similarly, given our teacher collaborators' schedules and workload at their schools, we often did not receive the real-time or end-of-iteration feedback we could have benefited from, with the exception of the teacher from Iteration Three. This was in part the result of our attempt at maintaining the delicate balance of welcoming as much investment as the teachers could provide while not asking for too much of their time.

Future iterations could examine how to create a more central role for mentors and teachers in the feedback and revision process.

In our iterative development of PurpleState, we benefited from a design-based research model in numerous ways. The knowledge that we would have multiple opportunities to refine and test the simulation enabled the team to take risks and to learn from our initial implementations. The iterative process also allowed us to draw from the perspectives of multiple team members over the course of the project. We believe these affordances allowed us to design a simulation more practical for classroom implementation that ultimately led to higher levels of student participation, deeper engagement, and more authentic collaboration. The DBR approach also helped us to develop a more powerful pedagogical model for promoting the epistemic practices associated with political communications. The design-based process allowed us not only to measure the outcomes of students' participation (as would occur in a traditional intervention study), but also to examine how and why students were engaging in particular ways. This information was vital for simulation development as well as theory-building.

Notes

1 This research and analysis was conducted while on faculty at the William & Mary School of Education. Funding was provided by the Spencer Foundation's New Civics Initiative.
2 Teachers in all three iterations established the groups for the simulation teams, but in Iterations One and Two those groupings were based more on social needs than on intellectual ones.
3 We did not embed audiovisual material in the WorkPro platform, although we did provide weblinks where possible.

References

Amiel, T., & Reves, R. (2008). Design-based research and educational technology: Rethinking technology and the research agenda. *Journal of Educational Technology & Society*, *11*(4), 29–40.

Barron, B. J. S., Schwartz, D. L., Vye, N. J., Moore, A., Petrosino, A., Zech, L., & Bransford, J. D. (1998). Doing with understanding: Lessons from research on problem- and project-based learning. *Journal of the Learning Sciences*, *7*(3–4), 271–311.

Brown, A. L. (1992). Design experiments. Theoretical and methodological challenges in creating interventions. *Journal of the Learning Sciences*, *2*(2), 141–178.

Cuban, L. (1986). *Teachers and machines: The classroom use of technology since 1920*. New York: Teachers College Press.

Cuban, L. (2001). *Oversold and underused: Computers in the classroom*. Cambridge, MA: Harvard University Press.

Dede, C. (2004). If design-based research is the answer, what is the question?, *Journal of the Learning Sciences*, *13*(1), 105–114.

Fredricks, J. A., Blumenfeld, P. C., & Paris, A. H. (2004). School engagement: Potential of the concept, state of the evidence. *Review of Educational Research*, *74*(1), 59–109.

Gould, J. (2011). *Guardian of democracy: The civic mission of schools*. Philadelphia, PA: Annenberg Public Policy Center of the University of Pennsylvania.

Henrie, C., Halverson, L., & Graham, C. (2015). Measuring student engagement in technology mediated learning: A review. *Computers & Education, 90*, 36–53.

Hess, D. (2009). *Controversy in the classroom: The democratic power of discussion.* New York, NY: Routledge.

Hess, D. E., & McAvoy, P. (2014). *The political classroom: Evidence and ethics in democratic education.* New York, NY: Routledge.

Kahne, J., Hodgin, E., & Eidman-Aadahl, E. (2016). Redesigning civic education for the digital age: in pursuit of equitable and impactful democratic engagement. *Theory and Research in Social Education, 44*(1), 1–35.

Lave, J., & Wenger, E. (1991). *Situated learning: Legitimate peripheral participation.* Cambridge, UK: Cambridge University Press.

Levine, P., & Kawashima-Ginsberg, K. (2017). *The republic is (still) at risk–and civics is part of the solution.* Medford: Jonathon M. Tisch College of Civic Life, Tufts University.

Margolis, J. (2008). *Stuck in the shallow end: Education, race, and computing.* Cambridge, MA: MIT Press.

Newmann, F., King, B., & Carmichael, D. (2007). *Authentic instruction and assessment: Common standards for rigor and relevance in teaching academic subjects.* Des Moines, IA: Iowa Department of Education.

Parker, W. (2003). *Teaching democracy: Unity and diversity in public life.* New York, NY: Teachers College Press.

Parker, W., & Lo, J. (2016). Reinventing the high school government course: Rigor, simulations, and learning from text. *Democracy and Education, 24*(1), Article 6. Retrieved from: http://democracyeducationjournal.org/home/vol24/iss1/6

Parker, W., Lo, J., Yeo, A. J., Valencia, S. W., Nguyen, D., Abbott, R. D., Vye, N. J. (2013). Beyond breadth-speed-test: Toward deeper knowing and engagement in an Advanced Placement course. *American Educational Research Journal, 50*(6), 1424–1459.

Raphael, C., Bachen, C., Lynn, K. M., Baldwin-Philippi, J., & McKee, K. A. (2010). Games for civic learning: A conceptual framework and agenda for research and design. *Games and Culture, 5*(2), 199–235.

Saye, J. W., & Brush, T. (2007). Using technology-enhanced learning environments to support problem-based historical inquiry in secondary school classrooms. *Theory & Research in Social Education, 35*(2), 196–230.

Shaffer, D. W. (2006a). *How computer games help children learn.* New York, NY: Palgrave MacMillan.

Shaffer, D. W. (2006b). Epistemic frames for epistemic games. *Computers & education, 46*(3), 223–234.

Stahl, G., Koschmann, T., & Suthers, D. (2006). Computer-supported collaborative learning: An historical perspective. In R. K. Sawyer (Ed.), *Cambridge handbook of the learning sciences* (pp. 409–426). Cambridge, UK: Cambridge University Press.

Stoddard, J. (2014). The need for media education in democratic education. *Democracy & Education, 22*(1). Retrieved from: http://democracyeducationjournal.org/home/vol22/iss1/4.

Stoddard, J., Banks, A., Nemacheck, C., and Wenska, L. (2016). The challenges of gaming for democratic education: the case of iCivics. *Democracy & Education, 24*(2), Article 2. Retrieved from: http://democracyeducationjournal.org/home/vol24/iss2

Stoddard, J., Swiecki, Z., & Shaffer, D. W. (2018). Behind the curtain: An epistemic design process for democratic media education simulations. In C. Wright-Maley (Ed.), *More like life itself: Simulations as powerful and purposeful social studies* (pp. 21–39). Charlotte, NC: Information Age Press.

Appendix 3.A

PurpleState Solutions, Inc. Virtual Internship Overview

Task 1: Entrance Interview and Online Environment Tutorial

- Interns complete an entrance interview (questionnaire/assessment).
- Interns read the Online Environment Tutorial, found in the resources section.

Task 2: PurpleState Campaign Design Manual Orientation (CDM)

- Interns review the Campaign Design Manual covering core concepts in political communications:
  1. Persuasive techniques in political advertising.
  2. How to conduct a media audit (e.g., review media sources, identify allies and earned media outlets).
  3. Role of polling in campaigns and limits on polling data.
  4. Media channels for reaching different target audiences (e.g., television ads, social media).
- Interns complete a task that asks them to apply what they have read.

Task 3: Media Audit Task

- Interns utilize their knowledge developed in Task 2 to "catalogue" sample political media for the PurpleState media database. They analyze three sample media for source, perspective, persuasive technique used, intended audience, and evidence. They also identify potential allies, friendly journalists, and outlets.

Task 4: CDM and Media Audit Reflection

- Interns participate in a synchronous discussion facilitated by their account manager (online mentor) to share their CDM research and Media Audit Task. The discussion covers how to plan media campaigns and the types of tasks interns will perform in their groups when developing their Campaign Design Proposal.

Task 5: Request for Proposals (RFP) Meeting (synchronous chat session)

- Interns read RFP resource to learn about the media campaign design proposal that they will be working on. The RFP comes from a special-interest group advocating a pro or con position on fracking (either New Energy Virginia or Clean Water Virginia).

- Account Manager runs a reflection meeting with interns to ensure understanding of the RFP. The meeting explores what the special-interest group is looking for, how to utilize previous research, and what interns need to consider as they design their campaign.

Task 6: Issue Research and Media Audit

- Interns research the policy issue (fracking) and voter demographics
- Individual students will submit campaign research memos to share with their group. Each member selects a task to complete:

    1. Polling: Consult polling data (or conduct original survey research) to understand current sentiment, to test the effectiveness of potential messages, and to discover interested demographic groups.
    2. Research arguments in favor of fracking: Research and identify compelling evidence. Identify likely allies (e.g., organizations, journalists, politicians) with a public following (local and national) to understand the angles that the public is most interested in.
    3. Research arguments against fracking: (Same as previous.)
    4. Identify stakeholders: Determine the political landscape, including the players on both sides and the organizations that support/oppose them.

Task 7: Initial Campaign Design Proposal (for Account Executive "John")

- The team of interns uses their research to design their proposal, using the PurpleState Campaign Design Process and Proposal Template (which also serves as the task rubric). Elements of the proposal include:

    1. Intended audience demographic to target/persuade.
    2. Selected strongest message for target audience.
    3. Selected media channels to best reach target audience demographic.
    4. Timing and location of media for target audience.
    5. Strongest evidence for/against on issue sample taglines, images, etc.
    6. Proposed budget.

Task 8: Initial Proposal Reflection Meeting (synchronous chat session)

- Interns review feedback on their initial proposal.
- Account Manager runs a meeting with interns to reflect on polling and interest-group feedback.
- In the reflection meeting, students plan changes to their proposal based on what they decide will please their clients.

Task 9: Campaign Design Proposal Final Draft

- Intern teams revise and resubmit their final Campaign Design Proposal for review.
- Optional Task: Groups develop a PowerPoint slideshow based on their proposal to pitch to the Account Executive "John."

Task 10: Exit Interview

- Interns complete exit interview (questionnaire/assessment).
- Mentors thank the students and say goodbye.

4

DEVELOPING AUTHENTIC PERFORMANCE ASSESSMENTS IN A CLASSROOM MINI-ECONOMY

Reflections on the Process of Design

Stephen Day and Christine L. Bae

Every year, dozens of elementary teachers in the state of Virginia transform their classrooms into miniature economies, or "mini-economies," in which students interview for jobs, earn imaginary income, analyze the classroom market, select production methods, manage resources, and ultimately create their own businesses. At the culminating Market Day held at a state university, students bubble with enthusiasm as they explain the benefits of their products to passersby before turning around to renegotiate prices and scout the competition. Throughout the experience, students are excited, proud, and engaged in meaningful economic decision-making.

Even though valuable opportunities like this exist, however, many teachers struggle to find the time in their curriculum to teach and assess economics content in relevant and powerful ways. The pressures of standardized testing can narrow the curriculum and incentivize teachers to focus only on a prescribed list of tested items. To address this problem, in 2014 the Virginia State Legislature opened the door for teachers to take advantage of opportunities like the mini-economy by passing an act mandating the use of authentic performance assessments (PAs) in place of standardized multiple-choice tests in Grades 3, 4, and 5 social studies (as well as in Grade 3 science and Grade 5 writing) (VDOE, 2017; Bland & Gareis, 2018). As a result of this mandate, social studies in these grades would no longer be assessed only by statewide standardized tests, but also by authentic PAs created by the school districts. Students would demonstrate social studies knowledge through real-life activities such as those involved in a classroom mini-economy.

As Wiggins (1989) has proposed,

> if we wish to design an authentic test, we must first decide what are the actual performances that we want students to be good at. We must design those performances first and worry about a fair and thorough method of grading them later.
>
> (p. 83)

Following Wiggins's sentiment, this chapter describes an effort to identify authentic student performances in elementary economics, to develop assessment tasks that elicit these performances, and to develop a fair and reliable method of grading the assessments. Each of these steps requires a research and development process that allows for frequent reflection and revision, in collaboration with practitioners. A design-based research (DBR) approach seemed an appropriate fit. Employing this method, a team of teachers and researchers envisioned and designed a series of lesson plans and PAs, and then iteratively tested, debriefed, and improved upon them in several third- and fourth-grade classrooms. The following year, an additional group of teachers not involved in the original design conducted a second round of field tests to establish ecological validity and reliability of the assessments.

The findings from this DBR study suggest that authentic PAs can capture a range of students' real-world economic thinking in the context of a mini-economy. This chapter draws on these results to establish design elements that future educators might incorporate when creating similar PAs for economics or other social studies fields. More significantly, it presents a detailed account of the procedure followed in creating the assessments. As McKenney and Reeves (2012) point out, contributing to the knowledge base on the curricular and instructional "design process" (p. 212) is an important affordance of DBR, but one to which few have devoted much effort. With that aim in mind, this chapter offers process-based suggestions for designing authentic PAs collaboratively with teachers, based on the experience of those involved in this project.

Authentic Performance Assessments in a Classroom Mini-Economy

A mini-economy (sometimes called a "mini-society") is a classroom simulation in which students have jobs, earn play money, and can buy goods at a class store. Many classroom mini-economies include a consensual political process as well, with students voting on class rules, writing a constitution, or establishing financial regulations (e.g., counterfeit prevention). A mini-economy can last from a few weeks to an entire school year. In the culminating Market Day, students create their own classroom businesses, eventually selling their goods and services in a large market consisting of several classrooms or even multiple schools. The Market Day in this study included more than a dozen schools and hundreds of students.

Several studies have demonstrated positive outcomes for classroom mini-economies. Kourilsky and Hirshleifer (1976) found that students were highly motivated to learn in such an environment. They also found fewer disciplinary issues among students using a mini-economy (even one not focusing on classroom management) than among students not using a mini-economy (see also Brown, 2010). Cassuto (1980) found significantly larger test-score gains in economics knowledge among elementary students who used the Mini-Society program (a form of mini-economy) than among those who learned from more traditional means (see Kourilsky, 1983). Mini-economies also have been shown to build girls' confidence in entrepreneurship and finance. Kourilsky and Ballard-Campbell (1984) found that before participating in one, girls were more likely to report that entrepreneurship was the domain of males, but after taking part, girls reported confidence in business and personal finance on an equal footing with boys. Finally, students who took part in the Mini-Society program were more likely to employ cost/benefit analysis (CBA) effectively when conceptualizing economic problems than were those who did not take part (Kourilsky & Graff, 1985).

In sum, the literature shows that mini-economies have the potential to elicit authentic intellectual work in economics, making them a prime context for the use of PAs. However, teachers have reported that the pressures of standardized testing dissuade them from using mini-economies, even when they receive training in how to do so (Carr, 2003). Despite the opportunities that mini-economies afford, teachers have been hesitant to incorporate authentic assessment into their curriculum unless they can justify it within the testing structure. Given the new state statute mandating the use of performance assessments in Virginia, the current project sought to capitalize on this new political climate to develop such assessments for use in classroom mini-economies across the state.

To summarize the project in broad strokes, a design team consisting of elementary classroom teachers and two university researchers created a series of authentic PAs that encouraged students to use economic thinking as they participated in a mini-economy. Each PA engaged students in pursuing a compelling question within the field of economics, for example: PA1, "What should our business produce?"; PA2, "Do we have the resources to make our product?"; and PA3, "What should I specialize in?" These prompts asked students to explain how scarcity affects decision-making and how decisions have opportunity costs, to conduct CBA, and to navigate situations with scarce productive resources. Students demonstrated their understanding through participation in group activities (e.g., gathering and discussing classroom market data), as well as through culminating essays—ultimately using their knowledge to create and improve their businesses. Theory and research on authentic intellectual work (Newmann, Marks, & Gamoran, 1996) and performance-based assessment (Wiggins & McTighe 2005; McTighe, 2015) guided the design of the PAs.

In the initial stages of the project, however, the researchers involved were hesitant to impose their own views of authentic assessment on the teacher participants. Rather, they hoped to build on the teachers' current practices, as all of them were already using mini-economies in their classrooms (though not necessarily for purposes of assessment). To this end they selected the College, Career, and Civic Life (C3) Framework (NCSS, 2013) to function as a set of design principles, an approach that would allow teachers to deepen and extend their own assessment practices as they implemented the PAs, while still providing a common language and set of concepts for the team to use.

The National Council for the Social Studies (NCSS) published the C3 Framework in 2013 to generate authenticity in the social studies classroom through the use of inquiry (Schwab, 1966; National Council for the Social Studies, 2013; Marri, 2016; Saye, 2017). More specifically, the Framework presents an "Inquiry Arc" consisting of four elements: (a) Developing Questions and Planning Inquiries, (b) Applying Disciplinary Concepts and Tools, (c) Evaluating Sources and Using Evidence, and (d) Communicating Conclusions and Taking Informed Action (NCSS, 2013). The design team reasoned that the inquiry arc would help the teacher participants create authentic PAs that sparked student curiosity, drew on disciplinary concepts, fostered analysis of evidence, and prompted real-world decision-making—all well-established components of authentic assessment.

Study Design

The study posed three main questions, about design *principles, processes,* and *products,* respectively:

> RQ1: What design principles facilitate the creation of high-quality authentic PAs in economics?
>
> RQ2: What design processes facilitate the creation of high-quality authentic PAs in economics?
>
> RQ3: Can locally developed PAs elicit authentic and measurable intellectual work in economics from elementary students?

The first question considered whether design principles drawn from the C3 Framework offered useful guidance for creating authentic PAs, or whether they provided too little coherence. The second question sets up the main storyline of this chapter: an inquiry into the affordances and constraints conferred by the process followed to create the PAs. The last question examines if the PAs, after several rounds of revision, fulfilled their intended purpose of eliciting authentic and measurable performances in economics.

The context for this research was a program run by a university center dedicated to economics education, directed by the lead researcher, Stephen Day (first author). He oversaw all portions of the current project, including professional development, design of instructional materials, field-testing, classroom observations, and analysis of data. Day recruited eight third- and fourth-grade teachers from a database of those taking part in a statewide mini-economy program. The email invitation advertised as the core aim of the study the creation of authentic PAs. Thus, all eight teachers had prior experience in using a classroom mini-economy and had committed to working to create PAs for use in that environment.

In planning out their approach for developing the PAs, the design team (consisting of Day and the eight teachers) sought to draw on the particular strengths of DBR methodology. For one, a teacher–researcher partnership would keep the work "close to the ground" while still maintaining structure. Second, the iterative nature of DBR would allow the team to catch mistakes in design early and often, and to address them through revision (Bryk, Gomez, Grunow, & LeMahieu, 2015). Third, observing use of the PAs in different classrooms at various stages in their development would allow the team to reflect on the efficacy of the design principles at work. Finally, proceeding through multiple iterations would allow the team first to consider data on the viability of the initial design, then on teachers' implementation, and lastly on student learning outcomes and rubric reliability (see McKenney & Reeves, 2012). In sum, the design team worked closely together to enact, test, and refine the PAs through iterative cycles of design and analysis—the hallmark of DBR (Cobb, Confrey, diSessa, Lehrer, & Schauble, 2003; Anderson & Shattuck, 2012; Design-Based Research Collective, 2003).

In the first iteration (year one, 2014–2015), the eight teachers participated in a planning workshop where they shared materials they currently used when they ran classroom mini-economies. The plan was for the team to develop these materials into PAs—although ultimately that did not work, as the design narrative below makes clear. Instead, Day ended up designing the PAs and revising them based on teacher feedback. Four of the teachers then implemented the PAs in their classrooms, with Day observing them. These four teachers and two new ones returned for a group interview to revise the PAs based on field-test results from year one.

In the second iteration (year two, 2016–2017), Christine Bae joined the project, as did a new group of four third- and fourth-grade teachers who had not participated in planning or field-testing during year one. The new teachers implemented the revised PAs in their classrooms, with Day and Bae observing. As the materials were meant to be made publicly available, it was important to test them in a "naturalistic setting" with teachers not involved in their design (see Barab and Squire, 2004; McKenney and Reeves, 2012). The second iteration focused on establishing interrater reliability on the assessment scoring rubric, as well as on evaluating the ability of the PAs to elicit authentic intellectual work (RQ3).

The researchers used constant comparative methods (Charmaz, 2006) to analyze qualitative data from the focus-group interviews, classroom observations, and students' writing in response to the PAs. In Iteration Two, the researchers triangulated students' written work against transcribed video of their peer-to-peer discourse in small groups as they completed the performance tasks. Analyzing students' real-time verbalizations and problem-solving offered insight into their thought process as they completed the various components of the PAs (see Ge & Land, 2003). The researchers also analyzed the correlation between two graders' scoring to help establish the reliability of the PAs and accompanying rubric.

Table 4.1 summarizes the design work, data collection, and analyses that occurred during each phase of each iteration (corresponding, respectively, to "micro-cycles" and "meso-cycles" in McKenney and Reeves's terminology; 2012, p. 78). The following sections share this design narrative in much greater depth, along with findings from Iterations One and Two.

TABLE 4.1 Project Timeline and Data Sources

Design phase	Data sources
Iteration 1	
1.1: Vision casting, professional development, and collaborative design	Field notes from professional development sessions Focus-group interview Research journal Rough drafts of lesson plans
1.2: Development of the authentic PAs	Second drafts of lesson plans, performance assessments, and scoring rubrics
1.3: Field testing, classroom observations, and teacher interviews	Class observations, field notes, student work samples, and teacher post-interviews from West End Elementary, East End Elementary, and Rural Elementary Schools
Iteration 2	
2.1: Reconvening the design team; expert panel	Focus-group interview Feedback from expert panel on performance tasks and rubrics
2.2: Establishing reliability and ecological validity of the PAs and scoring rubric	Classroom observations, video-recorded discussions, and student work samples from Oceanshore, South Side, Satellite, and River Road Schools. Rubric scores from two graders

Note: All names of teachers and schools are pseudonyms.

Design Narrative

Iteration One

The purpose of the first iteration was to design a viable set of PAs in as collaborative a manner as possible. Data collection and analysis focused on monitoring teachers' views of the assessments and underlying design principles to ensure the usability of the PAs within elementary classrooms. The team also monitored students' engagement with the assessment tasks helped to ascertain whether the PAs were in fact eliciting the kinds of economic reasoning the designers intended (RQ3). Such goals are typical for "alpha testing" of innovations (McKenney & Reeves, 2012, p. 137).

Phase 1.1: Vision casting, professional development, and collaborative design. At the outset of the project, the design team (Day and the teachers) met for two professional development sessions, with the shared goal of creating authentic assessments to use with classroom mini-economies. Rather than having experts or researchers develop the assessments in isolation and then disseminating them to teachers to implement, the design team sought to begin with the practices already in place in teachers' classrooms (Thornton, 1991; Thornton 2008). Toward this end, in the first workshop the team worked on building community, setting a shared vision, and agreeing on a design framework (the C3 Framework). Teachers also shared their current practices in running classroom mini-economies. Day then asked them to bring to the next session a lesson that they were already using in their classrooms. They received a book, *Teaching the C3 Framework* (Swan, Lee, Mueller, & Day, 2014), containing examples of lessons employing the Framework to study for the next meeting.

At the second professional development session, the teachers shared the lesson plans they brought. They then worked in groups to give the lessons a common format that followed the Inquiry Arc of the C3 Framework. Yet here the team encountered a caveat: While the lessons displayed many creative ideas, they did not count as authentic assessment. Rather, the lesson plans varied widely in their content and even disciplinary focus. For example, one was essentially an English literature lesson with mini-economy applications (based on the book, *The Hard-Times Jar*). Another was a lesson plan on Jamestown history, also with mini-economy applications, but again, not a performance assessment. Though the lessons appeared promising, altogether they lacked the coherence needed for a singular project. So the team switched from the day's original agenda to brainstorming what the assessment products should look like, writing ideas on a whiteboard, and reaching consensus on desired key features.

A focus-group interview with the team followed, in which the participants discussed the usefulness of the C3 Framework as a guiding instrument. In the end, the team decided that the Framework lent focus, direction, and structure to their planning and should be retained going forward. However, they delegated authority to Stephen Day to develop the PAs and accompanying rubrics, thus moving away from the initial bottom-up approach. The lesson plans they had shared became supporting materials for those assessments, available on the project website (www.vaminieconomy.org).

Phase 1.2: Development of the authentic PAs. Following the parameters set by the teacher participants, over the next month Day created several drafts of PAs for use in a classroom mini-economy. Each PA consisted of scaffolded tasks that led students through one step in creating a business and required them to use economics concepts in their answers. The three PAs field-tested in this project were as follows:

PA1: What should our business produce? Students analyze their personal wants and goals. They survey fellow classmates on their wants and goals and use this data to brainstorm classroom business ideas that could address people's stated wants. In groups, they then decide what their businesses will produce, using a decision-making model (a double cost/benefit analysis, or "decision tree") to guide deliberation. The task ends with a short reflective essay on the prompt, "How did the ideas of *wants* and *scarcity* help you decide what your business should produce?"

PA2: Do I have the resources I need to make my product? In their business groups, students categorize the natural, human, and capital resources they will need to create their product. They use a diagram to investigate the alternative uses for one of the resources (which gets at the opportunity cost of using it for their intended purpose). They then write a short reflective essay on the following prompt:

Explain which of the resources in your product will be the most difficult for you to get. Next, explain what you can do to solve this problem. For example, you could change how to make the product, find a different resource, or even pick a new product entirely.

Figure 4.1 shows the student handout for this assessment.

PA3: What should I specialize in? Students learn about specialization and division of labor through a classroom game. The game takes the form of a controlled experiment in which one group of students produces hamburgers using an assembly line while the other produces the hamburgers individually. In the assessment task, students critique in writing the use of an assembly line and explain how (or if) they can use specialization in their own businesses. They then create a diagram of their production process, noting the role of specialization and the uses of natural, human, and capital resources.

Day presented these assessments to the participating teachers, who discussed them and offered feedback. He then revised and shared them again, and each of teachers agreed to try them out in their classroom over the next few months.

Phase 1.3: Field testing, classroom observations, and teacher post-interviews. In this phase, the participating teachers implemented the designed PAs in their classrooms. Day observed and video recorded each implementation (six in total) and later transcribed, coded, and analyzed student performances qualitatively. After observing each class, he interviewed the teacher about how the lesson and assessment had gone.

The observations revealed that the teachers enthusiastically taught the lessons the team had worked on but spent little time on the performance assessments themselves. That said, students were still engaged in authentic work. For example, one class grew embroiled in a heated debate about the costs and benefits of the actions taken by a character in the book, *The Hard-Times Jar.* Another class took a structured approach to gathering market data on how much money consumers would pay for their products. These varying practices may have been a side-effect of the performance-assessment mandate not yet having uniform state benchmarks. Teachers were focused on how to create the best possible mini-economy experience for their students but were not yet accountable to their school districts to produce specific assessment products. The variation in teacher practice also stemmed from the planning team's own decision to allow them flexibility in implementing the PAs during the study.

Major findings from Iteration One. The first iteration yielded findings related to each of the three research questions. In regards to RQ1, "What design principles facilitate the creation of high-quality authentic PAs in economics?" analysis of the teacher interview data revealed that they began with a clear idea of what "authentic" meant and sought to adhere to it. Their definition essentially was "real-world" and "interdisciplinary." They used the C3 Framework as a means of staying true to this conception of authenticity. To that end, the Framework worked as a loose guide through each iteration of design—a set of suggestions to be emphasized or de-emphasized as expedient. The teachers used the Framework's Inquiry Arc as a guidepost rather than as a strict set of rules.

Name: _____

Do I Have the Resources I Need to Make My Product?

With a partner, think of all the resources that go into the production of your product. Think of as many as you can. *Examples: Capital resource—The truck that carried the paper you used to the store. Human resource— The truck driver.*

Natural Resources   Human Resources   Capital Resources

My product: _____

Next, choose one resource from a box above. Think about what else that resource could be used to produce if it wasn't being used in your product. Write down each of your answers in the six spaces provided.

The resource here...   Could have been used for...

Which of the resources in your product will be the most difficult for you to get, and is there anything you can do about this? For example, you could change how to make the product, find a different resource, or even pick a new product entirely.

You must use the following words in your answer: **scarce, opportunity cost,** and **resource**

Bonus: Write and record a skit! In the skit, some business owners are trying to decide between using their money for more advertising, for making more products, or for keeping as profit.

FIGURE 4.1 Student Worksheet for Performance Assessment 2.

Interestingly, while there was consensus that the C3 Framework was helpful for structuring inquiry in the mini-economy, the teachers' feedback varied as to which aspects of the Framework they found more helpful. One found that the Framework helped her focus on using primary sources more consistently. Another said that it reminded her to base her inquiry around a compelling question. Still another mentioned how it reminded her to focus on guiding students towards communicating their conclusions clearly.

The C3 Framework therefore turned out to be useful to everyone, but in different ways. This flexibility led the team to conclude that as a set of prescriptive design principles, the Framework lacked the specificity needed to yield a uniform set of authentic PAs reproducible on a broad scale. Moreover, many elementary teachers, who spend most of their time on literacy and math, may not value or be familiar with the C3 Framework's principles of social studies inquiry. In the next iteration, the design team de-emphasized the distinct characteristics of the Framework while retaining them in spirit, so as to avoid distracting teachers from the more central project goal of designing PAs for classroom mini-economies.

Another set of findings address RQ2: "What design processes facilitate the creation of high-quality authentic PAs in economics?" Rapid and early data analysis proved invaluable for setting the direction of the entire project. The initial design plan to have teachers share their current mini-economy practices and mold them into the PAs did not work, because the practices were too disparate and too teaching-oriented rather than assessment-oriented. Catching this problem early allowed for a change in direction before the project went too far astray. The team resolved instead to allow the project leader to design an original set of PAs based on the ideas put forth by the participating teachers.

The iterative, open-ended design process followed also alerted the team to another needed change in Phase 1.3. The classroom observations had revealed that, far from implementing the assessments in lock-step manner, each of the teachers had adapted them to fit within their existing practice—most often by incorporating interdisciplinary themes into the assessments. Teachers regularly infused children's literature into the lessons preceding the PAs and constantly referred back to the stories as a way of focusing students' attention. As for math connections, one teacher enthused about the opportunity the mini-economy provided for students to use numbers for "record-keeping." In another class, students used market surveys; the surveyors then tabulated and analyzed the responses to guide the setting of prices, in effect creating a demand curve. Teachers spoke of these sorts of practices as examples of interdisciplinary, real-world learning. One summarized how the teachers viewed mini-economies as an interdisciplinary vehicle for instruction and assessment:

> And so if you are a third-grade teacher, [and] you have to do a performance-based lesson, then you have all the tools right here, and it's a creative way to incorporate STEM and hands-on learning, and 21st Century Skills, so why not incorporate this as your performance-based assessment in third grade? It substitutes for your overall assessment for the year.

In sum, the process of vision-casting with teachers and then observing how they actually used the first drafts of the PAs, allowed the design team to learn how to better align the assessments with the teachers' goals. For the second iteration, the team revised the PAs and supporting lesson plan materials to fit more easily within an interdisciplinary context.

The first iteration also yielded insight into RQ3: "Can locally developed PAs elicit authentic and measurable intellectual work in economics from elementary students?" The classroom observations offered tentative evidence that they can. For example, as noted above, PA3 asked students to investigate the economic concept of specialization, first by engaging in an assembly-line experiment in which some students made Playdoh hamburgers using specialization while another group made them individually. The students then applied the lessons learned in the experiment to their own businesses, the goal being to consider whether specialization could help their businesses be more productive. In an observation at West End Elementary School, one group did switch to assembly-line production after taking part in the experiment. Another group told the researcher they had considered implementing an assembly line but had rejected the idea because they believed it ineffective for what they were producing. Still a third group reported that they were already using specialization in their group: One person made advertisements, one made the product, and one conducted market research. In all three of these groups, the students were accurately applying the targeted economic concept to their real-world performance, as well as coherently discussing the reasons for their choices.

Students also exhibited economic decision-making through cost/benefit analysis (CBA). In an adaptation of PA1 (see above), students at Rural Elementary School used CBA to analyze decisions facing migrant workers in the book, *The Hard-Times Jar*. For example, should the protagonist, hungry for learning, borrow a book from her school and return it later, even if her teacher forbade it? And should the girl use money from her parents' savings to buy books, thus furthering her education? Students weighed the costs and benefits of these decisions in sometimes heated moral argument. However, their written work often did not match the quality of their oral argumentation. After noting this trend, the design team later revised PA1 to provide more support for student writing and more explicit instructions.

Lastly, analysis of student work revealed a critical error in the design of PA3: It did not include any prompts that directly addressed the compelling question. The assessment was entitled, "What Should I Specialize In?" and the supporting lesson did address that topic. The prompts, however, asked students about opportunity cost and productive resources and did not lead them to address specialization beyond a basic definition. This is an example of how design flaws can be "hiding in plain sight" until after analyzing student work. It was through piloting the PAs in classrooms that this flaw was revealed.

In summary, by the end of the first iteration, the PAs had potential to elicit authentic intellectual work in economics but needed further refinement. Fortunately, early discovery of flaws in their design, before the PAs had been scaled up too far, allowed for revision for the next iteration. The findings suggested that this revision should focus on better aligning the PAs with objectives that teachers valued (such as interdisciplinary learning), on ensuring their ease of use in classroom mini-economies, and on structuring tasks and prompts to more directly elicit authentic disciplinary work in economics.

Complete results from year one can be found in summary form in Day's doctoral dissertation (2015). All materials, including a pacing guide, lesson plans, rubrics, and the performance assessments themselves, are posted on a free, public website: www.vaminieconomy.org.

Iteration Two

Whereas the first iteration had focused on refining the design principles and on establishing the viability of the new assessment under highly favorable conditions (i.e., in the classrooms of the teachers who helped design them), the second iteration examined how the assessments would fare under more typical circumstances—as is customary in product "beta testing" (McKenney & Reeves, 2012, p. 138). As the ultimate goal was to create resources for use in school districts across the state, the PAs needed to be tested with teachers who were not part of the original design team. The reliability and ecological validity of the scoring instrument also needed to be determined. The researchers established the former through an interrater check, and the latter by triangulating students' scores on the rubric against video footage of students' peer-to-peer discourse in small groups as they completed the PAs (see Ge & Land, 2003; Breakstone, 2014). The graded student work, the perspectives of different graders, the students' in-class conversations, and the comparisons across these datasets provided deep insight into the nature of students' disciplinary thinking as elicited by the PAs (RQ3).

Phase 2.1: Reconvening the design team; expert panel. To begin the second iteration, the design team reconvened (with two added members) to review the previous year's work, discuss research results, suggest further edits, and capture key insights in another focus-group interview. In the interview, teachers emphasized the importance of having classroom materials that aligned with both the mini-economy curriculum and with the state social studies standards. "Shame on me," said one teacher, "if I can't show you how what I'm doing in my class aligns with standards." Along similar lines, they discussed the ways that they justified the mini-economy to their school administrators—for example, as "enrichment," or as a part of instructional blocks in math, English Language Arts, or social studies. One teacher related that her district's administrator for curriculum and instruction expressed interest in encouraging teachers to explore use of PAs.

A panel then convened consisting of five experts in teaching and learning economics, drawn from university centers for economics education (such centers exist in 45 U.S. states). The panel reviewed the PAs (but not the accompanying lesson plans, which were judged to have received enough scrutiny to be kept as-is).

The expert panel also reviewed the rubrics Day had created for scoring the assessments, and ultimately recommended using one common rubric for all of them. As students would be expected to know the rubric criteria well enough to grasp what they were being graded on, the expert panel felt it would be too difficult for them to learn a new rubric for each assessment. Having a common rubric also could help students and teachers focus on building specific skills over time. Based on this advice, Day drew from the categories developed by Schug (1981) to create a common rubric, which he shared with the participating teachers (Figure 4.2).

Phase 2.2: Establishing reliability and ecological validity of the PAs and scoring rubric. The final phase consisted of another round of field testing and classroom observations with four teachers from four different schools (52 students in total). As noted earlier, the teachers selected for observation were

	Beginning (–4)	Proficient (5–8)	Mastery (9–10)
Economics knowledge	Student not able to accurately use economics content	Student uses economic content with few mistakes	Student uses economics content accurately; no mistakes
Application of economics knowledge	Student inconsistently applies knowledge of economics content to the business	Student accurately and usefully applies knowledge of economics when making decisions for the business	Student uses economics knowledge to make important improvements to the business
Helpfulness to real-world product/ business plan	Student work does not generally add much to the product or business plan	Student work adds value to the real-world product or business plan	Student work adds importantly to the real-world product or business plan
English/Language Arts skills: using evidence to support a thesis	Thesis (main point), details, or the link between them is unclear or missing	Thesis and supporting details are clearly linked	Supporting details support the thesis in a compelling way that adds significantly to the overall point
Data analysis skills* *Use for data collection, math, and/or decision-making models	Student does not accurately record or interpret data	Student accurately records and interprets data; the problem is solved correctly	Student correctly analyzes data in a way that adds significantly to the business project.

FIGURE 4.2 Common Scoring Rubric for Authentic PAs.

not part of the design team, so as to test the ecological validity of the PAs under more typical classroom conditions. Two kinds of data were collected: (a) students' written responses to the PA prompts, and (b) transcribed video footage of the small-group conversations that occurred as they engaged in the performance tasks. Triangulating these two datasets allowed the researchers to see the performance behaviors underlying students' written responses. A total of 15 students were observed in depth, yielding video footage of groupwork on several different days. Student discussion was transcribed, coded according to relevance to economic concepts, and graded using two dimensions (Rows 1 and 2) of the common scoring rubric for the PAs. Then, to test the reliability of the rubric, two experts (Day and an experienced elementary social studies teacher) scored students' written responses using four dimensions of the rubric for all but one PA, and all five dimensions for the final PA, with minimal communication beforehand.[1]

Major findings from Iteration Two. Findings from the second iteration mainly address RQ3, which asked about the capacity of PAs to elicit and measure authentic intellectual work in economics. In classroom observations, the researchers noticed several themes: First, students appeared interested and active in pursuing the compelling questions, which kept them focused on the disciplinary content. Second, they were using both the targeted economic concepts and the data gathered in class to answer the PAs' compelling questions (albeit with varying degrees of skill). Last, they were intensely excited about their mini-economy businesses, so much so that a few impassioned disagreements took place among group members who had differing visions of how to run their business.

There was considerable variation in students' rubric scores, which suggests that the PAs were capable of measuring different degrees of mastery. Students at Satellite Elementary School, for example, varied in the depth of their economic thinking both in their group conversations and in their written responses to the PAs. One group of students were responding to the prompt from PA1, "What should our business produce?" and were weighing the costs and benefits of two potential options using a "decision tree," which is a side-by-side CBA (Figure 4.3). The group was trying to decide between making magics (a kind of fabric accessory) versus maracas. Having completed the decision tree, one student referred to it in conversation to guide the group's thinking:

> *Student 4*: So magics have more in the benefits and less that we need here [in the costs]. So it's actually better because it has more benefit and less material so it would take less money. And over here [maracas] it's only two things [in benefits] so [magics] is more [beneficial]. So let's go with the magic.

This student assembled information about costs and benefits of two different products, organized the information into a diagram which she analyzed in a systematic fashion, and used her analysis to evaluate the group's options. The standards of authentic intellectual work are all present: She has used higher-order thinking, has

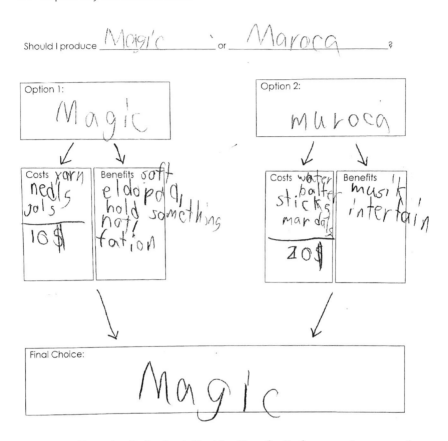

FIGURE 4.3 Example of a Student's Decision Tree for Performance Assessment 1.

begun to attain age-appropriate depth of knowledge, has engaged in substantive conversation, and has thereby helped her group form a real-world connection (Newmann & Wehlage, 1993). This student scored a 7 out of 10 on the "Economics Knowledge" portion of the rubric, and a 7, as well, on "Application of Economics Knowledge" (although she scored lower on other portions of the task).

As an example of a less-successful attempt at using economic thinking, consider the following conversation about wants, scarcity, and choice, also from PA1:

Researcher: How did you decide what your wants were?
Student 1: Because I ask my parents for all this stuff.
Student 2: If I got unlimited cash, if that was the only [thing I got], then I could just buy the other things . . . and then a phone. My mom won't let me get one until middle school.

In this example, the first student did not identify herself as a choice-maker, nor consider why she might want things. Her wants were simply the "stuff" she asked her parents for. The second student said that she could just acquire money as the gateway to other things. She did not grapple with the essential problem of scarcity; instead, in effect she wished it away. On the "Economics Knowledge" portion of the rubric, both students scored a 4 out of 10. On "Application of Economics Knowledge," both students scored a 3.

Similar variation occurred in students' written responses to the PAs across all four schools. As shown in Table 4.2, standard deviations ranged from 0.8 to 1.8 depending on the PA and scorer, indicating varied levels of student proficiency. Equally significant, most students scored in the "proficient" range, indicating that the PAs were indeed eliciting authentic economic thinking, at least according to the rubric.

The data also suggests that the PAs and scoring rubric can act as a reliable means of assessing economic reasoning. Although one rater tended to score PAs slightly higher than the other, the Pearson's r correlations between the two raters indicate moderate to high agreement, according to Landis and Koch's (1977) Benchmark Scale. Furthermore, standard deviations were similar across raters, with the possible exception of PA3, meaning that the two raters saw similar amounts of variation across the sample—another testament to the rubric's reliability. Overall, these outcomes suggest that, while attention must be paid to grader training as the use of PAs progresses, the assessments designed do appear to capture students' economic thinking with a level of objectivity or consistency.

To learn more about what lay behind these numbers, students' small-group conversations were scored independently of their written work on the PAs, using two dimensions of the rubric pertaining to "Economics Knowledge" (row 1) and "Application of Economic Concepts" (row 2)—that is, what they knew about economics and if they were able to use it. Each student received their own score based on their individual contributions to the conversation ($n = 15$). The average discussion score for these 15 students was 7.1 ("Proficient"), while the corresponding rubric scores for these same students' written work were 6.47 (knowledge) and 6.53 (application), respectively. The Pearson's r (correlation) between their conversations and their written PA scores was 0.71, demonstrating a strong linear relationship. Even though the sample here was small, the results

TABLE 4.2 Students' Performance Assessment Scores from Two Raters in Year 2

	n	Rater 1 score M (SD)	Rater 2 score M (SD)	Interrater correlation (Pearson's r)
PA1: What should our business produce?	41	6.5 (1.1)	7.76 (0.8)	.79
PA2: Do we have the resources we need to make our product?	28	5.8 (1.8)	6.2 (1.7)	.87
PA3: What should I specialize in?	22	6.4 (1.5)	8.0 (0.9)	.83

Note: The task was worth a total of 10 possible points. 1–4 = "beginning"; 5–8 = "proficient"; 9–10 = "mastery."

do suggest that what ended up on their sheets of paper reflected what they had talked about with their classmates in the live setting.

In sum, the results suggest that the design process the team followed to create the PAs succeeded in yielding a usable product. First, when responding to the PAs, students were engaged in the kinds of economic thinking that the design team had envisioned. Second, student work appeared to be at an appropriate level: few had achieved mastery, nor should they, given the amount of time teachers spent on the material (one to three days). Third, grading practices seemed consistent enough to work on a larger scale, given some additional fine-tuning. Scaling up was indeed planned as the next step, as the goal was to make the PAs available to teachers across the state.

Events intervened, however, to change the future plans of the design team. The State Board of Education updated its requirements for authentic PAs, providing local school districts with a set of quality criteria, along with guidelines for PA creation and reporting mechanisms. The upshot of this change was that any fine-tuning of the PAs would need to occur at the district level in coordination with teachers and administrators. Local districts would still need templates for PAs, but no one would be using materials "off-the-shelf." This actually put the current iteration of the PAs in just the right place: available for use as well-designed, scaffolded, field-tested starting points for districts that wished to use classroom mini-economies. However, the policy change also obviated the need for further design iterations in coordination with local districts.

Discussion

This study responded to a recognized need for authentic performance assessments that could measure student learning in economics and other social studies fields. Since so much of good design involves close interaction with the end user (teachers in this case), the project team selected a DBR approach to investigate the products created, processes followed, and design principles used in the study. This approach yielded significant findings that could aid future researchers and practitioners in developing similar types of assessments. The following sections discuss these results beginning with the third research question and ending with the second, so as to conclude with the study's most significant implications: those related to the process of design.

Can Locally Developed PAs Elicit Authentic and Measurable Intellectual Work in Economics from Elementary Students?

The PAs produced showed evidence of effectively eliciting and measuring student thinking in economics. Specifically, students did indeed use cost/benefit analysis, make decisions about how to use resources, adjust production procedures, and organize information when creating and implementing a classroom business. The second iteration of the study indicated that the PAs were functioning as intended and were ready for use on a broader scale.

What Design Principles Facilitate the Creation of High-Quality Authentic PAs in Economics?

The findings show that the C3 Framework can indeed serve as a coherent and useful basis for creating performance assessments, even in a complicated context like a classroom mini-economy. That said, the following refinements to the implementation of that Framework derive from this study's findings:

1. Inquiry-based performance tasks should emphasize the lesson's compelling question(s) to ensure alignment with the authentic objective of the PA (C3 Dimension 1).
2. Performance tasks should be fashioned to help students use disciplinary concepts as tools for answering the compelling question(s), rather than as ends in themselves (C3 Dimension 2).
3. Sources and evidence should be carefully chosen for both authenticity and ease of use (C3 Dimension 3). In the discipline of economics, students can collect their own primary source material in the form of real-world data.
4. Informed action can be aided by the presence of an authentic and interdisciplinary project goal (e.g., moral reasoning about the book, *The Hard-Times Jar*) (C3 Dimension 4). Educators should consider repurposing school-based projects that currently exist and that could be deployed as part of PAs.

The findings also show that the C3 Framework can operate "in the background" as a set of guiding principles, which can lend flexibility for teachers working in an interdisciplinary setting. The C3 Framework need not be used in a lock-step fashion, unless the user has reason to do so.

What Design Processes Facilitate the Creation of High-Quality Authentic PAs in Economics?

This study revealed several trade-offs inherent in the process of designing authentic PAs. The first of these is between freedom and coherence. The study design initially gave teachers the freedom to use their existing classroom practices as the basis for developing the PAs, but this strategy ultimately did not work and led to the researcher taking a stronger lead going forward. This pattern is well-documented in the professional development (PD) literature; for a strategy like that to work, teachers would need more time for initial PD (Banilower, Boyd, Pasley, & Weiss, 2006; Blank & De Las Alas, 2009). Iterations of professional development, observation, and reflection (through post-observation interviews) witnessed teachers improving in their ability to design and enact authentic PAs. Procuring extra time for PD at the beginning could have led to a more coherent and efficient process of PA development and implementation, yet doing so might have made the project more about what the researchers wanted to see and less about what the teachers were already doing.

A second trade-off is between ecological validity and statistical control. The shifting conditions under which the design team collected quantitative data offered insight into different classroom situations, but these conditions also limited the extent to which the team could draw causal claims. A further iteration could potentially address this limitation, but as noted above, most likely that will be left to school districts to undertake.

Keeping these tradeoffs in mind, the study illustrated how DBR can be used to bridge research and practice by fostering collaboration between university partners and teachers, working towards the common goal of designing new assessments. This collaborative approach facilitated teachers' sense of ownership over the reform efforts. As an unexpected result, they became ambassadors for the change from multiple-choice tests to authentic PAs. This became apparent in year two of the project as the researchers followed up with the original teachers on the design team to see how the PAs were being used. The teachers showed increased confidence in further developing and adapting the PAs, so much so that they had even begun sharing the assessments with their colleagues. For example, the participating teacher from Rural Elementary School subsequently created a schoolwide mini-economy Market Day and introduced the authentic PAs created in this project as a model for all third-grade teachers in her district. The same teacher presented at a summer institute hosted by the Center for Economic Education. A large school district that had teacher–leaders in attendance subsequently adopted mini-economies, along with versions of the PAs, districtwide as part of their assessment plan.

In another example, the two participating teachers from West End Elementary were later promoted to curriculum specialist and technology specialist, respectively, and subsequently introduced the PAs to other third-grade teachers in the district, one of whom participated in the field test of the PAs in Iteration Two. The work of these teachers in turn influenced a larger, neighboring school district to use the mini-economy PAs as part of their own districtwide efforts to create performance-based assessments. At Oceanside Elementary, when the participating teacher was switched to a different grade the year after her class was observed, she was careful to train her replacement to continue implementing the mini-economy activity and participating in Market Day. The fact that these teachers displayed leadership and ownership of the mini-economies and accompanying PAs, even expanding them to the district level, is evidence of the power of the DBR process this project followed.

In a year-one focus-group interview, the teachers reported unanimously that this capacity-building aspect was the best part of the process. Specifically, their participation in the study gave them ideas for lessons and assessments that they could take back to their respective districts and use to bring their colleagues on board. Because teachers were central to the design-based cycles from the conception of the project onward, the participants did not feel that they were being "talked down to" or required to follow a particular curriculum or assessment in a top-down fashion. Instead, teachers were provided with opportunities to share their best ideas through ongoing engagement in a community of professional practice (see Lo, Adams, Goodell, & Nachtigal, this volume).

In light of these successes attributable to our collaborative process of design, we present here a model encapsulating the main steps in this process that others can use in future efforts to develop authentic forms of assessment.

1. Professional development I: Creating a common vision for the designed assessments and for future PD.
2. Review of existing teaching practices and drafting of authentic PAs.
3. Professional development II: Learning how to implement the new PAs.
4. Revision of PAs based on teacher feedback.
5. Field-testing of assessments and analysis of classroom data.
6. Feedback from expert panel.
7. Revision of PAs based on field-test and expert panel.
8. Second field test and analysis of classroom data.
9. Professional development III: Reflecting on and revising the PAs.

Professional development, or capacity building, is the end goal of this design process, even though in real life the cycles of revision, analysis, and professional development may never end. The goal is not simply to "perfect" the performance assessments. This outlook keeps the experience of the teacher front-and-center. Authentic assessments work against the mass-produced bubble-sheet regime that keeps the tests under lock and key. As such, authentic PAs rely on a design process that involves teachers every step of the way. The iterative nature of DBR is what makes that model possible.

Conclusions

This study effectively ended when the school board policy changed, moving the PA development process into the hands of school districts. However, the project proved successful even as events changed. It helped grow teacher–leaders, build local capacity for PA creation, establish model PAs in economics, and lay out a design process that others could replicate.

Some general thoughts about design-based research methodology are also in order. Perhaps ironically, while DBR usually requires a long and drawn-out research process, each stage of data analysis can seem to come in a rush. Projects demand that the design team "iterate fast" in the initial stages of research and development so as to "constrain attempts to lose direction, motivation, and drive" (Funk, 2016, p. 358). Researchers must be prepared to begin analysis of new data immediately upon collecting it. They must plan for the rigmarole of data entry, transcription, coding, and revisiting literature if a DBR project is to maintain agility. If a full quantitative analysis is not feasible between each iteration, researchers must prepare some plausible step (e.g., recording analytic memos or collecting graded student work) that will allow for comparison across iterations. One way to lessen this burden is to keep the initial product simple. That is, the boundaries of the innovation being developed, tested, and revised must be clear and pragmatic. Researchers should be wary of building an entire set of educational materials before an initial round of testing.

Field-testing early also allows for glaring issues to be identified while they can still easily be addressed. As others have found, such oversights are easier to commit in assessment creation than one might expect (Breakstone, 2014). Perhaps more importantly, the DBR process has the potential to identify unforeseen opportunities for innovations in the design. After all, the point is not to avoid disasters, but to create ambitious innovations that push at the frontiers of educational practice.

Lastly, this study provided an example of how DBR can be used in the complex context of shifting educational policy, classroom practice, and assessment reform in elementary social studies. No matter how detailed the research plan was, the study was subject to changes based on external factors, such as the state legislature modifying its plan for assessment accountability, and school districts statewide having varying approaches to implementing the policy. DBR is enacted in real time. However, responding to real-time changes creates challenges for conducting rigorous, systematic research activities. It can be difficult to rein in the many moving parts and to organize them into coherent findings.

On the other hand, the unscripted nature of DBR is also an asset, for it allows the methodology to capture the world's uncertain realities. In traditional before-and-after research methods, a change in policy or inconsistency in implementation can doom a study. In DBR, it may simply be a new wrinkle in a design iteration, which carries with it the potential for more unexpected findings. In the case of this study, flexibility in product design led to widely differing local implementations. Though this was initially frustrating, the collaborative design-based approach allowed for both flexibility and continuity from school district to school district. Most importantly, the teachers on the design team brought their experiences home to their districts, becoming leaders and innovators in a more authentic approach to social studies assessment.

Note

1 The fifth criterion was "Data analysis skills" (see Figure 4.2). Only PA1 required that skill.

References

Anderson, T., & Shattuck, J. (2012). Design-based research: A decade of progress in education research? *Educational Researcher*, *41*(1), 16–25.
Banilower, E. R., Boyd, S. E., Pasley, J. D., & Weiss, I. R. (2006, February). Lessons from a decade of mathematics and science reform: A capstone report for the Local Systemic Change through Teacher Enhancement Initiative. Chapel Hill, NC: Horizon Research, Inc. Retrieved from http://www.pdmathsci.net/reports/capstone.pdf

Barab, S., & Squire, K. (2004). Design-based research: Putting a stake in the ground. *Journal of Learning Sciences, 13*(1), 1–14.

Bland, L. M., & Gareis, C. R. (2018). Performance assessments: A review of definitions, quality characteristics, and outcomes associated with their use in k-12 schools. *Teacher Educators' Journal, 11*, 52–69.

Blank, R. K., & De Las Alas, N. (2009). *The effects of teacher professional development on gains in student achievement: How meta analysis provides scientific evidence useful to education leaders.* Washington, DC: Council of Chief State School Officers.

Breakstone, J. (2014). Try, try, try again: The process of designing new history assessments. *Theory & Research in Social Education, 42*(4), 453–485.

Brown, A. B. (2010). *Middle school minisociety: Student achievement* (Doctoral dissertation, Walden University). Retrieved from ProQuest Dissertations and Theses. (Accession Order No. AAT 3412935)

Bryk, A. S., Gomez, L. M., Grunow, A., & LeMahieu, P. G. (2015). *Learning to improve: How America's schools can get better at getting better.* Cambridge, MA: Harvard Education Press.

Carr, M. M. (2003). *An investigation into implementation of the Mini-Society instructional program* (Doctoral dissertation, The University of Kansas). Retrieved from KU Scholar Works. (http://hdl.handle.net/1808/7773)

Cassuto, A. E. (1980). The effectiveness of the elementary school Mini-Society program. *Journal of Economic Education, 11*(2), 59–61.

Charmaz, K. (2006). *The construction of grounded theory: A practical guide through qualitative analysis.* Thousand Oaks, CA: Sage.

Cobb, P., Confrey, J., diSessa, A., Lehrer, R., & Schauble, L. (2003). Design experiments in educational research. *Educational Researcher, 32*(1), 9–13.

Day, S. H. (2015). *How elementary teachers use classroom mini-economies when guided by the C3 Framework.* (Doctoral dissertation, North Carolina State University). Retrieved from ProQuest Dissertations and Theses. (Accession Order No. AAT 10110536)

Design-based Research Collective. (2003). Design-based research: An emerging paradigm for educational inquiry. *Educational Researcher, 32*(1), 5–8.

Funk, M. (2016). Design and data: Strategies for designing information products in team settings. In P. Markopoulos, J. Martens, J. Malins, K. Coninx, & A. Liapis, (Eds.) *Collaboration in creative design.* Switzerland: Springer.

Ge, X., & Land, S. (2003). Scaffolding students' problem-solving processes in an ill-structured task using question prompts and peer interactions. *Educational Technology Research and Development, 51*(1), 21–38.

Kourilsky, M. L. (1983). *Mini-society, experiencing real-world economics in the elementary school classroom.* Reading, PA: Addison-Wesley Publishing Company.

Kourilsky, M. L., and Ballard-Campbell, M. (1984). Sex differences in a simulated classroom economy. *Sex Roles: A Journal of Research, 10*(1&2), 53–66.

Kourilsky, M. L., and Graff, E. E. (1985). Children's use of cost-benefit analysis: Developmental or non-existent. In S. Hodkinson and D. Whitehead (Eds.), *Economic education: Research and development issues* (pp. 127–39). Essex, England: Longman Group, Ltd.

Kourilsky, M. L., and Hirshleifer, J. (1976). Mini-society vs. token economy: An experimental comparison of the effects on learning and autonomy of socially emergent and imposed behavior modification. *Journal of Educational Research, 69*(10), 376–381.

Landis, J. R., & Koch, G. G. (1977). The measurement of observer agreement for categorical data. *Biometrics*, 159–174.

Marri, A. R. (2016). Fostering economic literacy for K-12 students through the College, Career, and Civic Life (C3) Framework. In M.B. Henning (Ed.), *Innovations in economic education: Promising practices for teachers and students, K–16* (pp. 171–184). New York, NY: Taylor & Francis.

McKenney, S. E., & Reeves, T. C. (2012). *Conducting educational design research.* New York, NY: Routledge.

McTighe, J. (April, 2015). What is a performance task? Retrieved from https://blog. performancetask.com/what-is-a-performance-task-part-1-9fa0d99ead3b

National Council for the Social Studies [NCSS] (2013). *Social studies for the next generation: Purposes, practices, and implications of the College, Career, and Civic Life (C3) Framework.* Maryland: NCSS.

Newmann, F., Marks, H., & Gamoran, A. (1996). Authentic pedagogy and student performance. *American Journal of Education, 104*(4), 280–312.

Newmann, F. M., & Wehlage, G. (1993). Five standards of authentic instruction. *Educational Leadership, 50*(7), 8–12.

Saye, J. W. (2017). Disciplined inquiry in the social studies classroom. In M. M. Manfra, & C. B. Bolick (Eds.), *The Wiley handbook of social studies research* (pp. 336–359). Malden, MA: Wiley and Sons.

Schug, M. (1981). What educational research says about the development of economic thinking. *Theory and Research in Social Education, 9*(3), 25–36.

Schwab, J. (1966). *The teaching of science.* Cambridge, MA: Harvard University Press.

Swan, K., Lee, J. K., Mueller, R., & Day, S. (2014). *Teaching the College, Career, and Civic Life (C3) Framework: Exploring inquiry-based instruction in social studies.* Washington, DC: National Council for the Social Studies.

Thornton, S. J. (1991). Teacher as curricular-instructional gatekeeper in social studies. In J. P. Shaver (Ed.), *Handbook of research on social studies teaching and learning* (pp. 237–248). New York: Macmillan.

Thornton, S. J. (2008). Continuity and change in social studies curriculum. In S. Levstik, & C. Tyson (Eds.), *Handbook of research in social studies education* (pp. 15–32). New York: Routledge.

Virginia Department of Education [VDOE] (2017). Performance Based Assessments. Retrieved from www.doetest.virginia.gov/instruction/professional-learning/performance-based-assessment/index.shtml

Wiggins, G. (1989). A true test: Toward more authentic and equitable assessment. *Phi Delta Kappan, 70*(9), 703–713.

Wiggins, G. P., & McTighe, J. (2005). *Understanding by design.* Alexandria, VA: ASCD.

PART II
Using and Producing Theory

5

APPLYING THEORY TO PROBLEMATIC PRACTICE

Lessons Learned from Two Implementations of a Unit on Gender

Jennifer Burke

Theory is vital to design-based research (DBR), since theory informs the initial design of an educational intervention and is then applied during data analysis. This chapter features a DBR project in which I (acting as both researcher and practitioner) used theory to uncover flaws in the implementation of a "critical gender " unit for elementary students, in which they were encouraged to challenge the gender binary through a series of "critical gender" lessons.

I selected this term "critical gender" as a label for my educational intervention since the intent was to get children to think critically about the ways they understood and experienced gender. I designed the critical gender unit to deepen young children's understanding of American gender stereotypes that are learned from peers, media, and society at large (Blakemore, Berenbaum, & Liben, 2009; Davies, 1989). The intervention aligned with the social justice goals I had previously pursued in my own elementary school classrooms. I hoped to combat the onslaught of stereotypical gender messaging that children receive from peers and society, by helping them learn to recognize and reject these limiting messages.

Theoretical Framework

Constructivist gender schema theory is used within developmental psychology to explain how a child's cognitive development combines with societal influences to create patterns of thought (schema) that prescribe "male" and "female" traits (Bem, 1981; Coyle & Liben, 2016; Hillard & Liben, 2010; Martin & Halverson, 1981). According to this theory, when a child experiences something that does not fit into their previously established schema, they experience cognitive dissonance (Festinger, 1968). At this point, children need to either change their initial gendered thought or dismiss what they are experiencing as an "incorrect" display of gender (Bem, 1981).

Feminist poststructuralist theory describes gender as a process that individuals engage in daily, and it questions the necessity of the male/female binary. In this theory, gender is something that one "does" through everyday social relations (Davies 1989; Paechter, 2007; Renold, 2005; Walkerdine & Lucey, 1989; West & Zimmerman, 1987). The selection of preferences, such as style of dress, toys, and recreational activities are all ways of children "doing" their gender. Much like gender schema theory, poststructuralist theory does not assume gender is bio-logical, nor that it is a socialization process imposed on young children by more knowledgeable adults (Davies, 1989; Paechter, 2007; Renold, 2005; Walkerdine & Lucey, 1989). Rather, children themselves are actively constructing their own understandings of gender through their discourse (socially organized frameworks of knowledge and meaning; Renold, 2005). Applying a feminist poststructuralist perspective, the students in this study constructed their concept of gender within their society, and were therefore limited by the discourse available to them. This discourse limited how they understood what it means to be masculine or femi-nine in the context of creating their own gendered identities (Davies, 1989; Connell & Messerschmidt, 2005).

The theoretical limitation here is also a practical one. How can an adult encourage children to see beyond the gender binary that permeates all of society? If children process information in terms of feminine and masculine, how can one get young children to see that those two categories are not necessarily the only two that exist? When children arrived in my elementary classroom, they had already had years of experience shaping their own gender schemas. As an educa-tor, I found myself struggling with ways to get students to challenge this binary because I did not have many available options for operating outside of it. This became highly problematic, as I will address in this chapter.

Recognizing and addressing the problems associated with stereotypical gender messages is important for many reasons. Children who feel atypical in relation to gender can experience psychological distress (Egan & Perry, 2001). Peers may aggravate this distress, pressuring each other to conform to specific gender roles. Decades of research indicate that young children see the world through a rigid male/female gender binary (Davies, 1989; Bem, 1981). Children themselves often police these boundaries. In a school setting, this is accomplished through verbal means, such as name-calling or rude comments, as well as through non-verbal means, such as exclusion from play activities or group conversations (Davies, 1989; Pahlke, Bigler, & Martin, 2014; Killen et al., 2002).

Another reason to implement a critical gender curriculum is to combat sexism—discrimination based on a person's sex or gender that is linked to ste-reotypes and gender roles. Sexism negatively impacts not only individual victims but everyone in society by being exclusionary. Sexism has been shown to impact which jobs children believe to be appropriate for a specific gender, thus limiting their future career trajectories from early childhood onward (Coyle & Liben, 2016). For example, in the United States there is widespread interest in the need to increase the number of women pursuing careers in science, technology, engineering, and mathematics (STEM), but disinterest in STEM begins in early childhood for many girls because they do not view these positions as feminine (Coyle & Liben, 2016). Sexism is not limited to social domains, but also impacts psychological domains, like the negative impact that exclusively encouraging aggression has on young boys' emotional development (Pascoe, 2007).

This study is also situated within feminist pedagogy, an overarching philosophy of education that aims towards social change. Feminist pedagogy stems from consciousness-raising groups starting in the late 1960s and 1970s and is now widely found in Women's Studies courses at the university level (Weiler, 1991). It has been applied to elementary students since at least the 1990s (Brady, 1995). Freire (1970/1993) and feminist educators understand that consciousness raising is the first step to creating revolutionary change (Weiler, 1991). Thus, my critical gender unit attempted to start by promoting consciousness raising among my students. Discussions about unfair stereotypes that the students and their families had encountered would allow my young learners to share their experiences and feelings. For instance, when I shared the stereotype that only men should work outside the home, the children were able to share countless examples from their own families of mothers, aunts, sisters, and grandmothers who worked outside the home.

All this theory and literature led to the creation of a DBR study, through which I aimed to document and describe the way children experienced gender when taught a critical gender curriculum. The following section describes this project.

Research Design

The study unfolded in several stages. It began with the initial review of relevant literature concerning educating young children on gender and societal inequities. In the second stage, I drew upon my 11 years of early-childhood teaching experience to construct a series of developmentally appropriate critical gender lessons. These interactive lessons aimed to foster students' questioning of society's rigid gender binary through exploration of stereotypes they commonly experienced (e.g., toys, sports, media) and by using children's literature to introduce the ideas of being transgender and gender expansive. In the third stage of the project, the researcher became the practitioner, as I implemented and video-recorded six weeks of critical gender lessons. The lessons ranged from 30 to 50 minutes in duration. I wrote daily field memos and used them to refine my future lessons and activities.

I taught two iterations of the educational intervention. The first was in a first-grade classroom and the second in a third-grade classroom. Both iterations took place in a suburban elementary school that served approximately 950 students from preschool to fifth grade. In both classrooms I worked as the special-education teacher in an inclusive, co-teaching model.

There were 17 students in the first-grade classroom: seven girls and ten boys. Nine students qualified for free or reduced lunch, and, at the time of the study, the school district identified one of the students as homeless. Four of the students qualified for special-education services. In addition, the children were racially and ethnically diverse. Four of the students were Latino, four were white, three were African American, three were multiracial, two were Indian American, and one student was Filipino American. The general education teacher in this classroom was a white woman in her late twenties. There were 21 students in the third-grade class, 12 girls and nine boys. Eleven students qualified for free or reduced lunch. Six of the students were Latino, eight were white, five were African American, one was biracial, and one was of North African descent. Both the general education teacher and I were white women in our early thirties.

Since I served as both the researcher and the educator in this study, some might label this action research. There are, in fact, many similarities between DBR and action research (see Kim, this volume). Anderson and Shattuck (2012) point out that both modes of research fall into the category of applied research. They state, "good science often leads to very practical outcomes while contributing to theoretical and basic understandings" (p. 17). The aim of this study was to document and describe how children experienced a critical gender curriculum, in the hope of contributing to understandings of educational interventions aimed at challenging children's ideas about the gender binary and the limitations of gender stereotypes.

The key difference between action research and this study is this study's firm grounding in a feminist poststructuralist perspective. The study was based on the feminist poststructuralist concept that individuals are simultaneously creating and enacting their gender identities through their discourse. This undergirded my aim to create a curriculum to allow for discourse within which students might question previously held gender assumptions. My intention was to "advance, uncover, explore, and confirm" (Barab & Squire, 2004, p. 5) how children experienced gender. Although constructed locally, gender is a global phenomenon; in addressing this broad theme, this project goes beyond action research, which tends to aim toward meeting a local need.

The lessons were recorded, then transcribed and coded using discourse analysis. I used microethnography, defined by Atkinson, Okada, and Talmy (2011) as "ethnographic microanalysis of audiovisual recordings [as] a means of specifying the learning environments and processes of social influence as they occur in face-to-face interaction" (p. 91). Microethnographic discourse analysis proved exceptionally useful because it was at this analysis stage of the project that problems in my practice became evident.

In line with the iterative nature of DBR, I identified problems between the first and second integration that allowed me to alter my approach. For example, the videos revealed that the first graders continually saw nothing harmful in gender stereotypes. In fact, even after the lesson they continued to police classroom behaviors among themselves, such as suggesting to the new boy in the classroom that boys should use blue paper and only girls should choose pink. This led me to increase the focus on stereotypes in the second iteration, and add an entire week's worth of lessons that explored the limitations of gender stereotypes.

Post-implementation, microethnographic discourse analysis from the second iteration allowed me to further apply theory to problematize my practice. This revealed deeper problems with my practice that could theoretically apply to all classrooms attempting to address gender inequities. I discuss these problems in the "Tales from the Classroom" section below.

Design Principles Driving the Intervention

The critical gender curriculum that I created and implemented in this study was built using Freirean critical pedagogy (1970/1993). Critical pedagogy focuses on questioning the established order of society so that education does not contribute to the reproduction of inequality, but instead can lead to social change. This curriculum pursued Freire's intention of liberation from oppression, and so the focus became students' lived experiences with gender stereotypes. I attempted to apply Freire's concept of conscientization, in which a new technique is learned that contains a critique of present circumstances in an attempt to overcome these circumstances (Gadotti & Torres, 2009). The intention was that by exploring the limitations of gender stereotypes, the students would undergo a "liberation process" where they would be able to recognize and rid themselves of the influences of the dominant consciousness. Ideally, after completing this unit, students would be able to recognize the gender inequality they faced in their lives. I had extremely high expectations for my young learners, and I hoped that once armed with insight gained from their critical gender discussions, students would refuse to allow this inequality to limit their thinking or alter their behavior to conform to current gender norms. They would also become more tolerant of peers who did not conform to those norms.

Derman-Sparks (2008; Derman-Sparks & Edward, 2010) notes that all children are harmed when spoken and unspoken messages about difference are absorbed without their being considered and questioned. In the critical gender curriculum, I applied this concept by constructing a series of lessons in which students discussed stereotypes they had experienced, and in which they debated the validity of these stereotypes with their peers.

Few research studies have focused on critical gender classroom experiences. Pahlke, Bigler, and Martin (2014) implemented elementary lessons focusing on gender-based exclusion, role-based stereotyping, and unequal gender relationships. Children were directly taught a phrase (or phrases) to challenge the type of bias they were learning about, such as "Give it a rest, no group is best!" or "There is no such thing as a girls' (boys')_____" (p. 130). Children in this study were able to identify sexism in media, such as a scene they were shown of *Rudolph* in which boy and girl elves perform a song for Santa in gender-separated groups.

Also notable is a single-class case study focusing on the use of anti-bias educational goals during a second-grade language arts unit (Allen, 1997). The unit began with a discussion of what it means to be "fair." The class then listened to different accounts of an event that happened on the playground. They used this experience to create definitions of bias and equity. All activities were built around the anti-bias goal of recognizing unfairness and appreciating various perspectives. Gender inequality was one aspect of fairness explored by Allen's class.

I drew on Allen's approach as I created the unit for my study. Specifically, I used children's literature as the vehicle for introducing complex topics of inequality (Copenhaver-Johnson, 2006; Hinton, 2004; Schieble, 2012; Boutte, Lopez-Robertson, & Powers-Costello, 2011). Although this was not a language arts unit—I created it to meet district and state social studies goals and objectives—I selected literature as the main mode of introducing the concept of gender and gender stereotypes.

I shared this literature via whole-class read-alouds, a teaching technique where the teacher sits in front of the entire class and orally reads a book with the students, stopping periodically to check for understanding. Morgan (2009) advocates the use of read-alouds because culturally authentic children's books contain difficult subjects that might be best examined with adult guidance. As teachers interact with students during read-alouds, they can lead discussions on concepts like race, culture, and discrimination. Focusing on these concepts can make them meaningful for young students (Banks, 1994). Adults can model respectful ways to discuss challenging topics and can serve as moderators to facilitate meaningful dialogue. When using literature, it is recommended that a combination of works of fiction and nonfiction be used to ensure that issues are not presented and viewed as unreal, and to provide concrete and authentic information (Boutte et al., 2011). When selecting works, I was careful to select authentic sources from multiple perspectives on topics pertaining to gender.

Despite the wide range of independent reading levels in the classroom, the children were able to have a shared experience to draw upon for the critical gender discussions that were an integral part of the intervention. Brookfield and Preskill (1999) and Rubin (2011) advocate discussion as an important pedagogical method essential to democratic citizenship. The first- and third-grade students were expected to verbalize their ideas. They developed this skill as they listened to their classmates and considered their perspectives while forming their own thoughts and opinions.

One structured-discussion technique used in the unit was the "take-a stand" discussion strategy. I used it to get children to share their relevant experiences by encouraging them to take both a literal and metaphorical stance on a continuum. In take-a-stand, the teachers pose questions, while students, who are standing, choose where to position themselves along a continuum according to how they feel about that issue. While standing, the students then take turns sharing their justification for why they took that stance. Most of the children in this study cited either their families or entertainment (TV shows or movies) as their sources of information. Often the conversations would grow contentious, as children disagreed about issues such as who could/should play professional sports. My co-teacher and I reminded them of the importance of hearing what their classmates were saying before interjecting their counterarguments. I could tell this approach was highly engaging to the learners because one afternoon I announced it was time for social studies and one student enthusiastically called out, "Great! Do we get to argue today?" Although she saw the take-a-stand activity as delightful arguing, I hoped it was fostering the students' ability to listen to peers and verbalize their own perspectives.

Sharing children's literature and child-centered discussions became the foundation of my critical gender curriculum and provided the data that led me to realize the problems with this particular approach to educating about gender.

Tales from the Classroom

In using microethnographic discourse analysis to explore how the children in my classroom were thinking about gender, I began to notice shortcomings in the intervention I had created—in both the first iteration (done with first graders) and the second iteration (done with third graders). The following sections detail these realizations.

Retaining a Gender Binary

The first phenomena that became obvious in iteration one was that the first graders were deeply entrenched in the gender binary. I saw this clearly during the whole class read-aloud of *10,000 Dresses* (Ewert, 2008). I had selected this picture-book as a read-aloud because it features a protagonist, Bailey, who is transgender. Despite Bailey's constant dreaming about dresses throughout the book, she is told, "You are a boy." Bailey insists, "I don't feel like a boy." The book has a happy ending, because Bailey finds an older girl who makes dresses with him. She tells Bailey, "You are the coolest girl I know." I selected this book to encourage the young learners to realize that some people do not wish to identify as the gender they are assigned. I also selected it to push children to realize that rigid gender-binary behavioral expectations limit the range of interests a person can have (i.e. girls are the only ones allowed to like dresses). The intent was to get children to dismantle their own gender-binary thinking and begin to see gender as more fluid and loosely defined.

As noted above, if a child witnesses a behavior that is incongruent with their gender schema, the child will often experience cognitive dissonance. I observed this with the first graders when I introduced *10,000 Dresses*. As always, I introduced the book by showing the children the cover. Immediately, brows furrowed, heads tilted, and some children pursed their lips as they struggled to understand the image on the cover. Most students found the character on the cover, with short spiked blonde hair and wearing long sparkly dress, to be too contradictory to comprehend. How could the two paradoxical accoutrements exist at the same time? Even before I began reading, the students were struggling to fit this image into their neatly defined gender binary. While some students were initially confused, others smirked, suppressed laughter, or giggled openly. When asked "What is so funny?" they pointed to the cover, saying, "He is wearing a dress!" Another student curled his lip and said, "Ew!"

These comments can be explained using gender schema theory. I had hoped the cognitive dissonance the students were experiencing was an opportunity to alter their previously held binary schema. I wanted them to see the protagonist and realize that not everyone fits neatly into the schemas they had constructed as "boy" or "girl." However, instead of making an accommodation and expanding their idea of appropriate gender behavior, these first graders pushed back against this change to their schema. They used mockery, laughter, and insults in an effort to eradicate the dissonance. Davies (1993) calls these behaviors *category maintenance* work. Category maintenance is how students reify the gender binary, and despite my intentions it was happening before I even began to read the book.

I remember being optimistic that after listening to the book and experiencing the main character's struggle, the first graders' category maintenance would cease. Yet the post-reading results were mixed. Some children ardently supported Bailey's right to choose her gender. One first grader declared, "She can be a girl if she wants to." But other first graders said the book was "bad" and suggested that Bailey's brother was justified in his threat to kick Bailey.

This result was horribly inconsistent with my original intention of getting the children to see the limitations of gender-binary thinking. Their responses, however, made sense when analyzed through a feminist poststructuralist perspective. The students had limited discourse available to them that was un-gendered. Even basic sentence structure became challenging, due to English language pronouns. When attempting to provide a summary of *10,000 Dresses*, for example, a first grader said, "No, he's dreaming that—no she's dreaming that she's a—no, he's dreaming that he's, no, she that—but he's a she. NO. He's dreaming that he's a she." This student was attempting to explain that the main character had dreams where "he" was able to be a "she" and wear beautiful dresses. While this first grader was perhaps cognitively capable of understanding this concept of a gender non-conforming character, he struggled to express it clearly because of the limitations of English gender pronouns, and of the binary categories they represent.

During the second iteration of the study (with third graders), I decided to place this lesson after a series of other lessons that addressed stereotypes. I felt that after the third-grade class had debated who should be allowed to wear various types of clothing and had identified the assumption that only girls should wear dresses and only boys should wear hats as problematic, that they would be better prepared to experience a protagonist who was transgender.

Even after these lessons, though, the conversations that occurred during and after reading *10,000 Dresses* to the third graders demonstrated to some extent the same cognitive dissonance evident in the responses of the first graders. While reading the book, the third graders could not come to terms with the fact that the protagonist did not fall neatly into their gender schema. They tried multiple means to determine the protagonist's gender, using hair (the character had short hair), clothing (the character dreamed of wearing dresses, but had shorts on in daytime illustrations), and first name (Bailey) as gender clues. As they struggled to fit Bailey into existing gender schema, one student called out, "I'm so confused! Is it a boy or a girl?" Another student, while reading, called out, "Oh my gosh! This is a dream," thinking that he could eliminate the gender inconsistency by classifying it as make-believe. Near the conclusion of the book, students were very upset that they had yet to place the character into the category of boy or girl. They called out things like, "Is she a boy or a girl?" and "When are you going to tell us?" Upon realizing the book was over, students shouted out, "What?!!" "This is horrible!" "But I'm confused!" and "I just can't!" The third graders' annoyance was palpable. The book did not conform to their gender schema, and their difficulty fitting Bailey into their preconceived ideas of boy or girl caused them great distress.

In that moment, I decided I needed to add another book that featured a gender nonconforming protagonist. The following day I read the third graders *My Princess Boy* (Kilodavis & DeSimone, 2010). This book is told from the point of view of a little boy's mother. The mother explains how much her son likes dresses and concludes by asking the reader if he or she will choose to laugh or play with a "Princess Boy." This book elicited an entirely different reaction than did *10,000 Dresses*. It caused no outbursts or issues; the children sat silently and listened. When I asked the class which book they liked better, they all agreed on *My Princess Boy*. When asked why, Daniella called out, "Because we know he is a boy that likes dresses. Fine." The students found this book more palatable because they understood that it was about a boy who liked dresses. There was no cognitive dissonance because they did not have to wrestle with gender ambiguity. They could choose to expand their gender schema for this individual, because the book made clear that it was the kind thing to do. Based on the book, the third graders seemed to understand that they should not laugh when they came across a "princess boy."

When I analyzed the third graders' responses to both books, I realized my presentation of *10,000 Dresses* was problematic. I was trying to break the children's binary thinking, so when they asked me questions like "Is it a boy or a girl?" I deliberately did not respond. I shrugged or said, "What do you think?" My attempt to dismantle the binary caused cognitive dissonance, which resulted in category maintenance that unintentionally reinforced the binary. To fit Bailey into their pre-established gender schema, the children paid close attention to the words and illustrations of *10,000 Dresses* in the hope that they would be able to determine the truth of the main character's gender. The students' annoyance at the end of the book signaled a failure in their ability to determine the gender, and my failure at dismantling binary thinking. If I were to implement a third iteration of the intervention, I would present the book differently and remove the ambiguity. I would begin with explaining that Bailey was assigned the gender "male" at birth, and so everyone thinks Bailey is a boy even though Bailey does not feel like one. Perhaps then I could accomplish the goal of getting the children to realize how limiting and damaging it can be to force an individual into the gender binary.

Classroom Constructions of Masculinity

According to feminist poststructuralist theory, the individual cannot stand apart from the societal implications of gender. Connell (2010; Connell & Messerschmidt, 2005) similarly contends that masculinities do not exist prior to social behavior. When I initially designed and implemented the first and second iterations, I did not really factor in masculinity. Historians and anthropologists agree that there are multiple masculinities in any given society depending on time period, social class, and ethnicity. However, usually there is one form of masculinity that is the most highly regarded. Connell (1995) labels this most prized form of male gender expression *hegemonic masculinity*. In Western society, the hegemonic masculinity that is valued is aggressive, heterosexual, and tied to athletic prowess (Pascoe, 2007). Although not a part of my initial design, hegemonic masculinity revealed itself as a very important factor during data analysis. This section will demonstrate how masculinity was constructed in my classrooms through a series of conversations on "tomboys."

Throughout the lessons on stereotypes, the third graders used the term "tomboy" to refer to a girl who did not choose to conform to feminine gender expectations. In both the first- and third-grade classrooms, the title "tomboy" was something most of the girls tried to prove they deserved. Third-grade students began using the term "tomboy" to label characters in books, movies, TV shows, classmates, or themselves. Since the third graders were using the term tomboy more than the first graders had in the first iteration, I decided to explore this term further with them during the second iteration of the curriculum. I positioned the third-grade students as "the experts" and asked them to help the teachers understand the term "tomboy."

When I first introduced the term, the students were very eager to help define it. I wrote the word on the whiteboard, and immediately there was a buzz about the classroom. One student called out, "I know that word." Other students remarked, "Oh, that word," and "Oh, I know what a tomboy means." Several girls were quick to self-identify as a tomboy. When I asked what one was, Taylor shouted out, "Hint! Hint! Me! Me!" Leeann explained, "What a tomboy does and looks like? They dress like a boy. And how they act—like how they say boys act like boys, instead girls act like boys instead of girls." Here Leeann used her gender schema to define a tomboy. According to her, there were boy-expectations for behavior, which were in contrast to girl-expectations. A tomboy was a girl who chose to exhibit the expected behaviors of a boy.

The children further defined what it means to be masculine by describing the male traits tomboys exhibit. Marshall suggested activities, saying, "Um, they like to go hunting and they also like to get muddy." Madelyn provided another layer on what tomboys like to do. "Um . . . it's kinda like a girl that only likes playing with boys and she likes being rough and playing a lot of sports." Here, the students were again using personal preference for activities and clothing as means of expressing the gendered identities of tomboys.

This pattern was seen also in the conversations they had while drawing images of tomboys later in the lesson, and in the drawings themselves (Figure 5.1). Clothing preferences viewed as boyish included athletic apparel and not dresses. Activity preferences included sports, Legos, hunting, getting muddy, interest in space, and playing with boys instead of girls. Once again, the children were reifying the gender binary by attributing specific preferences and characteristics to one gender, in this case males.

The children also used the term "girlie-girl." They defined this as the hyper-feminine opposite to the masculine behavior they were told to draw. In an attempt

FIGURE 5.1 Both Drawings Are from a Third Grade Boy. The Left Image Is of a "tomboy." The Right Image Is of a "tomgirl." The Caption on the Right Reads, "Tomgirl: A boy who lost his mind."

to unpack this term, I asked the class what "girlie-girl" meant. One student said, "It's a girl that acts like a girl." Another female student offered an impersonation where she twirled her hair and used a high-pitched voice, "and [they] go hah hah." I asked the class if they thought a girlie-girl was the opposite of a tomboy. Most students nodded their heads or verbally agreed. No one disagreed.

Since the class now had created two extremes, tomboy and girlie-girl, it seemed like a natural time to use the established classroom practice of staging a "take-a-stand" continuum discussion. On one side of the classroom, the term "tomboy" was posted, on the opposite side, "girlie-girl," with room for lots of variation in between. Taylor ran to the extreme left, where the tomboys were positioned. Every single girl (with the exception of Kimberly, who elected not to pick a position) positioned themselves in the middle or to the left near the tomboy side. No students self-identified as girlie-girl.

The girls were given a chance to explain why they selected their positions on the continuum. Taya, who stood near the middle, said, "Because I'm a girl and I do girl stuff but I also like to play sports a lot." Her response was androcentric, meaning that she assumed a male point of view was central and that "girl stuff" was a deviation (Bem, 1993). Taya and several of her classmates separated "girl stuff" as a sex-specific deviation from an allegedly universal standard. She liked to play sports, which she considered both a male behavior and something that deviated from "doing femininity" properly.

Many of the other girls also indicated that they enjoyed engaging in behaviors they considered masculine. Girls used their occasional desire to wear dresses as evidence of their femininity, but still indicated that they preferred male things. "I'm in both because usually in the summer I have, I wear, dresses sometimes and um . . . I do sports." By choosing to identify as both feminine and masculine, these girls were trying to reap the benefits of both genders. They realized as girls they were expected to "do" their gender correctly, which included occasionally liking "girl" things like dresses and playing with other girls.

According to her position on the continuum, Ariel was the most extreme girl, but even she was just slightly right of center. She explained, "Um because I'm a little bit of both, but I'm a little more like a girlier, like a little bit." Ariel often wore dresses to school and frequently talked about engaging in activities the children considered feminine, such as playing with dolls and doing crafts. Her desire to label herself as "a little bit of both" is evidence of the power of androcentrism in this classroom. There was no social status to be gained by strongly asserting femininity. On the contrary, selecting male items as a preference was a way for girls to achieve higher status.

For many of the girls in the classroom, identifying as a tomboy was liberating. Riley (almost all the way over near "tomboy" on the continuum) said,

> The reason why I am like a tomboy is because like, like sometimes my brother hands me hand-me-downs and I'm crazy and I like and I don't, and because, um, sometimes it—like I play a lot of sports, like I play basketball.

Riley's use of the term "crazy" implied a wildness that males are permitted to engage in and females are not. To be feminine is to show restraint, but to be wild and therefore "crazy" was a privilege only males are afforded, and therefore it was desirable for girls.

The third-grade girls showed a strong desire to identify as tomboys. To them, this label meant the freedom to engage in physical activities that they enjoyed but were labeled as "for boys." Through adopting these "for boys" behaviors, the girls could gain social standing among their peers. This shows that femininity in the classroom community was not as valuable as masculinity. Many of the girls desired the masculine label of "tomboy," but none of the males wanted to take on feminine traits.

Why did the boys not value femininity? The answer can be seen by further exploring the benefits of masculinity. While drawing a tomboy, third grader Michael declared, "I'm adding some other things, like smoking." When the teacher asked, "You think that tomboys smoke?" Michael started erasing because he thought he was "caught" drawing something inappropriate. It was interesting that his definition of masculinity involved elements he believed to be inappropriate. His drawing was consistent with his earlier definition of what it meant to be a boy: "Boys play hard and boys do sports. Stuff like that. And that's tomboy." Michael's language indicated that he defined masculinity as "tough" and even a little outside what was permissible in school (i.e., the "inappropriate activity" of smoking). Toughness was also reflected in his use of the term "play hard." Michael continued to define masculinity in terms of the freedom to break rules, to be reckless, and to destroy. As Michael explained, "Boys always do boy things, like they hang up, like they hang out whenever they want to, feel like doing. Being able to burn stuff down." Michael's definition of masculinity was consistent with those of other classmates, whose definition of hegemonic masculinity was a person who plays rough, engages in sports, and likes to be dirty.

In American society, there is a co-dependence between femininity and masculinity; neither can be fully understood in isolation from the other. They are seen as opposing forces (Davies, 1993; Reay, 2001; Connell & Messerschmidt, 2005). When masculinity is defined as reckless abandon and freedom, femininity is defined as the opposite: restraint and suppression. When that is the local understanding of gender, why would a young student choose the latter?

Reflecting on the Gender Continuum Activity

While implementing these take-a-stand activities, I thought I was pushing children to see the limitations of gender norms. In reality, I was acting counter to my own set purpose of getting children to dismantle the gender binary. It was not until I considered Kristeva's (1986) three tiers of the Women's Movement while engaged in data analysis that I realized my error. This feminist political framework describes a three-tier struggle, which both Davies (1989) and Kristeva see as simultaneous, necessary, and ongoing work. The first tier is a demand for access, which is the struggle for equality. The second is the need to use and subvert the male symbolic order (i.e. education and legal system). The third is to transcend the need for a rigid gender binary.

Davies (1989) argues that lack of progress in the third tier is due to the constant societal reification of the gender binary. It is tempting to say that the existence of tomboys is the beginning of this process. Through taking up the identity of "tomboy," some might argue that the girls were trying to achieve that third tier, in which multiple means of self-expression are possible. But a closer examination of the girls' language reveals that this was not the case. Tomboys are not operating outside of the patriarchal structure, but instead attempting to gain access to it by adopting male preferences. Gaining access is Kristeva's tier one. Tier one is still important for equity, because every individual should have access to whatever recreational activities they desire. However, the concern is that females are trying to achieve status by adopting patriarchal practices, for instance, in this classroom it was access to sports and adoption of a series of male preferences that led to the tomboy identity. This is not expanding access and creating multiple possibilities but is instead normalizing male patterns of behavior, attempting to achieve status through endorsing hegemonic masculinity. It is trying to "act male." This way of thinking is operating within the patriarchy, and not actively dismantling it.

When I was trying to get the third graders to discuss their gender during the take-a-stand activity, I asked the girls to line up according to how they self-identified. The students created the terms, with "tomboy" on one end of the spectrum and "girlie-girl" on the other. A third grader, Kimberly, added a further level of complication to this gender identification discussion when she asked, "What if you have no clue?" Since this lesson spontaneously evolved out of our discussion, I did not stop to apply feminist poststructuralist theory; I had not considered alternatives to the gender continuum that we had created. As Kimberly's teacher, I felt a strong instinct to avoid pressing her into assuming an identity she did not feel comfortable with. I complimented Kimberly for bringing up a "good point" and gave her the option of not participating, which she accepted. In hindsight, this hasty solution was exclusionary. Kimberly was isolated for her desire to function outside of the gender binary. In fact, she may have been demonstrating Kristeva's (1986) third tier and should have been celebrated rather than marginalized. I had created the unit to get children to recognize and speak up against rigid gender norms, yet in this situation I was so trapped by my own binary thinking that I failed to see Kimberly's resistance as the embodiment of what I was striving for. This insight was revealed to me months later during my data analysis.

What I did not account for while creating this study was that in trying to get children to expand their thinking about gender, I might inadvertently reify the binary. This became apparent during data analysis, particularly when reflecting on the continuum activities. By forcing children to position themselves along a boy–girl continuum, I was forcing them to make a choice about their gender identification and then display it in front of the entire class. Through this embodied activity, the gender binary may have become even more solidified in their cognition, contrary to my intentions.

So, how did this happen? For starters, the gender continuum activity began with separating the children into the two categories of boys and girls (since each gender lined up separately). The sheer act of sorting the children by gender reinforced for them that gender was a valid means of sorting individuals. It solidified the notion that gender came in binary options, "boy" or "girl," with no room for variation. This was also counter to my intention to highlight a range of gender possibilities and to expand students' thinking. Instead of stressing how fluid gender could be, I created two rigid categorizations.

The activity then forced children to consider their bodies and their own gender identities that they had constructed within the classroom community. Had they been presenting themselves in feminine clothing such as dresses? What did their hair length indicate? After considering how they physically embodied their gender, I then instructed them to physically stand before their classroom community as a representative of their gender. This would have been extremely problematic for any student questioning their own gender identity, such as a transgender child. But even for children who identify as the gender they were assigned at birth, this activity confirmed a binary understanding of gender.

Words matter. By defining femininity as somewhere on the continuum of "super girlie-girl" and "100% tomboy," the students and teachers were defining (and therefore limiting) the behavioral range of femininity. What had begun with the intention of encouraging students to explore their gender identities and see the limitations of projecting the gender binary onto their bodies and their identities had ended up having nearly the opposite effect. The take-a-stand activity forced female students into binary thinking (by having boys and girls line up as separate groups) and limited their range of behaviors by allowing peers to define correct ways of displaying femininity.

The activity also failed in its treatment of the male students. Masculinity is defined by dominance and control, and to assert their own masculinity boys engage in "fag discourse" (Pascoe, 2007). In Pascoe's study, fag discourse resulted when high-school students were insulting each other for doing something feminine. The boys in my classroom had already asserted that any boy who acted "like a girl" was defined as "crazy" or "had lost their mind."

Since I had heard this slightly sanitized third-grade version of the fag discourse, I should have realized that I was asking males to do something very difficult. By standing anywhere on the continuum besides the extreme hegemonic masculine side, I was setting children up to be objects of ridicule. Even if a boy had enjoyed playing with dolls at home with his cousins, he most likely would not have felt comfortable revealing this in a classroom where feminine behaviors had been constructed as inappropriate for boys.

Although this continuum activity did lead me to deep realizations about how children understand gender, it completely missed the original intention of the intervention: expanding children's thoughts beyond the binary. Analysis showed that the anti-bias curriculum failed to perform several important functions for the children that Freire (1970/1993) would have considered part of "ridding themselves of the dominant consciousness." First, the children in this study had a lot of difficulty expanding their binary view of gender. Even after reading about transgender individuals, they struggled with the idea that gender could be fluid, or that there were multiple gender options available. Students continued to express that, for gender, the only options were "boy" and "girl." How you "did" that gender was a matter of personal preference, but only those two fixed categories existed.

Conclusion

DBR's unique capacity to blend theory and practice while promoting cycles of improvement was central to this project. DBR requires the researcher to reflect back on the intervention through "retrospective analysis" (Edelson, 2002, p. 116; see also Wang & Hannafin, 2005). In these reflections, I drew on feminist poststructuralist theory, which allowed me grapple with the complexities of engaging and shifting young children's (and my own) taken-for-granted understandings of gender. Employing feminist poststructuralist theory ultimately allowed me to see where the curriculum I had created failed to align with my original goals of expanding students' understandings of gender and interrupting binary thinking.

If there were a third iteration of this study, I would alter the focus of the intervention to directly teach the children about the limitations of the gender binary. It is impossible to get children to think outside the gender binary unless you teach them what it is and explain how it impacts them. In addition to placing the emphasis on stereotypes and ranges of femininity and masculinity, I would also teach them the definition of "gender binary" and provide examples of how it positions males and females as opposites. The class would then explore how that is problematic, using insights from the fields of sociology and psychology. We would explore examples from children's literature of characters trapped in gender-specific behavior as a result of the binary, and children would have ample opportunities to share and compare their own experiences to raise their consciousness of the limitations of both the gender binary and gender stereotypes. I would encourage students to point out when they experienced the gender binary in their daily lives; hopefully this would interrupt binary thinking instead of reifying it.

References

Allen, A. (1997). Creating space for discussions about social justice and equity in an elementary classroom. *Progressive Education in Conservative Times*, 74 (7), 518–524.

Anderson, T., & Shattuck, J. (2012). Design-based research: A decade of progress in education research? *Educational Researcher*, 41(1), 16–25.

Atkinson, D., Okada, H., & Talmy, S. (2011). Ethnography and discourse analysis. In K. Hyland and B. Paltridge (Eds.), *Continuum companion to discourse analysis* (1st ed.) (pp. 85–100). New York, NY: Bloomsbury.

Banks, J. (1994). *An introduction to multicultural education.* Boston, MA: Allyn and Bacon.

Barab, S., & Squire, B. (2004). Design-based research: Putting a stake in the ground. *Journal of the Learning Sciences, 13*(1), 1–14.

Bem, S. L. (1981). Gender schema theory: A cognitive account of sex typing. *Psychological Review, 88*, 354–364. DOI:10.1037/0033295X88.4.354

Bem, S. L. (1993). *The lenses of gender: Transforming the debate on sexual inequality.* New Haven, CT: Yale University Press.

Blakemore, J. E. O., Berenbaum, S. A., & Liben L. S. (2009). *Gender development.* New York, NY: Taylor & Francis.

Boutte, G., Lopez-Robertson, J., & Powers-Costello, E. (2011). Moving beyond color-blindness in early childhood classrooms. *Early Childhood Education Journal, 39*(5), 335–342.

Brady, J. (1995). *Schooling young children a feminist pedagogy for liberatory learning.* Albany, NY: State University of New York Press.

Brookfield, S., & Preskill, S. (1999). *Discussion as a way of teaching; Tools and techniques for democratic classrooms.* San Francisco, CA: Jossey-Bass.

Connell, R. W. (1995). *Masculinities.* St. Leonards, New South Wales: Allen & Unwin.

Connell, R. W., & Messerschmidt, J. W. (2005). Hegemonic masculinity: Rethinking the concept. *Gender and Society, 19*(6), 829–859.

Connell, R. W. (2010). *Schools & Social Justice.* Philadelphia: Temple University Press.

Copenhaver-Johnson, J. (2006). Talking to children about race: The importance of inviting difficult conversations. *Childhood Education, 83*(1), 12–22.

Coyle, E. F., & Liben, L. S. (2016). Affecting girls' activity and job interests through play: The moderating roles of personal gender salience and game characteristics. *Child Development, 87*(2), 414–428.

Davies, B. (1989). *Frogs and snails and feminist tales: Preschool children and gender.* Sydney: Allen & Unwin.

Davies, B. (1993). *Shards of glass: Children reading and writing beyond gendered identities.* Cresskill, NJ: Hampton Press.

Derman-Sparks, L. (2008). Why an anti-biases curriculum? In A. Pelo (Ed.), *Rethinking Early Childhood Education* (pp. 7–12). Milwaukee: Rethinking Schools.

Derman-Sparks, L. & Edwards, J. O. (2010). *Anti-bias education: For young children and ourselves.* Washington, DC: National Association for the Education of Young Children.

Edelson, D. C. (2002). Design research: What we learn when we engage in design. *Journal of the Learning Sciences, 11*(1), 105–121. DOI: 10.1207/S15327809JLS1101_4

Egan, S., & Perry, D. G. (2001). Gender identity: A multidimensional analysis with implications for psychosocial adjustment. *Developmental Psychology, 37*, 451–463.

Ewert, M., & Ray, R. (2008). *10,000 Dresses.* New York: Seven Stories Press.

Festinger, L. (1968). *A theory of cognitive dissonance.* Stanford, CA: Stanford University Press.

Freire, P. (1970/1993). *Pedagogy of the oppressed* (Rev. ed.). New York, NY: Continuum.

Gadotti, M., & Torres, C. A. (2009). Paulo Freire: Education for development. *Development and Change, 40*, 1255–1267. DOI: 10.1111/j.1467-7660.2009.01606.x

Hillard, L. J., & Liben, L. S. (2010). Differing levels of gender salience in preschool classrooms: Effects on children's gender attitudes and intergroup bias. *Child Development, 81*(6), 1787–1798.

Hinton, K. (2004). "Sturdy black bridges": Discussing race, class, and gender. *English Journal, 94*(2), 60–64.

Kilodavis, C., & DeSimone, S. (2010). *My princess boy: A mom's story about a young boy who loves to dress up.* New York: Aladdin.

Killen, M., Lee-Kim, J., McGlothlin, H., & Stangor, C. (2002). How children and adolescents evaluate gender and racial exclusion. *Monographs for the society for research in child development, 67*(4). Oxford, England: Blackwell Publishers.

Kristeva, Julia (1986) 'Women's time', in Toril Moi (Ed.), *The Kristeva Reader* (pp. 187–213). New York: Columbia University Press.

Martin, C. L., & Halverson, C. F. (1981). A schematic processing model of sex typing and stereotyping in children. *Child Development, 42,* 1119–1134. DOI:10.2307/1129498

Morgan, H. (2009). Using read-alouds with culturally sensitive children's books: a strategy that can lead to tolerance and improved reading skills. *Reading Improvement, 46*(1), 3–8.

Paechter, C. (2007). *Being boys, being girls: Learning masculinities and femininities.* Maidenhead: Open University Press.

Pahlke, E., Bigler, R. S., & Martin, C. L. (2014). Can fostering children's ability to challenge sexism improve critical analysis, internalization, and enactment of inclusive, egalitarian peer relationships? *Journal of Social Issues, 70*(1), 115–133. DOI: 10.1111/josi.12050

Pascoe, C. J. (2007). Dude, you're a fag: Masculinities and sexuality in high school. Berkeley, CA: University of California Press.

Reay, D. (2001). "Spice girls", "nice girls", "girlies" and "tomboys": Gender discourses, girls' cultures and femininities in the primary classroom. *Gender and Education, 13*(2), 153–166.

Renold, E. (2005). *Girls, boys and junior sexualities: Exploring children's gender and sexual relations in the primary school.* London: Routledge.

Rubin, B. (2011). *Making citizens: Transforming civic learning for diverse social studies classrooms.* New York: Routledge.

Schieble, M. (2012). Critical conversations on whiteness with young adult literature. *Journal of Adolescent & Adult Literacy, 56*(3), 212–221.

Walkerdine, V., & Lucey, H. (1989). *Democracy in the kitchen: Regulating mothers and socialising daughters.* London: Virago.

Wang, F., & Hannafin, M. J. (2005). Design-based research and technology-enhanced learning environments. *Educational Technology Research and Development, 53*(4), 5–23.

Weiler, K. (1991). Freire and a feminist pedagogy of difference. *Harvard Educational Review, 61*(4), 449–475.

West, C., & Zimmerman, D. (1987). Doing gender. *Gender and Society, 1*(2), 125–151.

6

FROM PRACTICE TO THEORY

Ontological Innovation in a Ninth-Grade History Classroom[1]

Eric B. Freedman

In a traditional experiment, the researcher makes a prediction and then examines data that bear on it, leading to the prediction's confirmation or refute. This procedure fits with the skeptical orientation of the scientific enterprise. At minimum, science strives to avoid the creation of myth: Better to say nothing than to advance a theory lacking evidence in support. The American philosopher Charles S. Peirce, however, asked a provocative question about the experimental method: Where do scientists' predictions come from?

Peirce called the act of prediction "abduction," as distinguished from "deduction" (applying a general rule to a specific case) and "induction" (generalizing from a case to a rule). Peirce's views on the nature of abductive reasoning evolved over time, but his most mature statement was as follows:

> The surprising fact C is observed.
> But if A were true, C would be a matter of course.
> Hence, there is a reason to suspect that A is true.
>
> *(Peirce, 1902, p. 159)*

As an example, if someone grabs an umbrella on the way out the door, an observer could abduce that it is raining outside. Scientists derive such predictions from various kinds of stimuli: other people's work, unexpected experimental results, late-night conversations over wine, even dreams. The essential element is the advancement of a supposition that, if true, would explain why a given phenomenon assumes certain patterns.

Duckworth (2006) describes abductive reasoning as follows:

I once had what struck me as a great insight, derived from Piaget's work: "All the rest of the world passes us by unless we think of thinking about it in that way." . . . Nobody until Einstein thought of thinking about space and time as interdependent variables, though once he had done so, other physicists were able to think that way too. . . . Nobody until Piaget, for that matter, thought of thinking about how children thought about conservation problems. Until he did, that whole part of the world passed all of us by.

(p. 41)

Duckworth's thoughts highlight just how important abductive reasoning is. The act of advancing a theory—or, as she puts it, "think of thinking about it in that way"—sets the scientific process in motion. For theories must exist before they can be confirmed or refuted (see Habermas, 1971).

Experiments sometimes do yield new theories. For example, when psychologists discovered that smaller, not larger, degrees of reinforcement often yielded more robust changes to behavior, it helped lead to the invention of attribution theory and to the notions of intrinsic and extrinsic motivation. Yet experimental research by itself is ill-equipped to generate new theory in this way, for it was not designed to do so. Experiments aim to confirm or refute theories, not to create them.

Design-based research (DBR) holds a different sort of potential. Compared to randomized controlled trials or other experimental methods that test whether a given design works as intended, DBR is far more open-ended. With DBR, the design need not be fully worked out in advance, ready for final testing. Rather, the designers tinker with the product, adding new features, removing or modifying others, and observing what happens as a result. This design space is fertile ground for the generation of theory. As Edelson (2002) puts it,

Through a parallel and retrospective process of reflection upon the design and its outcomes, the design researchers elaborate upon their initial hypotheses and principles, refining, adding, and discarding—gradually knitting together a coherent theory that reflects their understanding of the design experience.

(p. 106)

This chapter offers a case example of this sort of theory construction through design. I explain how designing and field-testing an intervention that aimed to help students connect the past to the present led to the development of a theory of positivistic versus critical historical reasoning (Freedman, 2015). The chapter offers a phenomenological reconstruction of the thought process through which I arrived at these theoretical constructs, in order to illustrate how design work can contribute to the generation of theory.

Generating Theory through Design

"Theories," diSessa and Cobb (2004) observe, "have always displayed a principal part of the power and elegance of science" (p. 79). The authors go on to describe the nature of theoretical constructs, the building blocks of theories:

> Science needs its own set of terms or categories to pursue its work . . . "force," "gene, "natural selection," "molecule," "element," "catalyst." The process of creating such categories, however, is far more complicated than writing down a definition. . . . Instead, defining the technical terms of science is more like finding and validating a new category of existence in the world. . . .
>
> Scientific terms must "cut nature at its joints." That is, they must make distinctions that really make a difference, ignore the ones that prove to be inconsequential, and enable us to deepen explanations of the phenomena of interest. We must develop theoretical constructs that empower us to see order, pattern, and regularity in the complex settings in which we conduct design experiments.
>
> *(p. 84)*

DiSessa and Cobb label this type of theorizing *ontological innovation*, "the invention of new scientific categories, specifically categories that do useful work in generating, selecting among, and assessing design alternatives" (p. 78). Yet the authors also acknowledge the difficulty of generating such constructs. Those that seem obvious today—force, gene, molecule—took centuries to discover or invent.

Qualitative researchers have long recognized the deficiencies in the ability of experimental methods to generate theory. The alternatives they advance, such as ethnography, case study, or grounded theory methodology, all aim towards "thick description" that delineates the essential features of a phenomenon or setting. Geertz (1973) offers the classic example of distinguishing between an involuntary blink and a conspiratorial wink, each with profoundly different social meaning. Categories such as these, "wink" versus "blink," allow people to make sense of and act in the world. Traditionally, though, qualitative research is conducted in natural settings and aims to generate categories of understanding about the world that already exists.

In contrast, DBR allows for theory generation within engineered contexts. As Cobb, Confrey, diSessa, Lehrer, and Schauble (2003) put it, "Design studies are typically test-beds for innovation. The intent is to investigate the possibilities for educational improvement by bringing about new forms of learning in order to study them" (p. 10). Engaging in design offers opportunities for piecing together new theories. As Edelson (2002) puts it:

> First, the practical demands of design require that a theory be fully specified. . . . [Otherwise], it cannot meet the needs of designers. Second, the process of design reveals inconsistencies more effectively than analytical

processes . . . because the theory will provide the designer with conflicting guidance. Third, the goal-directed nature of design provides a natural focus for theory development. Where theoreticians often have little more than Occam's razor to guide their choice among alternative theories, designers have practical considerations such as resources, goals, and constraints to guide them.

(pp. 118–119)

I would imagine that most people who have designed something can relate to this sentiment. In my forays into videogame development with my brother, I can remember the late-night drafting sessions fueled by grand ambitions, only to discover the next morning when we tried programming the computer to do the thing we had envisioned, that our plans were indeterminate or infeasible. We would return to the drawing board and rethink our plan. Similarly, in DBR the requirement that the intervention must be built and then used in a live setting serves as a "reality check" that forces clearer theorizing.

These observations apply not only to theories about designs themselves, but also to theories about the contexts and outcomes of design. McKenney and Reeves (2012) distinguish between two types of DBR. The first, research "on interventions," focuses "explicitly on characteristics of the design of the intervention, and how the intervention works, with whom, under what conditions" (p. 23). By contrast, in the second type, research "through interventions," the designed artifact "serves more as the research context or as a complex treatment, whose primary purpose is to provide a means for studying specific phenomena that are related to, but not the same as, the intervention itself" (p. 23). In the second type no less than the first, DBR creates opportunities for the generation of theory. In Edelson's (2002) terminology, a *context theory* "characterizes the challenges and opportunities presented by a class of design contexts" (p. 113). For example, in a design project focused on historical investigation in a fifth-grade class, VanSledright (2002) observed that the students appeared to possess an "encyclopedia epistemology" (p. 72), in which the answer to historical questions lies waiting in some textbook. His efforts to promote a more constructivist view helped him recognize and name the epistemic impediments that stood in the way.

DBR also can yield an *outcomes theory* that "characterizes a set of outcomes associated with some intervention" (Edelson, 2002, p. 113). As a visionary form of research, DBR aims to produce new forms of thinking or acting, which it then seeks to characterize and explain. Occasionally, DBR also yields unintended outcomes, worth understanding precisely because of their all-too-common yet unfortunate occurrence. As Edelson puts it, "the problems exposed through formative evaluation or the eventual failure of a design effort can contribute important information about undesirable outcomes, which can also contribute to an outcomes theory" (p. 113). This chapter explores one such undesirable outcome in the field of history education and contrasts it to a more desirable outcome seen less often.

Applying Grounded Theory Methodology in DBR

While design researchers have expounded on the methodology's potential for generating theory, they have been more reticent about the analytic tools that might facilitate that process. Grounded theory methodology offers one highly useful set of tools. Glaser and Strauss (1967) originally developed the approach as a means of uncovering the "basic social processes" (Glaser, 1978, p. 93) that occur in a given domain or locale. In classical grounded theory, the researcher or "analyst" records fieldnotes and conducts interviews, and then combs through the data in search of themes and patterns. Analytic observations are recorded as codes, or categories of human action—such as "keeping one's cool" or "social valuing." After inducing initial codes, the analyst returns to the field to seek out additional examples of the coded categories, in a process that Glaser and Strauss (1967) call "theoretical sampling." Once numerous instances of each code have been recorded, the analyst looks across each instance of a single code, in a technique called "constant comparison," to determine under what conditions the phenomenon tends to occur and to what effects. Often the codes are revised during this process—some added, others dropped or redefined. In this way, the analyst builds from the ground up a theory that explains and predicts phenomena in a given domain.

Grounded theory methodology emerged from sociology, a field that operates most comfortably in natural settings, but many aspects of the approach readily apply to DBR. The two methodologies, in fact, share a similar history. As suggested earlier, DBR was conceived as a means of generating usable products and theory through exploratory yet systematic tinkering, in opposition to the experimental model that verifies preformed theories through randomized trials. Similarly, grounded theory was intended to free sociologists from the field's obsession with verifying the "grand theories" of giants like Durkheim or Weber. As Glaser and Strauss (1967) explain:

> By making generation [of theory] a legitimate enterprise, and suggesting methods for it, we hope to provide the ingredients of a defense against internalized professional mandates dictating that sociologists research and write in the verification rhetoric, and against the protests of colleagues who object to their freedom in research from the rigorous rules of verification (so stifling to the creative energies required for discovering theory).
>
> *(p. 7)*

In short, both traditions emerged as alternatives to the "verification rhetoric" that privileges the confirmation of theory over its generation. Yet while DBR methodology only vaguely specifies how to derive theoretical constructs from the data, grounded theory methodology offers highly elaborate analytic tools, such as inductive coding, theoretical sampling, and constant comparison. As this chapter aims to illustrate, these tools can be of enormous benefit to design researchers.

Design of the DBR Study

This section outlines the conception and design of the DBR study that will serve as a case example of ontological innovation. In describing its various components, I highlight the unscripted, serendipitous nature of DBR. Plans often needed to be scrapped, but the new tactics that emerged in their place yielded unforeseen insights that helped facilitate the generation of theory.

Design Principles

Inspired by analogous work in math and science, many recent reform initiatives in history education have sought to promote disciplinary expertise (e.g., De La Paz et al., 2017; Nokes, Dole, & Hacker, 2007; Reisman, 2012b; VanSledright, 2002). Nearly all of these efforts draw on the work of Wineburg (1991), who compared how historians and high-school students interpret accounts of past events. He identified three heuristics that the historians used far more often than the students did: "sourcing," or considering how an author's motives and identity might affect what is written; "corroboration," or comparing multiple accounts; and "contextualization," or placing an account within its temporal and geographic context (see also Leinhardt & Young, 1996; Shemilt, 1987). When asked why students need to learn such skills, given that so few of them will grow up to be historians, some advocates of disciplinary approaches (e.g., Nokes et al., 2007) suggest that the skills could transfer to situations requiring analysis of present-day accounts, for example, a news article or campaign speech (cf. Wineburg, 1999). Yet if that were the main rationale, why even study history, instead of current issues all along?

The present study drew on a theoretical model that links past to present more explicitly (Figure 6.1). The model posits that the basic question democratic citizens must answer is, "What is to be done?" or in other words, "In this particular situation, what will or should I do, or what should we as a society do?" The model delineates two ways that the study of history can help answer that question (see Seixas, 1994): by illuminating the root causes of current issues (historical antecedents), and by providing analogous situations for comparison (historical analogies). The model also incorporates Barton and Levstik's (2004) distinction between the *analytic stance* and the *moral response stance* to history education. With both antecedents and analogies, students can pose empirical (i.e., analytic) questions ("What happened, why did it happen, and to what effect?"), as well as moral questions ("What should have been done at the time?"). The present study aimed to develop and field-test an 11-week curriculum that took this approach to exploring the past not just for its own sake, but to shed light on the present (Freedman, 2009).

Each of the curriculum's five units of instruction engaged students in answering one or more of the types of questions specified by the model (Table 6.1).

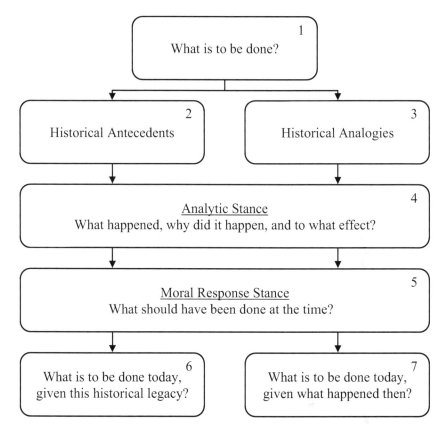

FIGURE 6.1 Model for Linking Past to Present.

For example, in the third unit, "How successful was the Civil Rights Movement in desegregating American public schools and in creating educational equality?" students traced the antecedents to a current social issue by exploring the long-term impact of decisions made in the past, as well as the morality of those decisions as they bear on the present (Figure 6.1, boxes 2, 4, 5, and 6). The data featured in this chapter come from the curriculum's second unit, on the Vietnam War, in which each student crafted a three-page history of the war's peak years (1964-1971) from 12 conflicting accounts (Figure 6.1, box 4).

The project also drew on the idea from critical theory that even an inquiry-based curriculum can never be politically neutral (Apple, 2004; Ellsworth, 1989; Freedman, 2007; Freire, 1970/1993; Shor, 1992). As Duckworth (2006) suggests, we can only inquire about what "we think of thinking about"; everything else "passes us by" (p. 41). In other words, we can never ask all the possible questions about a given topic that would shed light on all the possible responses to it (let alone interrogate all the possible topics that exist).

TABLE 6.1 The Designed Curriculum

Unit of Instruction	Mode of Reasoning
Pre-curriculum mini-unit: Should the U.S. government grant reparations to the descendants of African slaves today? Mini-unit designed to introduce students to reparations in preparation for the pre-curriculum essay. They discuss a short reading and then write a five-paragraph essay responding to the unit question. (3 class periods)	What is to be done today, given this historical legacy? (Figure 6.1, boxes 2 and 6)
Unit 1: Who primarily caused the Cold War? Students read two competing answers to the unit question, and hear a guest lecturer (a Cold War historian) present a third. They then write and revise an essay responding to the unit question. (9 class periods)	What happened, why did it happen, and to what effect? (box 4)
Unit 2: What happened during the final eight years of the Vietnam War? Students analyze primary accounts (e.g., letters, diary entries, government resolutions, and a personal interview), which they use to write a three-page history of the war to share with classmates and compare with their textbook's account. (18 class periods)	What happened, why did it happen, and to what effect? (box 4)

Unit 3: How successful was the Civil Rights Movement in desegregating American public schools and in creating educational equality? Students consult selections from the video, *Eyes on the Prize*, an article by Kozol (2005) arguing that schools are still separate and unequal, and a lecture on the legal history of school desegregation. They then write an essay on the unit question. (9 class periods)

What happened, why did it happen, and to what effect? (boxes 2 and 4)

Unit 4: How successful were feminists in transforming everyday relations between men and women? Students discuss current gender roles and expectations and read a primary and a secondary source on second-wave feminism. They then create a cartoon strip responding to the unit question, based on the readings and one student-selected source. (5 class periods)

What happened, why did it happen, and to what effect? (boxes 2 and 4)

Unit 5: What, if anything, should be done to combat poverty and economic inequality in the U.S.? Students consult Lyndon Johnson and Ronald Reagan's competing approaches to poverty, as well as a set of readings by proponents of laissez–faire economics. They participate in a town-hall simulation on a proposal for universal basic income and then write an essay responding to the unit question. (9 class periods)

What is to be done today, given what happened then? (boxes 3, 4, 5, and 7)

Furthermore, different questions serve different political ends—or at least, can be shown to hold different political ramifications. In this sense, the theoretical framework or "method of analysis" that informs the questions posed and the means of arriving at answers puts a political spin on the nature of inquiry (Freedman, 2007). Other scholars have turned to the historical discipline for the source of the analytic methods taught. The disciplinary heuristics they select, such as sourcing, contextualization, and corroboration, can indeed serve as useful tools for historical analysis, but they do not go far enough. As Parker (2003) puts it, reasoning skills such as these allow students to engage "in social problem solving without enabling them to think about which problems are worth solving, according to whom, to what ends, and in whose favor" (p. 46; see also Barton & Levstik, 2004).

The current project thus adopted a more prescriptive framework, *critical multiculturalism*, to guide the selection of inquiry questions and analytic approaches. Critical multiculturalism examines the ways that race, class, gender, and other social categories structure people's life chances, both in the past and in the present (Steinberg & Kincheloe, 2001). Its selection can be justified by democratic theory: In a society devoted to political equality, the public schools should present a story of the nation (and world) that speaks to the experiences of the multiple groups that comprise it (Banks, 2008; Parker, 2003). Importantly, though, the curriculum presented evidence that both supported and opposed the specific dictates implied by the framework (such as fully desegregating the nation's schools). In the interest of avoiding indoctrination, critical multiculturalism informed not the answers provided to students, but the questions posed and the analytic frames endorsed (see Freedman, 2007).

Study Participants

The original plan was to locate three teachers to implement the curriculum during the 2007–2008 school year. After six months of recruitment, however, I found none willing and able to participate. Finally, Andria Thompson, a public schoolteacher recommended by a university professor, agreed to sign on.[2] Ms. Thompson had six years of teaching experience, carried a bachelor's degree in political science, and was completing her master's in curriculum and instruction at the time of the study. A screening interview suggested that she possessed the required familiarity with inquiry and multiculturalism. As she later explained, "I agreed to sign on . . . to get kids to think about the bigger issues that transcend the historical period. . . . [I wanted to] have them make sense of information and come to their own conclusions" (A. Thompson, interview #2, June 18, 2008).

Ms. Thompson wavered at the last minute, then finally joined with just enough time remaining in the school year to teach the curriculum. This meant that most of the preparatory work planned for the summer and fall had to occur on the fly. Fortuitously, however, Ms. Thompson had a scheduled planning period in between her two sections of ninth-grade history, meaning that she and I could talk nearly every day about what occurred in the first-period class and decide what to change for third period. The two class sections thus functioned as akin to successive iterations, with considerable tinkering in between.

The public high school where Ms. Thompson taught was located in a rural Midwestern community. As she described in our second interview, "It's a rural district with small town roots to it." The principal, she added, "pretty much allows us to develop our own curriculum, to try new things . . . [and] parents pretty much respect the school district for the most part." She also indicated that the students "are pretty accountable to their parents," implying that they compete assignments and care about their academic marks. In this sense, the school climate favored an ambitious curriculum like the one we designed.

Of those enrolled in her two sections of ninth-grade U.S. History, 40 (or 85%) consented to participate in the study: 10 boys and 30 girls, ages 14–15. Both classes were racially homogenous (96% white) but socioeconomically and ideologically diverse (see Freedman, 2015). Both were also of mixed ability, although Ms. Thompson remarked that they were stronger academically than in previous years. Third period contained two English-language learners and a handful of students with exceptionalities. Course grades ranged from A through F. First period averaged a B (3.16 out of 4) and third period a B– (2.56).

Data and Analysis

The 11-week field-test of the designed curriculum sought to answer four questions:

1. Did the curriculum work as intended?
2. What did students learn from it?
3. How did the students and teacher respond to the pedagogy employed?
4. Did the curriculum succeed in teaching a critical multiculturalist method of analysis while avoiding indoctrination?

I observed nearly every class session, kept daily field notes, and audio-recorded discussions, which were then transcribed. I also collected all student assignments and interviewed the teacher and just over half the students. For the most part, I planned the major assignments and activities, and Ms. Thompson taught, but at times she amended my ideas or I helped facilitate class discussion. As Ms. Thompson had conducted Socratic seminars infrequently in the past, she was eager to see how another teacher approached them. The second-period prep time afforded ample opportunity for co-planning and debriefing.

A pair of essays at the beginning and end of the curriculum were intended to serve as a pre/post assessment. The pre-essay capped the introductory mini-unit on reparations for American slavery, while the post-essay dealt with possible responses to the problem of poverty, the topic of the fifth and final unit (see Table 6.1). Student interviews were originally planned to take place directly after they had completed these essays, with the protocol prompting them to expand on what they had written. Due to scheduling difficulties, however, I did not complete the first round of interviews until about halfway through the curriculum. Furthermore, time constraints pushed the post-essay onto the final exam, leaving no opportunity for a second round of interviews. In the end, the pre- and post-essays turned out to be too incongruent to indicate change in student thinking over time.[3] However, the fact that the interviews occurred midway through the curriculum benefitted the study in another way: Students were still able to talk about their pre-essays (which they reread directly beforehand) but could also discuss the Vietnam unit currently underway. These interviews ended up providing some of the richest data on students' historical reasoning in response to the curriculum—as well as a prime occasion for ontological innovation.

To increase participation levels, I allowed students to enter the study without agreeing to an interview, and in that case only their written work and in-class comments were used as data. In total, 22 students (55%) agreed to an interview, which lasted 25–40 minutes each. The interviews were semi-structured; I often asked follow-up questions or moved quickly through certain prompts when time was running short.

To analyze the data, I employed the techniques from grounded theory methodology described above: inductive coding, theoretical sampling, and constant comparison (Glaser, 1978; Glaser & Strauss, 1967; Richards, 2005). The software program I used—Nvivo 8—allowed for the generation of a great many codes. Whenever I identified a new phenomenon of interest, I created a code for it. Later I combined redundant codes and moved those that never reappeared to extra folders for storage. Although over 100 codes still exist in the data file, those used for final analysis add up to less than 30. As I coded each piece of data, I created a memo recording my observations and hunches (see Glaser, 1978). I also made frequent use of Nvivo 8's matrix feature to create charts comparing the frequency of different codes in different documents—for example, how often students "trivialized racism" in the pre-essays versus the civil rights essays. In keeping with the spirit of grounded theory, I continually looked for emergent patterns in the data—though the research questions helped determine the types of patterns I looked for. In later stages, I also employed deductive coding—for example, to track students' use of sourcing and corroboration.

Results from this analysis appear in several reports and publications (Freedman, 2009, 2015, in review). Rather than summarize them again here, the remainder of this chapter examines how the use of a grounded theory data-analytic approach in this design study facilitated the generation of new theoretical constructs.

Ontological Innovation in a Ninth-Grade History Classroom

The Vietnam Unit

In its original conception, the foreign policy portion of the curriculum was to comprise three units covering the early Cold War, the Vietnam War, and the Iraq War. As the Vietnam unit drew into its third week, however, it grew clear that the Iraq unit would need to be cut, meaning that students would lose the chance to ask, "What is to be done?" about a current foreign-policy dilemma.[4]

Still, the Vietnam unit contained several unique elements. Many recent reform initiatives pose open-ended questions about past events that students are to answer using varied sources of evidence (e.g., De La Paz et al., 2017; Reisman, 2012a). Such tasks engage students in a kind of empirical analysis: Given this evidence, what do you believe happened?[5] Historiographic debates, though, often revolve not just around empirical matters like these, but also around matters of framing: Which slices of the past will receive attention? What questions will be asked? Whose stories will be told? (see Cronon, 1992; Novick, 1988). The Vietnam unit defined students' task broadly enough that they could not get by solely with determining empirically what happened in a given time and place; they would also need to tackle a framing dilemma (Freedman, 2015).

Students received 12 primary accounts, including government documents, public speeches, diary entries, letters, and film, representing the range of viewpoints contained in the documentary record (although, in hindsight, the set placed greater credence in perspectives opposing the war; see Freedman, 2015). Their assignment was to "write a history of the Vietnam War based on the primary source documents that you have read," focusing on the years 1964–1971. Since we allowed them only three pages to tell their story, they would need to decide which topics to emphasize or omit. Should they dwell on the antiwar movement or the Tet offensive, civilian casualties or the communist threat?

To establish background knowledge, we began the unit with a presentation on the clash between communism and capitalism, and distributed a packet on the history and geography of Vietnam. On days two and three, we analyzed Ho Chi Minh's Vietnamese Declaration of Independence of 1945 as a class, and on days three and four, Ms. Thompson lectured on the early years of the war (1945–1964). Over the next six days, students worked in cooperative groups of four to analyze the sources. Twice we provided them opportunities to synthesize their emerging ideas in a whole-class discussion. We treated these sessions as Socratic seminars, where students are expected to support their assertions with evidence and to respond to each other's contributions.

A worksheet called the "Document Analysis Slip" that students completed for each source served to scaffold their analysis. It began with six questions intended to help students apply Wineburg's (1991) sourcing and contextualization heuristics: When was the account written? By whom? What values, assumptions, and interests might the author have? Who was the intended audience? Why did the author write it? How might the author's identity, the intended audience, and the document's purpose affect what was written or depicted? To encourage corroboration, the worksheet then asked students to compare the source to others they had read. The final two questions focused their attention on the framing dilemma: "How much space in your 3-page history of the Vietnam War does this author's perspective merit? Justify your answer." The worksheet thus prompted students to attend to matters of both empirical credibility and framing, though it placed greater emphasis on the former (seven questions versus two).

Following Bain (2006), we waited until students had finished writing their histories before asking them to read and critique their textbook's treatment of the war. On the day the histories were due, students swapped papers and compared what they had written. "Try to *account* for these similarities and differences," the handout instructed. "To do this, you will likely need to ask each other *why* you interpreted things a certain way or chose to emphasize certain documents." For homework, students were to read a chapter from their textbook (Dallek, Garcia, Ogle, & Risinger, 2008, pp. 385–395) and "evaluate [the authors'] treatment of the Vietnam War." Here we assumed that the experience of constructing original histories from primary accounts would set students up to critique their textbook from a position of intellectual authority (Engle & Conant, 2002).

In summary, the unit aimed for students to grapple with the moral drama surrounding this controversial war. They would learn about hardships faced by soldiers on both sides, the case for containing the spread of communism, and the righteous indignation of antiwar figures like Dr. Martin Luther King. From these conflicting perspectives, students would need to piece together their own synthetic narrative.

Moral Investment in the War

Originally, Ms. Thompson and I had not planned for a whole-class discussion on the morality of the war. The writing assignment posed an analytic question, not a moral one: "What happened during the war?" not "Where do I stand on it?" (see Figure 6.1, boxes 4 versus 5). Class time was to focus on having students interpret the documents and determine what to include in their histories. However, we soon realized they were pursuing the moral question whether we intended it or not, so eventually we provided them a forum to do so publicly. To retain the unit's original focus, we planned to ask later in the discussion how their stances on the war should or should not factor into the composition of their histories. As it turned out, though, students grew so engrossed in the moral discussion that scant time remained to pursue this other prompt. That occurrence proved fortuitous, for it provided the first clue leading to the generation of theory.

We began the period with a journaling exercise, then opened the floor for discussion. Almost immediately, students expressed that U.S. involvement violated the principle of self-determination. As an example, consider the following exchange from the first-period discussion:

Lilly:	I think the U.S. formed their own government, and . . . they thought you should not be ruled by someone else. You should form your own government. That's what the Vietnamese people did. That's what the people wanted. They wanted a communist government, so we should have let them have what government they want.
Ms. Thompson:	Alright. Agree? Disagree?
Female Student:	Agree.
Female Student:	Agree.

A little later, I stepped in to push students' reasoning:

Mr. Freedman:	What if they wanted Nazism? What if they voted to install a leader that was like Hitler, who was gonna oppress the minority in the country. . . ? Would that be a justification to go to war. . . ?
Arla:	The governments are different. It depends on what they want. If they wanted something like what Hitler was doing with the Nazis, then yeah, people should step in and do something about it, so history doesn't repeat itself. . . . Maybe we had some issues with Russia, but Vietnam is a small country, and they want communism, so we should just let them have it instead of creating a big war for a stupid reason.

(Class session transcript, April 23, 2008)

As Lilly and Arla saw it, if Ho Chi Minh's communist government represented the will of the Vietnamese people, then the U.S. had no business meddling in that country's internal affairs. These two students were not alone. Several others in both sections objected either orally or in writing to what they saw as imperialist ambitions on the part of the United States.

Students' case against American involvement, however, went beyond abstract support for self-determination. The primary sources they had examined showed in vivid colors the war's human toll. They had learned that Ho Chi Minh had wide support among South Vietnamese peasants, and that U.S. soldiers thus never knew whom they could trust. To root out the enemy, the soldiers burned down whole villages and resorted to extracting information through torture. Learning these facts strengthened students' opposition to American involvement. At the same time, they came to recognize the moral complexities of the war. Some were torn over whether to support it, because they believed in the importance of containing communism but still objected to the harm inflicted on civilians.

The following fragment from the third-period discussion highlights the depth of their engagement on this topic:

Ms. Thompson:	All right, so the pressing question . . . was where are you at on this war? What are you thinking about? What's your opinion about the U.S. being in Vietnam. . .?
Chris:	. . . I'm against it because a lot of fatalities were civilians, especially with children or younger people. I thought burning down their homes was kind of not a very good thing to do, just because it's where they live . . . Also, the video, and the speech, and the letters kind of showed me how awful we treated them . . .
Ms. Thompson:	Thank you. Kevin.
Kevin:	I said I was in the middle because they said they were killing a lot of innocent people, but what else could we do? We had to stop communism.

A bit later, Ms. Thompson intervened to challenge comments made earlier (similar to those in first period) about the right of Vietnam to determine its own future:

Ms. Thompson:	Dustin made a comment, and I want us to kind of flesh this out a little bit . . . He said if a country wants our help, we should help them out. Were there people in South Vietnam that didn't want communism?
Dustin:	I thought there were.
Male Student:	Yeah. . .
Male Student:	Yeah.
Dustin:	I thought it was half-and-half.
Ms. Thompson:	Right . . . were there people in Vietnam, and especially in the south, that wanted the U.S. to be there?
Male Student:	Yes.
Male Student:	Yes.
Dustin:	Because then, on the video, they showed people greeting them with flowers.
Ms. Thompson:	Flowers, right? Alright . . . if some people wanted us there and some people didn't . . . what should have been our role? Scott.
Scott:	But they wouldn't want them there if they would get all their houses burned down and stuff after. They'd probably rather have communism than getting all their stuff burned down and all that stuff.

A few turns later:

Veronica:	Like with the thing that people wanted the U.S. there, I think that even though some people did, I think the U.S. mistreated that opportunity to help them because [of] all the bad stuff they did there, like burning down their houses. . .

Ms. Thompson:	Okay, thank you. Lara.
Lara:	. . . Hurting little kids and babies and stuff, they're not gonna be part of the VC. Their parents might, but they're not. They're not gonna be able to help out yet. So I think they at least shouldn't have hurt them. Let them be. And when we saw that picture of . . . [the man] bleeding in his head, I thought that was really horrible. . .
Veronica:	I totally agree children are totally mistreated, but my grandpa was telling me that when he was . . . in Vietnam . . . they saw a kid, he was really small or something, and he was holding a bag. He was by a U.S. truck, and they just thought he was walking around eating or something, and then he left, and then I guess a few minutes later the bag was under the truck or something, and the truck blew up. So he planted a bomb, and he was a kid . . .
Erika:	The man I interviewed, he said the soldiers . . . made friends with people in Vietnam. Some of them were supportive of the U.S., he said, and they just became really good friends.

(Class session transcript, April 23, 2008)

As the class period wound to a close, the room still bristled with energy.

I share these snippets of conversation to illustrate students' emotional invest-ment in this topic. To them, the Vietnam War involved flesh-and-blood people with their very lives and livelihood at stake. To them, the prompt for the unit, "What happened during the Vietnam War?" required more than a disinterested perusal of evidence; it required deep engagement in questions of right and wrong. By the time they sat down to write their histories, the students had already staked out impassioned stances in this moral debate.

Pursuing Objectivity in Historical Writing

Given the moral investment students displayed in the discussion, it surprised me greatly to discover that when it came time to write, they set out to produce a balanced, objective account of the war. The interview protocol included several questions on matters of positionality and bias in historical inquiry. One asked which topics they planned to focus on in their Vietnam histories and why, while another asked if their personal stance on the war should affect their choice of focus. In some cases I also asked if textbooks intended for U.S. classrooms should present a pro-American point of view, or if they should present a balanced or even a pro-Vietnamese point of view. Students' answers to these questions stood in stark relief to the passionate views they had expressed in the moral discussion—and provided the second clue towards the generation of theory.

When I asked students what they focused on in their histories and why, many could offer no explanation. Others offered a vague response, like Tina who said,

"The stuff that stuck out to me, that I remembered learning about, and the stuff that I thought really just made sense to put together." In total, seven of 19, or 37% of those asked, gave nebulous responses like this or said they were unsure how they allotted space to different topics. Other students (seven in total) selected sources for inclusion based on their perceived credibility. Such an approach aligns with the practices of historians, who do try to base their narratives on the most reliable evidence available. Yet surely when deciding whose accounts to include, historians consider more factors than this. A third approach (taken by three students) was to choose sources that produced a coherent story. For example, Brenda said she excluded the protest movement because she was unsure "how to transition from the protest back to the war." Maintaining coherence would seem another reasonable method for selecting material, but it too skirts the dilemma of deciding which coherent story to tell.

By far their most common response was to say they intended to give equal voice to all points of view. Katherine offers a prime example:

> I want to get everyone's opinions out there so everyone can get every point of view . . . I got the Gulf of Tonkin Resolution . . . I got this, and that, and that. . ., and I'm even putting the nurse's journal in there to see what the nurses did. And like I have a section called the antiwar movement, also, to get that view of people and to see not everyone was for it.

When I asked why it was important to include all these perspectives, she replied:

> Well, I know that I don't want just one biased person—one point of view . . . I need to know a lot about a topic, and other people's opinions, and what other people have found out before I can really believe anything, so I guess I just want to get that through in my history, also.
>
> *(Katherine interview, April 24, 2008)*

Here Katherine suggested that because no one alone knows the full story, diverse accounts must be woven together to produce the most credible narrative. Sixteen students in total (84%) said similarly that they strove to include "both sides" or "all sides" of the story.

At times, students elaborated further on the reasons to tell both sides. When I asked Becky if a textbook intended for U.S. schoolchildren should present a pro-American point of view, she replied: "You can't just say, 'Oh, U.S. is the best, we don't do anything wrong.' I think both sides need to be developed. . ., because what happened is what happened—it needs to be told." Here, Becky suggested that the darker actions of the U.S. government should not be hidden from public view, that historians have a moral responsibility to tell the full story.

Tina elaborated on this argument, asserting that to withhold perspectives from the history books breeds arrogance and naiveté:

Mr. Freedman:	Some people might say that in the United States it's good to have a history that focuses on U.S. perspectives or that presents kind of a pro-U.S. view. What do you think?
Tina:	Well, I think that just makes us full of ourselves.
Mr. Freedman:	Really?
Tina:	Yeah, because we've done bad things. It's just no one likes to look at it. We just want to be like, "Oh, whatever, let's not even think about it." But we shouldn't do that. We did bad things.

(Tina interview, April 25, 2008)

Tina rejected a nationalist narrative and implied that a more inclusive story would foster humility, perhaps even self-reflection. Chris offered another reason for including multiple perspectives: to compensate for the past practice of excluding them—an explanation Kelly (1986) has called "ideological affirmative action" (p. 118). In these instances, students argued for a balanced narrative not only to ensure empirical integrity, but also to promote humility and wisdom, or to compensate for imbalanced narratives told elsewhere. This was the closest students came to framing their narratives deliberately to achieve a social or political aim.

Several students took the notion of balance one step further and argued that personal or political motives should in no way influence decisions about whose perspectives to emphasize. Melissa provides one example:

Mr. Freedman:	Is there anything that stands out in your mind about the war that strikes you as particularly important that you'd want people to know about?
Melissa:	Nothing that I'm not strongly opinionated about, so it wouldn't really be history, it'd be more of my opinion.

(Melissa interview, April 24, 2008)

Chris's view was similar. When asked how his personal stance on the war should affect his narrative, he replied, "I think it should be just the things that happened, and your opinions of those events shouldn't affect it because everyone needs all the facts to come to a conclusion of how they feel." Like Chris and Melissa, 11 students in total (79% of those asked) said they wished to purge their subjectivity from their narratives.

Not everyone assumed that objectivity would come naturally, however. Eight students acknowledged that their personal biases might interfere with their plans to stay impartial. Ellen said, "I'll probably try not to lean towards one side and just try to state the facts, but I know my opinion might get in there and start changing my facts around a little bit." Kristen, who spoke strongly against the war in class discussions, said in her interview, "I would write stuff, and then I would realize that my opinion was way too much in there, so I'd rewrite to make it more neutral. I didn't want to go one way or the other." These students wished to craft an impartial narrative but acknowledged the difficulty of accomplishing that feat.

Veronica displayed perhaps the most nuanced understanding of personal bias. When I asked if her stance on the war influenced what she wrote, she replied, "It's probably obvious . . . that I was against it." She later explained that it is "good to have . . . both bias and just plain facts because the bias puts more emphasis on maybe [certain] things. But I think it's also good to know what is the bias. . . . I think it's good to see and know about it." Here Veronica suggested that bias might not be the historian's enemy, that personal beliefs and motives, if properly disclosed, could help shape a narrative in productive ways.

Veronica was in the extreme minority, however. Every other student, save one, who broached this topic said they wished to craft an objective account by including both sides, or all sides, of the story. In effect, they refused to view any aspect of the war as more significant than any other aspect, or to view any group's perspective or experience as particularly pertinent. For them, the goal was an impartial narrative, untarnished by the personal beliefs of the historian. Seeing this pattern in the data after witnessing students express such passionate stances in class discussion surprised and perplexed me. Their view of historical inquiry contrasted with that of critical theorists and figures like E. H. Carr (1961), who hold that historians' subjectivity has a vital and legitimate role to play. The data pointed to a theoretical distinction absent in the literature on history education.

Accurate Yet Biased

Before describing that theory, let me share one other slice of data that fed into it. To assess students' skill at sourcing and corroboration after participating in the unit, two questions from the interview protocol asked students to identify which of the 12 Vietnam documents they found the most and least credible and why (see Wineburg, 1991). A written assignment at the end of the unit asked them to assess their textbook in a similar way: "Based on what you know from the primary sources, how *accurate* is [the textbook's] account?" It then asked, "How *comprehensive* is their account? What topics (and whose perspectives) do they omit that you feel they should have included? What do they include that you or your classmates omitted?" Finally, it asked students to "come up with some reasons for the textbook's accuracy/inaccuracy, focus, and bias." Student responses to these oral and written prompts offered a third clue towards a theory delineating two contrasting conceptions of historical inquiry.

In their responses to the interview prompt, most students showed they could assess source credibility with admirable skill. On average, the 22 students interviewed assessed five documents each; they employed sourcing in 88.1% of these assessments and corroboration in 38.5%. For example, five students wondered if the Winter Soldiers (Doc 9) had cherry-picked or distorted facts to construct a case against the war. "I think that they might try to find the worst stories, the worst testimonies, and show those instead of the other ones. . ." said Chris, "because they want everyone to think that war is terrible, and they don't want us to have war at all." On the flip side, the fact that the Winter Soldier testimonies involved public self-deprecation led 11 students to find them more trustworthy. As Lilly put it,

> They would feel bad about what they did, torturing the Vietnamese. Also, they would probably want to hide that or not say that, but they're telling it to the public so people can know what really happened, so I think that's pretty reliable.

Whether they found the account suspect or believable, students in each of these cases referenced the author's knowledge, identity, audience, or purpose. In summary, they showed they understood that accounts can be biased, in what ways, and for what reasons—a central component of historical reasoning, yet one that many students their age seldom exhibit (cf. Stahl, Hynd, Britton, McNish, & Bosquet, 1996; Wineburg, 1991).

The students even turned a critical eye towards their textbook. Of the 28 who submitted written analyses of the book chapter, 75% employed sourcing and 93% employed corroboration. For example, Collin used the sourcing heuristic when he wrote,

> [T]hey make it sound like only the Viet Cong was doing horrible things when we were doing horrible things also. I think that they left out some of the information maybe to persuade the nation's youth that the war was a right thing to do and that we kind of had no choice.

As the assignment called for, the students corroborated the textbook with the primary sources they had already read, listing specific events that they felt the book covered in greater depth, less depth, or omitted altogether. Four observed a lack of attention to Martin Luther King's antiwar position. Five felt it glossed over American soldiers' experiences, while six felt it sidelined or ignored Vietnamese experiences. Lilly concluded,

> The book . . . did not include anything about the controversy surrounding the Gulf of Tonkin. It made the issue sound like it was agreed on by everyone. This was not true, and I think they should have included both sides of it.

Such assertions reveal an understanding rare among high-school students: that textbooks have authors, an intended audience, and a message the authors seek to convey (cf. Paxton, 1999).

At first, I took these findings as an encouraging sign. True, students were not making connections between past and present as originally intended, but the Vietnam unit was not set up well to accomplish that objective. Instead, it focused on historical analysis of the type that Wineburg (1991) and others had described, and on that front it appeared to be succeeding—that is, until I encountered another baffling trend. Despite the frequent accusations of bias, the vast majority of students—22 of the 25 who broached the issue—concluded that the textbook was accurate or mostly accurate. In fact, many of the same students who found the book empirically accurate also saw bias in its pattern of emphasis.

For example, Caitlin wrote, "the book did not give any opinions of the Vietnamese people because of course they focused on the U.S.'s history." But then she added, "The book company probably had real historians and nonbiased factual documents." In a similar vein, Chris wrote:

> The book is fairly accurate, it basically reiterates what all our documents said, but in a more clear and less shadowy way. But, I'm tired of hearing about the U.S. and how we were always doing it right, and how it was what we had to do. I don't care, I want to hear how the Vietnamese government interpreted all this, and I want to read about how the Vietnamese civilians lived all of this through our terrible torture.
>
> *(Chris textbook analysis, May 1, 2008)*

In total, 14 students (50%) suggested as Caitlin and Chris did that the book was accurate yet biased. Seven additional students who found the book accurate did not accuse it of bias but still commented on its pattern of emphasis. Thus, 21 students in total (75%) asserted that the textbook adequately accounted for the evidence yet still differed from their histories in its selection and omission of topical material.

In sum, the data suggested that at the end of the unit, the students could apply the sourcing and corroboration heuristics not only to the 12 primary documents, but also to the textbook itself. Oddly, though, they found the book accurate despite its pattern of bias. What did this mean? And how did it relate to the other surprising finding, that they held strongly opinioned views on the war but felt these had no place in a historical narrative?

From Practice to Theory

Historians have long debated what Novick (1988) calls "the objectivity question." Some maintain that personal commitments should never color the scholarship historians produce. Yet others disagree. As Carr (1961) maintains, "The facts speak only when the historian calls on them: it is he [sic] who decides to which facts to give the floor, and in what order or context" (p. 9). Later he adds, "this reciprocal action also involves reciprocity between present and past, since the historian is part of the present and the facts belong to the past" (p. 35). The evidence suggests that the students in this study did not share Carr's view. To them, the historian's subjectivity has no legitimate role to play.

As I considered this finding, I began to realize the curriculum may have set students up to reach that conclusion—or at least, did little to combat it. The Document Analysis Slip contained seven questions prompting an assessment of the bias of each source, but only two that asked how the source should factor into the larger story of the war. Nor did we model the strategies historians use to frame their narratives in this way. For example, we could have organized a session around the guiding question, "Why write history?" that explored how historians investigate different aspects of the past that follow from their aims and interests. We could have examined the introduction to *A People's History of the United States*, where Zinn (2001) describes how he aims to retell American history from the perspectives of the dispossessed, and compared his approach to those taken by historians who focus on women's experiences, military strategy, or the lives of presidents. An activity like this one might have prompted students to think more deeply about whether historical inquiry can and should be objective.

Ours is not the only curriculum, though, that fails in this regard. In Wineburg's (1991) original study, he implied that the critical apparatus supplied by sourcing, corroboration, and contextualization could be used not only to analyze primary sources, but also to expose the interpretive frames embedded in scholarly texts. In the experiment, though, Wineburg himself—not the study participants—determined the topic of investigation: "What happened at Lexington Green on the morning of April 19, 1775?" (p. 75). The participants could formulate their own theories about what happened on that day, but relying mainly on the evidence that Wineburg provided. Moreover, they were not asked to reflect on why this topic might be worth investigating, or if, perhaps, it might better be left to the dustbin of history. In short, his participants encountered a historical problem already framed by someone else.

Numerous curricula have been developed based on this model: (1) an open-ended historical question is posed; (2) models and scaffolds for interpreting sources of evidence are provided; (3) students consult multiple sources to arrive at an answer to the question (e.g., De La Paz et al., 2017; Nokes et al., 2007; Reisman, 2012a). Such an approach presents historical inquiry as essentially an empirical affair, the point of which is to arrive at the most defensible answer to a given question. In the Vietnam unit, the writing prompt was broad enough to prompt consideration not only of empirical matters, but also of philosophical questions concerning how to frame the overall story—questions about which topics and whose perspectives to emphasize or omit. Yet the unit still failed to scaffold this framing element for students or to model how historians themselves approach it.

This realization led me to draw a theoretical distinction between critical and positivistic forms of historical reasoning, and to delineate the pedagogical supports that might foster one or the other (Table 6.2). *Critical historical reasoning* refers to the cognitive strategies and epistemic beliefs that would enable someone to understand historiography as Carr (1961) does: as a continuous dialogue between the "historian and his [or her] facts" (p. 35). Critical historical reasoning

TABLE 6.2 Elements of Critical Versus Positivistic Historical Reasoning

Critical Historical Reasoning	Positivistic Historical Reasoning
(a) Considers historical scholarship partial and subjective.	Considers primary sources subjective, but historical scholarship potentially objective.
(b) Recognizes that historians' aims and assumptions frame their investigations, leading to points of emphasis and omission.	Does not recognize the role that framing plays in historical inquiry.
(c) Assesses both the empirical integrity of historical narratives, as well as their pattern of emphasis and omission.	Assesses empirical integrity, but not the pattern of emphasis and omission.
(d) Consciously and deliberately frames one's investigations to achieve certain goals.	Strives for objectivity when conducting an investigation or crafting a narrative.

Source: Freedman (2015)

requires recognizing that historians frame their investigations through the questions they pose and the theories they advance. It requires analyzing the empirical integrity of historical narratives, yet also their pattern of emphasis and omission that derives from the author's choice of frame. Finally, critical historical reasoning entails striving not for pure objectivity, but for conscious awareness of the frame one has adopted and the affordances and constraints it imposes.

By contrast, *positivistic historical reasoning* involves viewing historical scholarship as potentially objective, deemphasizing or ignoring the issue of framing, and assessing a narrative's empirical integrity but not its pattern of emphasis and omission. Few contemporary scholars, if any, have endorsed this positivistic view explicitly. Yet scholarship on the teaching and learning of history—particularly in North America—has rarely explored how to build students' knowledge and understanding of framing. As a result, teachers educated in the current paradigm may unwittingly foster positivistic forms of reasoning in their classrooms, just as we did.

This distinction between positivistic and critical historical reasoning gives meaning to the patterns observed in the data. On criterion (a) (see Table 6.2), the students leaned in the positivistic direction, considering primary sources subjective but historical scholarship potentially objective. On criteria (b) and (c), they showed greater proclivity toward the critical, in their recognition that the textbook could be empirically accurate yet biased in its pattern of emphasis and omission. On criterion (d), they clearly endorsed the positivistic goal of assembling an objective account of the war.

Note that this theoretical formulation, generated through the design and testing of a new curriculum, functions as both a context theory and an outcomes theory (see Edelson, 2002). Positivistic tendencies could exist as part of the context to which an intervention responds. Or they may appear, like we saw, as an unintended result—a situation that could grow increasingly common as approaches compatible with positivistic forms of reasoning gain prominence. The theory also points to strategies for pushing students in the critical direction, and in this sense functions in Edelson's terms as a *design framework* (p. 114).

Conclusion

This chapter described how DBR offers prime opportunities for the generation of theory. When researchers engage in iterative design, they encounter unanticipated impediments to the intended functionality, or, as in our case, they encounter unintended outcomes. Careful documentation and reflection on these occurrences prompts abductive insight: "The surprising fact C is observed. But if A were true, C would be a matter of course" (Peirce, 1902, p. 159). In this way, design research offers fertile ground for *ontological innovation*—the generation of new theoretical constructs (diSessa & Cobb, 2004).

Tools from grounded theory methodology can help facilitate this process. In this study, these tools helped reveal the patterns that prompted the formulation of the theory. For example, in looking across the student interviews, I kept seeing the "including both sides" code appear again and again. Students' positivistic outlook in this regard was revealed by the constant comparative method. I admit, though, that the theory of critical historical reasoning did not derive solely from the data. Elements of it were embedded in the project's initial design principles— i.e., in the notion that no inquiry can be politically neutral. They also find echoes in the theoretical frame for this chapter. There is a clear connection between abductive reasoning and the framing of historical inquiry: In both, the investigator sets the inquiry in motion through some insight, curiosity, or prediction, exerting a measure of control over the inquiry's direction even before any data or evidence is collected. Yet even if the theory of critical historical reasoning derived not only from the data itself (as grounded theory purists would have it), the data tipped me off to its full articulation.

Following conventions of academic writing, the journal article that first presented the theory (Freedman, 2015) implied that I had it in mind all along when designing the unit. That is not accurate, either, though I suspect I am not the only scholar to misrepresent matters in this way. At the outset I grasped the notion of framing, but not well enough to plan instruction that would teach it effectively. The DBR process facilitated the molding of half-formed ideas into a full-fledged theory. Beyond the creation of usable products, that may be the methodology's most important function.

In closing, I also want to highlight the serendipitous aspect of DBR. As we saw, numerous plans proved ineffectual, such as the pre/post essays for measuring student growth. Others proved infeasible, such as completing the Vietnam unit with enough time remaining to study the war in Iraq. Some of these contingencies derive from the short duration of the project (only one true iteration) or from my own inexperience (a doctoral student completing my dissertation at the time). Yet I also suspect they are not uncommon. DBR allows for unplanned surprises. The project was intended to test a model for linking past to present, but the unit that strayed furthest from that aim ended up yielding some of the most evocative findings. The formulation of new theoretical constructs may well depend upon that kind of freedom.

Notes

1 Portions of this chapter appeared in the journal, *Cognition and Instruction, 33*(4), 357–398 (Freedman, 2015), in slightly altered form. The material is reprinted here with gracious permission of the publisher.
2 To protect anonymity, this chapter uses pseudonyms for the teacher and students.
3 Had both essays covered the same topic, they could have been used to measure growth in content understanding. Had they both dealt with topics not covered by the curriculum, they could have measured growth in thinking or writing skills (cf. De La Paz et al., 2017). As it was, the pre-essay covered a topic dealt with very briefly (slavery reparations), while the post-essay covered one they had studied for more than a week (poverty in the U.S.), making the essays less useful for measuring student growth.
4 In 2008 when the curriculum was taught, the Iraq War had not yet ended.
5 Some of the historical inquiries in these initiatives depart from this formula, but the implications of asking different kinds of questions (e.g., moral versus analytic) has not received much attention in published reports of the work (see Barton & Levstik, 2004).

References

Apple, M. W. (2004). *Ideology and curriculum* (3rd ed.). New York, NY: Routledge.
Bain, R. B. (2006). Rounding up unusual suspects: Facing the authority hidden in the history classroom. *Teachers College Record, 108*(10), 2080–2114.
Banks, J. A. (2008). *An introduction to multicultural education* (4th ed.). Boston, MA: Pearson.
Barton, K. C., & Levstik, L. S. (2004). *Teaching history for the common good.* Mahwah, NJ: Lawrence Erlbaum.
Carr, E. H. (1961). *What is history?* London, England: Macmillan.
Cobb, P., Confrey, J., diSessa, A., Lehrer, R., & Schauble, L. (2003). Design experiments in educational research. *Educational Researcher, 32*(1), 9–13.
Cronon, W. (1992). A place for stories: Nature, history, and narrative. *Journal of American History, 78*(4), 1347–1376.
Dallek, R., Garcia, J., Ogle, D. M., & Risinger, C. F. (2008). *American history: Reconstruction to the present.* Evanston, IL: McDougal Littell.
De La Paz, S., Monte-Sano, C., Felton, M., Croninger, R., Jackson, C., & Piantedosi, K. W. (2017). A historical writing apprenticeship for adolescents: Integrating disciplinary learning with cognitive strategies. *Reading Research Quarterly, 52*(1), 31–52. DOI:10.1002/rrq.147
diSessa, A. A., & Cobb, P. (2004). Ontological innovation and the role of theory in design experiments. *Journal of the Learning Sciences, 13*(1), 77–103.
Duckworth, E. R. (2006). *"The having of wonderful ideas" and other essays on teaching and learning* (3rd ed.). New York, NY: Teachers College Press.

Edelson, D. C. (2002). Design research: What we learn when we engage in design. *Journal of the Learning Sciences, 11*(1), 105–121. DOI:10.1207/S15327809JLS1101_4

Ellsworth, E. (1989). Why doesn't this feel empowering? Working through the repressive myths of critical pedagogy. *Harvard Educational Review, 59*(3), 297–324.

Engle, R. A., & Conant, F. R. (2002). Guiding principles for fostering productive disciplinary engagement: Explaining an emergent argument in a community of learners classroom. *Cognition and Instruction, 20*(4), 399–483.

Freedman, E. B. (2007). Is teaching for social justice undemocratic? *Harvard Educational Review, 77*(4), 442–473. DOI:10.17763/haer.77.4.hm13020523406485

Freedman, E. B. (2009). *Inquiry and ideology: Teaching everyday forms of historical thinking.* (Doctoral dissertation), University of Wisconsin, Madison, WI.

Freedman, E. B. (2015). "What happened needs to be told": Fostering critical historical reasoning in the classroom. *Cognition and Instruction, 33*(4), 357–398. DOI:10.1080/0 7370008.2015.1101465

Freedman, E. B. (in review). *How discussions succeed or fail: A comparative study of productive disciplinary engagement in two history classrooms.* Manuscript under review.

Freire, P. (1970/1993). *Pedagogy of the oppressed* (Rev. ed.). New York, NY: Continuum.

Geertz, C. (1973). *The interpretation of cultures.* New York, NY: Basic Books.

Glaser, B. G. (1978). *Theoretical sensitivity: Advances in the methodology of grounded theory.* Mill Valley, CA: Sociology Press.

Glaser, B. G., & Strauss, A. L. (1967). *The discovery of grounded theory: Strategies for qualitative research.* Chicago, IL: Aldine.

Habermas, J. (1971). *Knowledge and human interests.* Boston, MA: Beacon.

Kelly, T. E. (1986). Discussing controversial issues: Four perspectives on the teacher's role. *Theory and Research in Social Education, 14*(2), 113–138.

Kozol, J. (2005, September). Still separate, still unequal: America's educational apartheid. *Harper's Magazine, 311,* 41–54.

Leinhardt, G., & Young, K. M. (1996). Two texts, three readers: Distance and expertise in reading history. *Cognition and Instruction, 14*(4), 441–486.

McKenney, S. E., & Reeves, T. C. (2012). *Conducting educational design research.* New York, NY: Routledge.

Nokes, J. D., Dole, J. A., & Hacker, D. J. (2007). Teaching high school students to use heuristics while reading historical texts. *Journal of Educational Psychology, 99*(3), 492–504.

Novick, P. (1988). *That noble dream: The "objectivity question" and the American historical profession.* Cambridge, England: Cambridge University Press.

Parker, W. C. (2003). *Teaching democracy: Unity and diversity in public life.* New York, NY: Teachers College Press.

Paxton, R. J. (1999). A deafening silence: History textbooks and the students who read them. *Review of Educational Research, 69*(3), 315–339.

Peirce, C. S. (1902). In C. Hartshorne & P. Weiss (Eds.), *The Collected Papers of Charles S. Peirce* (Vol. 5). Cambridge, MA: Harvard University Press.

Reisman, A. (2012a). The 'Document-Based Lesson': Bringing disciplinary inquiry into high school history classrooms with adolescent struggling readers. *Journal of Curriculum Studies, 44*(2), 233–264.

Reisman, A. (2012b). Reading like a historian: A document-based history curriculum intervention in urban high schools. *Cognition and Instruction, 30*(1), 86–112.

Richards, L. (2005). *Handling qualitative data: A practical guide.* London, England: Sage.

Seixas, P. C. (1994). Students' understanding of historical significance. *Theory and Research in Social Education, 22*(3), 281–304.

Shemilt, D. (1987). Adolescent ideas about evidence and methodology in history. In C. Portal (Ed.), *The history curriculum for teachers* (pp. 39–61). London, England: Falmer.

Shor, I. (1992). *Empowering education: Critical teaching for social change.* Chicago, IL: University of Chicago Press.

Stahl, S. A., Hynd, C. R., Britton, B. K., McNish, M. M., & Bosquet, D. (1996). What happens when students read multiple source documents in history? *Reading Research Quarterly, 31*(4), 430–456.

Steinberg, S. R., & Kincheloe, J. L. (2001). Setting the context for critical multi/interculturalism: The power blocs of class elitism, white supremacy, and patriarchy. In S. R. Steinberg (Ed.), *Multi/intercultural conversations: A reader* (pp. 3–30). New York, NY: Peter Lang.

VanSledright, B. A. (2002). *In search of America's past: Learning to read history in elementary school.* New York, NY: Teachers College Press.

Wineburg, S. S. (1991). Historical problem solving: A study of the cognitive processes used in the evaluation of documentary and pictoral evidence. *Journal of Educational Psychology, 83*(1), 73–87.

Wineburg, S. S. (1999). Historical thinking and other unnatural acts. *Phi Delta Kappan, 80*(7), 488–499.

Zinn, H. (2001). *A people's history of the United States, 1492–present.* New York, NY: Perennial Classics.

PART III

Collaborating with Educators

7

INTERSECTING GOALS IN AN ELEMENTARY SOCIAL STUDIES DESIGN PROJECT

Confessional Tales of Teacher and Researcher Relationships

Kathryn M. Obenchain, Julie L. Pennington, and Maricela Bardem

This chapter explores an understudied dimension of design-based research (DBR): the collaborative relationship between researchers and classroom teachers. Using reflexive autoethnography, we (the three authors) examine our changing relationship as we collaborated on a DBR study exploring young students' understanding of civic virtue and civic engagement.

Democracies require members to participate in community improvement for the betterment of their lives and the lives of others. In representative democracies such as the United States, this includes citizens' responsibility to hold elected officials accountable. Social studies educators have an obligation to prepare students to be "informed and reasoned" participants in their communities (Parker, 2003, p. 32). The way citizenship is taught can influence the manner and extent of young people's civic participation.

Scholars note that democratic societies best achieve their foundational principles when citizens adopt a critical perspective. Parker (2003) and Castro (2013) argue that critical citizenship operates from the assumption that democracy is unfinished. Democratic states, institutions, and the individuals who manage them require citizens' constant vigilance. Similarly, as societies evolve over time, particular institutions within democratic states also need to evolve to remain true to democratic ideals. Abowitz and Harnish (2006) suggest that critical citizenship includes discourses that "raise issues of membership, identity, and engagement" (p. 666). A vision of democracy as unfinished and evolving, as opposed to a unity perspective that focuses on preserving the status-quo, is beneficial for citizenship development (Abowitz & Harnish, 2006; Miller-Lane, Howard, & Halagao, 2007; Westheimer & Kahne, 2004). Critical citizens question and analyze, critically think, are informed, and commit to combatting injustice (deGroot, 2017; Johnson & Morris, 2010; Westheimer & Kahne, 2004).

These understandings and skills require a particular type of citizenship education that challenges sanitized and over-simplified narratives of individuals and the decisions they make. Social studies education can help foster this approach to civic life. The National Council for the Social Studies (2010) notes that "young people who are knowledgeable, skillful, and committed to democracy are necessary to sustaining and improving our democratic way of life, and participating as members of a global community." It can be challenging, however, to implement a critical civic approach in elementary classrooms where social studies is often not taught.

Continuing pressure to increase test scores in math, reading, and science have contributed to the de-emphasis or absence of social studies in the elementary school curriculum (Heafner & Fitchett, 2012; Vogler et al., 2007). Evidence indicates that some elementary teachers are uncomfortable with their own understandings of the content and purpose of social studies (VanFossen, 2005). If teachers do not see civic competence as a goal or recognize the importance of critical civic approaches, there are additional hurdles to overcome.

To address these challenges, the first two authors, Kathy and Julie, worked with Maricela, the third author, and an elementary teacher, to co-create a series of integrated social studies and literacy units built on the tenets of Critical Democratic Literacy (CDL) (Obenchain & Pennington, 2015). The three of us developed, implemented, and studied the CDL units using a qualitative adaption of DBR. We chose DBR for our collaboration because it allowed us to work with Maricela to bring CDL into her classroom in a flexible and responsive way. Given Maricela's expressed interest in expanding her students' social studies experiences and making sustained changes in her social studies teaching, as well as our shared interest in critical approaches, collaborating through DBR was appropriate. Collaboration is an essential component of the methodology, as researchers and teachers work together to better understand the contexts in which learning occurs.

Over the course of this two-phase CDL DBR study, however, our roles were altered as the broader institutional context surrounding Maricela's classroom changed. While the first phase was highly collaborative in planning, teaching, and assessing, the school administration redefined Maricela's responsibilities in the second phase, repositioning our roles in the classroom and the research. This chapter focuses on how and why our relationship changed, as well as the effects this repositioning had as we taught the CDL units. The relationship between researcher and teacher in DBR is an under-studied dimension of DBR and one that we address in this chapter. In this post-study analysis of our roles, we utilized autoethnography (Ellis, 2004; Reed-Danahay, 1997) to examine our relationship as co-teachers and researchers. Specifically, we conducted critical co-constructed autoethnography, which provides "a way for collaborating activist researchers to reflect on the tempo, uncertainty and complexity of research relationships" (Cann & DeMeulenaere, 2012, p. 146). Given the importance of researcher and teacher collaboration in the DBR model, a lack of attention to those relationships, as well as how they may evolve, has the potential to alter DBR work. Enacting critical perspectives and engaging in social-justice-oriented work in an era where set curriculum is preferred requires an in-depth understanding of the local context, the school, the classroom, and the teacher.

We focus on how the nature of our collaboration evolved over time and played a key role in understanding the broader educational contexts of the research study and the role of DBR in actual practice. This is important for DBR researchers in social studies to consider, because this level of collaboration opens up a space for the discussion of critical issues that potentially puts teachers and researchers in the position of challenging or contradicting current curricula.

Theoretical Framework

Critical Democratic Literacy

Our classroom DBR intervention was framed around the tenets of Critical Democratic Literacy (Obenchain & Pennington, 2015). CDL is a type of literacy comparable to scientific and mathematical literacy (Alexander, Walsh, Jarman, & McClune, 2008). It is dependent on the disciplinary content knowledge required for critical citizenship, including knowledge of history, political science, geography, and economics, as well as the methodological approaches used by scholars in these disciplines (e.g., analyzing primary sources, chronological thinking).

The critical element of CDL relies on critical theory (Kincheloe, 2004) and its call for disrupting the status quo in education and in the communities where students live, for the purpose of changing power relationships and dismantling institutions of oppression (Giroux, 1980; Macedo, 1993). A critical perspective recognizes that the ideals of democracy cannot be achieved without recognizing the need for collective action to address injustice (Tyson, 2003). This includes confronting categories of oppression such as those described by Young (1990), including exploitation, marginalization, powerlessness, cultural imperialism, and violence, at both individual and institutional levels. Similarly, Montgomery (2014) notes that "critical democracy explicitly promotes values of equality and social justice and works not only to address, but also to redress, issues of oppression" (p. 200). Beginning with this perspective on democracy, CDL aligns with critical conceptions of civic education (e.g., DeJaeghere, 2009; Swalwell, 2015; Westheimer & Kahne, 2004), in which students learn to question injustice and engage in work to benefit the common good.

CDL requires a particular type of literacy, consistent with a critical approach (Endres, 2001; Janks, 2000). It directly challenges the reduction of literacy into a set of discrete skills, a functional view that does little to prepare citizens to work for equity and justice (Obenchain & Pennington, 2015, p. 19). Bringing together democracy and literacy and situating them within a critical frame require citizens' engagement for the overt purpose of working for justice. The power of CDL comes from teaching in integrative ways that promote elementary students' awareness of injustices, past and present, as well as their commitment to contesting injustices imposed on themselves and others. The integrative approach in CDL "builds a needed resiliency to navigate, understand, and evaluate political and civic information via new literacies in order to remain an engaged and informed participant in society" (Obenchain & Pennington, 2015, p. 24). We suggest that CDL can be fostered in developmentally appropriate ways in early elementary settings. To explore this assumption, the three of us worked in Maricela's classroom for two semesters over a two-year period to explore the question, "How does elementary students' understanding of civic virtue and engagement evolve within a critical democratic literacy curriculum?"

Teacher–Researcher Collaboration in Design-Based Research

Design-based research (DBR) continues to grow in popularity as a research method in educational contexts, particularly in the U.S. (Anderson & Shattuck, 2012). DBR is dedicated to improving classroom teaching and learning in reliable and sustainable ways, while attending to the evolving classroom context. We used a qualitative adaptation of DBR to examine how elementary students understood civic virtue and engagement within a CDL-integrated unit. We employed notions of DBR and design-based implementation research (DBIR) due to their focus on classroom collaboration, with room for the continual iterative design and redesign of the study (Penuel, Fishman, Cheng & Sabelli, 2011; Wang & Hannafin, 2005). This attention to collaboration positioned Kathy, Julie, and Maricela as both researchers and teachers, sharing a philosophical affinity for CDL and each bringing particular knowledge and skills to the study and classroom.

The role of the classroom teacher varies across DBR studies (McKenney & Reeves, 2012). Anderson and Shattuck's (2012) review of a decade of DBR did not provide details on teachers' experiences or involvement, but it did highlight the importance of understanding the context in which the intervention occurred. Often, collaboration refers simply to researchers gaining access to teachers' classrooms to design and implement their intervention (e.g., Joseph, 2004). Alternatively, researchers can collaborate with classroom teachers in curricular design and iteration, with the researcher serving as the intervention instructors (e.g., Crompton, 2017; Suswandari, 2017; Wang & Hsu, 2017). Finally, researchers and teachers can collaborate throughout, with the teachers involved in the intervention's design, implementation, revision, and assessment (e.g., Fazio & Gallagher, 2018; Hultén & Björkholm, 2016). Often, this last structure involves some type of teacher professional development. MacDonald (2008) specifically called for the use of a Community of Practice structure in

DBR studies to better understand teachers' experiences, strengthen collaboration, and contribute to the sustainability of the intervention. Given the goals of DBR, we find this last structure to be the most beneficial.

Few studies have explored teachers' and researchers' experiences with collaboration in DBR. Brown, Taylor, and Ponambalum (2016) used DBR to study the transition experiences of vulnerable students, as well as teachers' experiences using lesson study to design and implement an intervention. They concluded that collaboration was essential to both the success of the intervention and its sustainability. Thein et al. (2012) determined that the collaborative elements of DBR strengthened the professional development experiences of teachers. The lead researcher also reflected on her own deepened understanding of the complexities of teachers' work and the necessity of a "true balance between theory and practice" (p.133) in DBR studies. Similarly, Joseph (2004) noted how her DBR study "provided a strong intellectual resource for my decision making as a teacher" (p. 241) by pushing her to more deeply explore her own understanding of learning and motivation theories that she had uncritically relied on. This literature highlights the importance of meaningful collaboration and of respecting teachers' expertise and knowledge of the context in which learning occurs (see also Lo, Adams, Goodell, & Nachtigal, this volume).

In this chapter, we use autoethnographic methods to examine the evolving relationship between the researchers and the classroom teacher in our CDL DBR study. In the following section, we briefly describe our roles as co-teachers and researchers, followed by our findings regarding student learning during the study. We then detail our post-study critical co-constructed autoethnographic (Cann and DeMeulenaere, 2012; Hughes & Willink, 2015) examination of the unexpected evolution in our relationship across the two years of the study.

Overview of the Original DBR Study

The original aim of the study was to explore ways to develop and refine a CDL curriculum that fostered elementary students' understandings of civic virtue and civic engagement. Kathy (a social studies researcher) and Julie (a literacy researcher) collaborated with Maricela (an elementary teacher) in her multi-grade elementary classroom over two years. We adopted DBIR's notions of "persistent problems of practice," a "commitment to iterative, collaborative design," and "developing theory related to classroom learning" (Penuel et al., 2011, p. 331), in planning out the study. The persistent problem of practice in the CDL DBR study was the impact of the accountability movement on social studies and literacy instruction. Therefore, the iterative, collaborative design of the study was linked to the need to study the CDL-based classroom instruction in collaborative, flexible, and responsive ways to examine how elementary students understood the concepts of civic virtue and civic engagement.

Persistent Problems of Practice

Two persistent problems of practice—limited time for social studies in elementary classrooms (Heafner and Fitchett, 2012; Leming, Ellington, & Schug, 2006) and a lack of a social justice orientation in elementary curricula, textbooks, and academic standards (Au, 2009)—were reflected in Maricela's classroom. In the first year of the study, her instructional guide was the Common Core State Standards' (National Governors Association, 2010) focus on reading more informational texts, with a constant awareness of the relationship between her reading instruction and the state's mandated assessments. Maricela's school district adopted and provided her with a series of nationally published elementary social studies textbooks (Scott Foresman, 2011) that she used for independent student work during a portion of her reading time.

Maricela, who taught from a social justice and critical literacy perspective, stated that the textbooks did not support her goal of social justice. For example, the textbook devoted one page to describing the life and historical significance of Harriet Tubman. Maricela found excerpts like this one limited in scope, as she believed in the importance of a social studies curriculum and wanted to use it to support her social justice aims. However, tasked with teaching all subjects to her multi-age students, Maricela had limited time to search for curricular materials to supplement the textbooks. She found a few books on Harriet Tubman for her students and they did book reports, but she had limited confidence in her own background knowledge in social studies, particularly as it applied to designing and implementing lessons beyond those from the textbooks. She positioned herself as limited in her knowledge of social studies instruction and accompanying content knowledge (see Fitchett, Heafner, & Lambert, 2014).

A collaborative DBR study based on CDL provided an opportunity for the three of us to find time for social studies instruction in Maricela's class through the effective integration of social studies into Maricela's reading time. In addition, given CDL's critical focus, we sought to identify content, pedagogy, and resources that would align with her social justice orientation, while still allowing Maricela to meet the mandated, state academic standards. Addressing these problems of practice was the impetus for our collaboration as co-teachers and researchers in her classroom.

Iterative and Collaborative Design

In order to foster a collaborative relationship among the three members of the study team, we initially created opportunities for frequent and ongoing discussion and review of student learning, curriculum, planning, and assessment. Prior to any lesson development, the three of us talked extensively about Maricela's goals for her students in social studies and literacy learning. This was particularly important given the varied interpretations of the purpose and contents of the social studies curriculum (Adler, 2008). As we began our discussions, it was clear that Maricela was already teaching from a critical stance and was drawn to the conceptual ideas within CDL. She taught her students to think critically and engaged them actively in her classroom through read-alouds and discussions of enduring critical issues and current events. We elected to work with Maricela to further develop these practices in a multi-year study, beginning with her first-grade students.

The study was conducted in two phases: (1) in 2014 with seven first graders, and (2) in 2016 when the same students were third graders. Both phases examined how a CDL approach could build students' understandings of the concepts of civic virtue and civic engagement. During phase one, Julie and Kathy proposed teaching from a conceptual standpoint and, at Maricela's request, worked on constructing instructional units on important figures in the textbook related to Black History Month. While we collaboratively created these unit plans in advance, we modified lessons daily in response to our ongoing assessment of student learning. In 2016, we taught about that year's election within the context of the history of U.S. presidents and the philosophical foundations of the U.S. political system. During both phases, we examined how students learned the concepts of civic virtue and civic engagement through integrated literacy lessons. As we evaluated student learning in our ongoing meetings, we began to refine and adjust our lessons and to narrow our research focus to understanding how CDL, a relatively new model, could be operationalized in the elementary classroom.

Data Collection, Analysis, and Main Findings

We videotaped lessons and collected student work (e.g., texts, writing samples, drawings). We used open coding and analysis of all the data, including student artifacts, transcripts of discussions, and assessments related to an understanding of civic virtue and civic engagement. Open coding indicated that students were articulating their knowledge of the civic concepts in their class discussions and their writing samples. We then identified key events and artifacts that provided rich detail and particular examples of ways students described their understanding of civic virtue and civic engagement.

Our analysis revealed the students' abilities to apply the concepts of civic virtue and engagement to various situations and contexts (e.g., historical, current). For example, students understood that Harriet Tubman demonstrated civic virtue because she took action to help herself as well as others. At the same time, they determined that astronaut and physician Mae Jemison, while a good role model, did not necessarily demonstrate civic virtue through her actions of becoming an astronaut. Students articulated the actions each figure had taken, as well as actions they personally could take to demonstrate civic virtue, such as standing up to a bully. Overall, students demonstrated a conceptual understanding of civic virtue, civic engagement, and civil disobedience, with the ability to evaluate examples and non-examples (Pennington et al., in review). These findings suggested that direct instruction in CDL can occur within the literacy instructional time, and expand beyond the district-provided textbook. Building on these findings and our successful collaboration, we began to plan for phase two with a new CDL topic, while maintaining the concepts of civic virtue, civic engagement, and civil disobedience. However, as we transitioned from phase one to phase two, a shift occurred in the roles that we played in the study. The examination of these shifts is the focus of the remainder of this chapter.

Reflexive Autoethnography: A Tool for Examining Researcher and Teacher Positioning in DBR

While DBR is used as a method to conduct classroom research, it does not explicitly address the interpersonal relationships and the nature of the intimate work co-researchers and teachers conduct. To examine the change in our collaborative relationship over the course of our study, we relied on autoethnography, which centers the self as the focus of study within various socio-cultural contexts (Hughes & Pennington, 2017). Autoethnography derives from broader movements in qualitative research that press for reflexivity throughout the research process (Ellis, 2004; Denzin & Lincoln, 2011; Reed-Danahay, 1997). Autoethnographers such as Ellis advocate for reviewing how researchers change as they engage in fieldwork. We adopted this approach in explicating how our relationship among the three of us shifted during the second phase of the study.

Critical Co-constructed Autoethnography

One type of autoethnographic work is critical co-constructed autoethnography (Hughes & Willink, 2015), which is a "process of collectively reflecting together about our work" (Cann & DeMeulenaere, 2012, p. 153). Our data consisted of shared discussions and reflections on our work together, in the form of emails, annotated lesson plans, and meeting notes. The three of us met, revisited our experiences, and checked our understandings of critical conversations and events that had occurred over the course of the study. During these meetings, we compared and discussed the significance of each event from our individual perspectives. We focused our analysis on the ways our DBR methodology, specifically our collaborative configuration, changed over time. Shifts in the context of Maricela's teaching life, in the roles the three of us played, and in the nature of our working relationship were central to these post-study analyses.

While representations of autoethnographic work range from traditional academic writing to poetry (Hughes and Pennington, 2017), our representation takes the form of a "confessional tale" (Van Maanen, 1988), where the researchers reveal aspects of their work not often shared with those outside of the research process. As Jonsen et al. (2012) put it, "The autoethnographic lens adds a rich account of the processes and team dynamics involved, including the events and uncertainties that take place as the collaboration unfolds" (p. 407). Our inquiry focused on how and why our professional relationship changed over time, from a collaborative and integrative working relationship to one with limited connections between the researchers and classroom teacher.

Moving from a Cohesive Triumvirate to a Split Trichotomy

Our autoethnographic analysis revealed that our collaborative relationship changed from a triumvirate and equal partnership to a disjointed trichotomy, although we remained close personally. Our shared commitment to educating students with a CDL focus continued to bind our relationship despite the changes in the study configuration. We posit that the shifting educational context in which we worked was responsible for the changes in our working relationship that we assumed would remain stable. As Anderson and Shattuck (2012) point out, DBR studies "provide rich descriptions of the contexts in which the studies occurred, the challenges of implementation, the development processes involved in creating and administrating the interventions, and the design principles that emerged" (p. 22). Between phase one and phase two of the study, the educational context changed considerably and became a challenge during implementation. By the end of the study, we were repositioned in several ways that altered the collaborative nature of our work, as well as adding a new dimension to Julie and Kathy's roles as researchers.

The Initial Triumvirate

Our original decision to collaborate using DBR rested on our shared commitment to teaching young children from a critical perspective. The three of us knew one another prior to conceptualizing and embarking on the DBR study. Julie and Kathy had co-authored manuscripts related to CDL and integrating literacy and social studies. Maricela had been a graduate student in courses that Julie and Kathy taught, providing her with opportunities to discuss scholarship on teaching and learning. Over the years, we had all come to know one another's shared philosophical beliefs about education and critical democratic literacy. We believed in developing and nurturing students' disposition to learn. Maricela relied on her growing knowledge of research from her master's coursework to infuse these ideas into her teaching. She was an exemplary teacher, committed to meeting the needs of all her students. We had a mutual respect for the experiences and expertise of one another, along with a mutual trust in one another. These shared beliefs were compatible with a DBR approach in terms of emphasizing collaboration, the importance of context, and persistent problems of practice.

Initially, we all participated equally in curriculum planning and engaged in instruction and student assessment. Our relationship focused on how to best teach the students to be engaged, virtuous, and critical citizens, and can be characterized as a triumvirate where we worked as a coalition. This was evidenced by our informal discussions, where the dialogue patterns were informal as we brainstormed ideas, asserted our ideas, and shared concerns and issues. Working from our established relationship, we discussed how we could meet state literacy and social studies academic standards through a CDL approach. We searched through available resources, including the textbook, possible supplemental materials (e.g., children's literature, websites, and videos) and sources for our planning. Kathy stepped in when questions about social studies, citizenship education, and conceptual learning were raised, and Julie brought expertise in critical literacy and integration, as well as her numerous prior years as an elementary teacher.

Maricela was the most knowledgeable about the literacy and social studies knowledge of her students, their cultural backgrounds, the available curricular materials, and the expectations of her school leadership. Her perspective on how she created a classroom environment that encouraged critical thinking with a focus on social justice across the entire curriculum positioned Maricela as instrumental in conceptualizing student learning goals for the project. Julie and Kathy frequently deferred to Maricela in light of this expertise. For example, Kathy said in a team meeting, "You know your students better than us, so we need to follow your guidance here. How should we frame our discussion with the students tomorrow about the connections they brought up today between civic engagement and bullying at school?" In another instance, Julie asked Maricela, "This is your class; how should we introduce civic virtue to students? What background knowledge do they have that we can connect to that concept?" And later, "How would a focus on storytelling support your goals for their learning?"

Kathy was a social studies teacher educator and civic education scholar. Julie and Maricela positioned her as the expert on the social studies curriculum and content. For example, Kathy noted that the students had assumed that everyone under study in phase one had been enslaved because they were Black. The students were unable to place the individuals within their historical context. Julie and Maricela asked questions such as, "How do we get students to understand that Tubman, Carver, and Jemison lived in different time periods?" Recognizing the need to explicitly teach the historical skill of chronology, Kathy then worked with Julie and Maricela to address this skill and add a timeline activity to clarify each person's historical placement.

As Julie was a literacy scholar, Kathy and Maricela positioned her as the expert in literacy teaching and learning, as well as an expert in integration. They drew on her expertise with questions such as, "How should we work with the students who are not at the reading level of this text?" and "How accessible are these informational texts to the English Learners in class?"

Figure 7.1 illustrates how the relationship was balanced as we functioned jointly. We worked together well, as evidenced by our informal style of cross-talking,

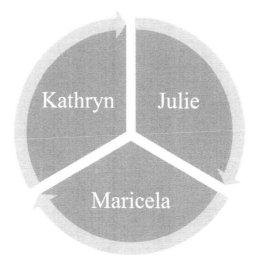

FIGURE 7.1   Triumvirate: Coalition of Three Functioning Jointly.

interspersing common ideas within discussions, and deferring to individual areas of positioned expertise when particular questions were raised. Each decision was negotiated, and consensus was easy and commonplace. Ideas were co-constructed as we shared the teaching, each stepping in when appropriate. We worked together in this way throughout phase one of the study, focusing on the CDL goals and student learning. As described above, results from this first year indicated that the students were able to understand the civic concepts and could apply them to personal, historical, and current examples. They were able to distinguish between examples and non-examples of the concepts and displayed appropriate dispositions and behaviors consistent with civic virtue in their own lives (Pennington et al., in review). Further, we learned that a CDL approach could complement existing academic standards in social studies and literacy, that it could be implemented successfully in an integrative manner within a literacy block in the classroom, and that young students could learn ideas that promoted critical citizenship.

The Eventual Trichotomy

In the second phase of the study, the relationship among the three of us altered due to a shift in Maricela's responsibilities. Her school was under pressure to improve their test scores, and the teachers for each grade level were required to meet together and coordinate their instruction. Maricela was now required to spend all of her planning time with her school colleagues rather than meeting and planning with Julie and Kathy, eliminating our debriefing and planning time. In addition, Maricela's planning with her school team included a requirement to teach E. D. Hirsch's *Core Knowledge* (2018) curriculum for social studies. At Maricela's urging and with the administration's continued support, we continued the study, but instead of working with the entire multi-age class as planned, Maricela asked Julie and Kathy to work only with the third graders from the first phase of the study.

The collaborative conversations that characterized the triumvirate stage of our DBR study disappeared as Julie and Kathy shared their work intermittently and hurriedly with Maricela. Instead of co-planning with Maricela, Kathy and Julie operated independently of her and the students in her class. Julie and Kathy developed and implemented a 12-week unit on the founding of the United States and the electoral process (Obenchain, Pennington, & Carter, 2018). As part of the school mandate, all of Maricela's lessons needed to be reviewed by the administrators to ensure that they met the state's academic content standards. Each week Kathy and Julie provided lesson plans for Maricela to submit. Maricela mentioned that her lesson plans received feedback from her administrators about what her curriculum did and did not include with respect to *Core Knowledge*. Maricela never brought any comments to Julie and Kathy about the lesson plans they submitted. During phase two, when Julie and Kathy taught, Maricela was always in the classroom, but she was working with other small groups concurrently. The opportunities to watch and support one another, to co-teach, and to debrief on the lessons disappeared, and this affected the collaborative nature of our DBR work. All of these shifts repositioned us significantly. Figure 7.2 illustrates the change in our relationship.

This trichotomy represents how the relationship altered and repositioned us as researchers by putting Julie and Kathy in a position of teaching and researching independent from Maricela, similar to more traditional studies that are not focused on collaborating with classroom teachers. Julie and Maricela

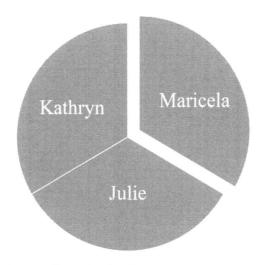

FIGURE 7.2 Trichotomy: Separation into Parts.

communicated intermittently, and informally checked in with each other just to make sure the study was proceeding smoothly. No conversations covered details of student learning or how to plan follow up lessons. Julie and Kathy would complete a lesson and wave to Maricela as she taught a reading group in the corner of her classroom. A few times during the semester, Julie and Kathy would ask the students to share their ideas with Maricela later in the day. During this period, Julie and Kathy were in constant daily communication evaluating the lesson for the day and modifying the next day's lesson. They sent weekly lesson updates to Maricela via email. Maricela often apologized for lacking time to meet with them, and she did not have time to read their plans. Maricela's time was spent attending trainings, planning with her team, and assessing her students on the mandated literacy and math tests.

Maricela began to share her frustrations with the new emphasis on mandated curriculum and testing, and asked for Julie and Kathy's help in navigating the requirements. She expressed her ideas about wanting to use materials and methods beyond what the new mandated curriculum offered. Julie and Kathy began to draw on their expertise in social studies and literacy instruction to provide ideas for instruction that she could implement on her own. Seeing Maricela as a colleague and as an excellent teacher, Kathy and Julie wanted to support her. They engaged in informal discussions with Maricela about how to teach in ways that aligned with current research. In particular, Julie shared examples of how she had navigated similar tensions in her own K-12 teaching experiences (Pennington, 2004) and talked about examples from the academic literature. Maricela was accustomed to creating or modifying her instruction and materials to suit her goals. She was adept at relying on research to justify her work, and she utilized many informal formative assessments as she taught, much in the same way we had operated during phase one.

There was a different collaborative nature to these new conversations. While Maricela still positioned Julie and Kathy as colleagues and educational experts, Julie and Kathy repositioned themselves as advocates for Maricela, for her ways of teaching, and for her students. Over the ensuing months, in addition to asking her advice on navigating the mandated curriculum, Julie and Kathy wanted to support Maricela by bringing in research that illuminated strategies consistent with CDL and teaching for social justice. Clearly, a social justice perspective permeated our views of rigid curriculum programs, and the content of our CDL work had solidified our shared identities as educators who critically examined goals and materials. Now, faced with tightly bound teaching expectations, we found ourselves in different positions within the CDL DBR study. First, we were positioned differently in teaching. Second, we were positioned differently with respect to the curricular requirements that Maricela now faced. Kathy and Julie could not challenge those district requirements. The two researchers were not employed by the school; rather, they worked at universities whose academic expectations aligned with critical work.

Unpacking the Relationship Shift

During this second year, while Julie and Kathy continued the CDL DBR study with the support of the school administrators, Maricela's role in the study was minimized, affecting our ability to continue a collaborative DBR study. The shift from collaboration to parallel work thwarted our ability to bring more social-justice-focused social studies into Maricela's classroom through integration with literacy (see Table 7.1).

Julie and Kathy found themselves in new territory and in a position that they had unintentionally created. The three of us had conceptualized the study and the CDL curriculum we planned to teach, and had talked a great deal about the role of education in preparing critical, engaged citizens who worked for social justice. In planning, we positioned ourselves in alignment with social justice issues, and we talked about our teaching lives, the current divisive political climate, and accountability pressures that we all thought were detrimental to a meaningful education. Our work in education was a form of advocacy and how we wanted to prepare students and teachers to become advocates for a more just world. These ideas directly applied to Maricela standing up for her own ideas as a teacher, using the knowledge, skills, and dispositions needed to recognize injustice and speak out against it. As standing up for oneself and others was part of the CDL-based curriculum we taught, so advocating for Maricela's autonomy as a teacher was part of our role beyond the classroom instruction. In the original intent of our DBR study built around the ideas of critical democratic literacy (CDL), this positioning was appropriate and meaningful. Now, however, we were faced with enacting these critical notions within an environment that was inflexible, particularly for Maricela.

The Consequences of Shifting Roles: Reflexive Autoethnographic Analysis

There were consequences for each of us as we worked through the changing context of the study. The navigation of issues of justice beyond the CDL DBR study as it related to curriculum became a focus of the autoethnographic analysis of our collaboration within DBR. After completion of the study, Kathy and Julie vacillated between advocating for Maricela's ideas and worrying that they were agitators pushing her to call for change at her school. As advocates, they supported and agreed with Maricela's view of education and for what she wanted her students to learn. As possible agitators, they agreed that Maricela should be allowed to rely on her professional judgment as a well-educated and experienced teacher to make classroom decisions that she knew to be best for her students. They agreed with her desire to participate in research opportunities as a way to improve her practice, to contribute to the knowledge base of classroom-based research, and to create a space for educational researchers to work in classrooms.

TABLE 7.1 Consequences of Dissolving the DBR Collaboration

Collaborative DBR: Year One Triumvirate		Non-Collaborative Classroom Research: Year Two Trichotomy
Maricela, Kathy, and Julie met during teacher planning time to co-design integrated lessons based on their shared goals, academic standards, social justice focus, and student progress.	Planning Time	Collaborative co-planning time was eliminated. Maricela unable to meet during her planning time. Kathy and Julie planned together and sent lesson plans to Maricela.
Maricela, Kathy, and Julie co-taught small-group and whole-class lessons.	Instructional Time	Co-teaching was eliminated. Kathy and Julie co-taught lessons (without Maricela) to one small group. Maricela taught other small groups of students.
Maricela brought in additional content and materials, and taught additional lessons during times when Kathy and Julie were not present to reinforce the DBR study's academic CDL goals.	Instructional Time	Maricela taught the district-mandated, compartmentalized curriculum that was separate from the DBR study's focus on social justice and CDL.
Maricela, Kathy, and Julie met and discussed student progress and adapted lessons accordingly.	Student Assessment	Collaborative reflection time on assessment, including areas to reteach, was eliminated. Kathy and Julie shared student progress intermittently with Maricela via email and informal conversations. Kathy and Julie continued adapting lessons based on their evaluation of student progress.

Kathy and Julie were urging Maricela to rely on her professional judgement to teach in ways that she knew to be best practices. They were encouraging her to break from established norms in her educational context. In some instances, they encouraged Maricela to speak up.

However, in encouraging Maricela to advocate for herself and her work, Kathy and Julie possibly placed her in a difficult position. Their role as university researchers could add credibility to her cause, or it could make the situation worse for her. Maricela knew she had their support and asked for their advice on how to advocate for herself with her administrators. Maricela attempted to challenge some of the curricular requirements by asking questions about using other materials and methods. She was told to use the school curriculum without modification. From a critical reflexive autoethnographic perspective, Kathy and Julie recognized their responsibility to critique their role in the DBR process. Their presence in Maricela's classroom positioned them as agitators rather than advocates.

Implications: Point of Entry and Curricular Challenges of DBR

There are two implications from this study: the importance of a point of entry for a collaboration, and the impact of how curriculum is viewed within particular school contexts. Teacher collaboration in DBR studies may be supported or hindered by the collaboration's point of entry. Points of entry include top-down orientations, such as the school district or the school site, and bottom-up orientations that are initiated at the classroom level. Each offers different opportunities and obstacles. We initiated our collaboration with the teacher, while other DBR studies may enter the collaboration at the district or school level. Entering at the classroom level met our goals and gave us the opportunity to adjust the curriculum based on student learning in a meaningful and recursive way, with the full support and continual input from the teacher. Maricela wanted to do this work and was invested in the outcome. On the other hand, since we were not collaborating at district and school levels, we had no control over the required curriculum or how Maricela spent her time. We obtained IRB permission to conduct the study from both the university and the school district, as well as permission from school administrators. However, permission is not collaboration; our collaboration was with the teacher, and that was our intent. If we had entered our collaboration at the institutional level, our CDL intervention work would have been controlled from the top administrative level.

This suggests that researchers should pay attention to both where they are entering the collaborative relationship and how they are defining collaboration. Researchers should be aware that if they enter the collaboration at the classroom level, it is possible that curricular demands dictated by the district or school administration will affect the collaboration and DBR study. Further, we must honor the institutional context that classroom teachers navigate, including how the context affects their ability to engage in DBR. While collaboration is a stated goal of DBR, the level of the classroom teacher's involvement varies greatly. DBR is not a simple activity implemented in a static environment. Bringing new ideas to classrooms and teachers requires careful attention to possible reactions and changes based on external goals removed from the study.

A second, related implication is that DBR practitioners need to be aware of how the planned curriculum might be viewed within the broader school context. Implementing a recognized, packaged curriculum might be more attractive to administrators who are under accountability and testing pressures. A predetermined curricula ensures that all teachers in the grade level or subject area are teaching the same material in the same way, with the expectation that all students will perform consistently and reliably on predetermined assessment measures. Curriculum decisions are typically made at the district or school level rather than by classroom teachers. In the case of our CDL DBR study, once *Core Knowledge* (2018) was established as the social studies curriculum, teacher grade-level planning groups were required for uniform curricular implementation.

While the CDL curriculum met and in fact exceeded the state social studies standards, it was not a pre-packaged, scripted, and exportable program that could be dropped into any classroom. Rather, CDL rests on standards and conceptual instruction with flexibility for students and teachers. Sustainability was not based on the program fidelity and scripted replication of lessons which can create tension in school contexts with packaged programs. DBR collaborations with teachers provide a means for working beyond social studies curricula (e.g., textbooks, packaged programs) that do not attend to teacher expertise and student knowledge. As Brophy and Alleman (2009) state:

> There are problems with this reliance on textbooks . . . the content does not consist of networks of connected information structured around big ideas (which would make it both worth learning and relatively easy to learn). Instead, it consists of parades of disconnected facts that provide a "trivial pursuit" or "mile-wide but inch deep" curriculum.
>
> *(p. 359)*

DBR acknowledges and purports to attend to the unique context of each classroom, and CDL works well with that approach. Yet, the same elements that make the research process authentic can also open up areas that must be navigated with care. This is especially true when the collaborators are committed to going beyond packaged curriculum and advocating for justice, and when the work is at odds with district mandates. Teachers and researchers must continually evaluate their roles and the power structures and contexts within which they work. These relationships are in perpetual motion and can morph depending on the evolving immediate context, as well as the broader institutional context.

We argue that design researchers should maintain clear and open relationships with the classroom teachers with whom they work, and remain aware of how the classroom intervention affects not only the students under study but also the teachers' notions of their own pedagogy and knowledge. This may be particularly challenging when studies are initiated at the institutional level and teachers are not at the center of the design. The top-down and bottom-up entry points have advantages and disadvantages for both researchers and teachers, and researchers must determine how far they are willing to go to support their research goals as they work with teachers.

Clearly, the complexity of each unique classroom context does not allow us to call for specific prescriptions for researchers to follow; rather, we propose guiding questions for researchers contemplating classroom-based DBR. Answers to these questions depend upon each researcher, classroom, and school context, and attend to the point of entry and the type of curriculum and instruction proposed.

Questions Regarding Point of Entry

DBR offers opportunities for attending to the changing classroom context that is inherent in every school. However, our research calls attention to the importance of the point of entry for DBR studies. The point of entry into collaboration is an important yet overlooked dimension in DBR. Attending to the consequences of the point of entry is often noted as a simple procedural aspect of planning. Whether collaboration begins at the district, school, or classroom level, we advocate involving teachers in all aspects of the intervention's design, implementation, and assessment, while also paying attention to the institutional attitudes and policies that influence collaborative work. Teacher collaboration as it relates to the institutional context is essential for achieving the promised results of DBR. Understanding the political landscape of the school is key. The following questions provide insight when considering a study's point of entry:

- Who generated the idea for the study?
- Are the teachers involved in the study willing participants, and how do you know?
- Who is making the curricular space for the intervention?

Questions Regarding Curriculum

DBR as a research method relies on a deep awareness of local and national issues as they relate to curriculum. In the continuing high-stakes accountability environment, many studies focus on large data sets and not on individual classrooms. The continued pressure from multiple stakeholders (e.g., school district, policymakers, parents) to raise test scores may find teachers working in contexts with narrow and prescribed curricular mandates, offering little time for experimentation. Alternatively, some studies may align with prescribed curriculum or pedagogy, placing teachers on the margins of participating in co-constructed inquiry by requiring fidelity to that curriculum. We propose the following questions to consider in regards to these curricular issues:

- What curriculum requirements does the school have?
- How are teachers positioned by the instruction and assessment requirements of the DBR study?
- Are the teachers positioned as knowledgeable or are they simply asked to implement a pre-existing program or intervention from the top down?
- What is the role of school administrators in the study?

Being able to conduct research in classrooms is crucial for fostering sustainable change. DBR is an excellent method for framing collaborative work in classrooms with teachers and students, but it should be continually reviewed and refined in ways that do not privilege top-down points of entry. Critical perspectives, such as CDL, drive innovative instruction and assessment, yet can be seen as a risk by school administrators or outside observers. DBR can be a valuable method for bringing teachers into the research process by building close collaboration and trust. However, when the research brings critical content and methods into the classroom and teachers' lives, researchers must consider if they are to be advocates or agitators of the status quo as they move the field forward.

References

Abowitz, K. K., & Harnish, J. (2006). Contemporary discourses of citizenship. *Review of Education Research*, *76*(4), 653–690. DOI: 10.3102/00346543076004653

Adler, S. (2008). The education of social studies teachers. In L. S. Levstik & C. A. Tyson (Eds.), *Handbook of Research in Social Studies Education* (pp. 329–351). New York, NY: Routledge.

Alexander, J., Walsh, P., Jarman, R., & McClune, B. (2008). From rhetoric to reality: Advancing literacy by cross-curricular means. *The Curriculum Journal*, *19*(1), 23–35.

Anderson, T., & Shattuck, J. (2012). Design-based research: A decade of progress in education research. *Educational Researcher*, *41*(1), 16–25.

Au, W. (2009). Social studies, social justice: W(h)ither the social studies in high-stakes testing? *Teacher Education Quarterly*, *36*(1), 43–58.

Brophy, J., & Alleman, J. (2009). Meaningful social studies for elementary students. *Teachers and Teaching*, *15*(3), 357–376

Brown, C., Taylor, C., & Ponambalum, L. (2016). Using design-based research to improve the lesson study approach to professional development in Camden (London). *London Review of Education*, *14*(2), 4–24.

Cann, C. N., & DeMeulenaere, E. J. (2012). Critical co-constructed autoethnography. *Cultural Studies: Critical Methodologies*, *12*(2), 146–158.

Castro, A. J. (2013). What makes a citizen? Critical and multicultural citizenship and preservice teachers' understanding of citizenship skills. *Theory and Research in Social Education*, *41*(2), 219–246. DOI: 10.1080/00933104.2013.783522

Core Knowledge Foundation. (2018, December 14). *Core Knowledge*. Retrieved from https://www.coreknowledge.org.

Crompton, H. (2017). Using mobile learning to support students' understanding in geometry: A design-based research study. *Educational Technology & Society, 20*(3), 207–219.

DeGroot, I. (2017). Mock elections in civic education: A space for critical democratic citizenship development. *Journal of Social Science Education, 16*(3), 84–96.

DeJaeghere, J. G. (2009). Critical citizenship education for multicultural societies. *Interamerican Journal of Education for Democracy, 2*(2), 223–236.

Denzin, N. K., & Lincoln, Y. S. (2011). *The SAGE Handbook of Qualitative Research.* Thousand Oaks, CA: Sage.

Ellis, C. (2004). *The ethnographic I: A methodological novel about autoethnography.* Walnut Creek, CA: Altamira Press.

Endres, B. (2001). A critical read on critical literacy: From critique to dialogue as an ideal for literacy education. *Educational Theory, 51*(4), 401–413.

Fazio, X. & Gallagher, T. L. (2018). Bridging professional teacher knowledge for science and literacy integration via design-based research. *Teacher Development, 22*(2), 267–280.

Fitchett, P. G., Heafner, T. L. & Lambert, R. G. (2014). Examining elementary social studies marginalization: A multilevel model. *Educational Policy, 28*(1), 40–68.

Giroux, H. A. (1980). Critical theory and rationality in citizenship education. *Curriculum Inquiry, 10*(4) 329–366.

Heafner, T. L., & Fitchett, P. G. (2012). Tipping the scales: National trends of declining social studies instructional time in elementary schools. *Journal of Social Studies Research, 36*(2), 190–215.

Hultén, M., & Björkholm, E. (2016). Epistemic habits: Primary school teachers' development of pedagogical content knowledge (PCK) in a design-based research project. *International Journal of Technology & Design Education, 26*, 335–351. DOI: 10.1007/s10798-015-9320-5

Hughes, S. A., & Pennington, J. L. (2017). *Autoethnography: Process, product, and possibility for critical social research.* New York, NY: Sage.

Hughes, S.A., & Willink, K. (2015). Engaging co-reflexive critical dialogues when entering and leaving the "field": Toward informing collaborative research methods at the color line and beyond. In J. Flores Carmona & K. V. Luschen (Eds.), *Crafting critical stories: Toward pedagogies and methodologies of collaboration, inclusion and voice* (pp. 95–114). New York, NY: Peter Lang.

Janks, H. (2000). Domination, access, diversity and design: a synthesis for critical literacy education. *Educational Review, 52*(2), 175–186.

Johnson, L., & Morris, P. (2010). Towards a framework for critical citizenship education. *The Curriculum Journal, 21*(1), 77–96.

Jonsen, K., Butler, C. L., Makela, K., Piekkari, R., Drogendijk, R., Lauring, J., Lervik, J. E., Pahlberg, C., Vodosek, M., and Zander, L. (2012). Processes of international collaboration in management research: A reflexive, autoethnographic approach. *Journal of Management Inquiry, 22*(4), 394–413.

Joseph, D. (2004). The practice of design-based research: Uncovering the interplay between design, research, and the real-world context. *Educational Psychologist, 39*(4), 235–242.

Kincheloe, J. L. (2004). *Critical pedagogy.* New York, NY: Peter Lang.

Leming, J., Ellington, L., & Schug, M. (2006). The state of social studies: A national random survey of elementary and middle school social studies teachers. *Social Education, 70*, 322–327.

MacDonald, R. J. (2008). Professional development for information communication technology integration: Identifying and supporting a community of practice through design-based research. *Journal of Research on Technology in Education, 40*(4), 429–445.

Macedo, D. P. (1993). Literacy for stupidification: The pedagogy of big lies. *Harvard Educational Review, 63*(2) 183–206.

McKenney, S. E., & Reeves, T. C. (2012). *Conducting educational design research.* New York, NY: Routledge.

Miller-Lane, J., Howard, T. C., & Halagao, P. E. (2007). Civic multicultural competence: Searching for common ground in democratic education. *Theory and Research in Social Education, 35*(4), 551–573.

Montgomery, S. E. (2014). Critical democracy through digital media production in a third-grade classroom. *Theory and Research in Social Education, 42*(2), 197–227. DOI: 10.1080/00933104.2014.908755

National Council for the Social Studies. (2010). National curriculum standards for social studies: A framework for teaching, learning, and assessment. Silver Spring, MD: National Council for the Social Studies. Retrieved May 29, 2018 from https://www.socialstudies.org/standards/execsummary.

National Governors Association Center for Best Practices, Council of Chief State School Officers. (2010). *Common core state standards for English language arts.* Washington, DC: National Governors Association Center for Best Practices, Council of Chief State School Officers.

Obenchain, K. M., & Pennington, J. L. (2015). *Educating for critical democratic literacy: Integrating social studies and literacy in the elementary classroom.* New York, NY: Routledge.

Obenchain, K. M., Pennington, J. L., & Carter, H. (2018). *Moving beyond civic rituals: Elementary students' understanding of civic life in the 2016 election.* Paper presented at the College and University Faculty Assembly of the National Council for the Social Studies Annual Conference, Chicago, IL.

Parker, W. C. (2003). *Teaching democracy: Unity and diversity in public life.* New York, NY: Teachers College Press.

Penuel, W. R., Fishman, B. J., Cheng, B. H., & Sabelli, N. (2011). Organizing research and development at the intersection of learning, implementation and design. *Educational Researcher, 40*(7), 331–337.

Pennington, J. L. (2004). *The Colonization of Literacy Education: A Story of Reading in One Elementary School.* New York, NY: Peter Lang.

Pennington, J., Obenchain, K., Carter, H., & Bedford, M. (in review). "We have the right to stand up": Elementary students' conceptual understandings of civic virtue and engagement. Unpublished manuscript.

Reed-Danahay, D. (1997). *Auto/ethnography: Rewriting the self and the social.* New York, NY: Berg.

Scott Foresman Social Studies. (2011). *A Social Studies Curriculum.* New York, NY: Pearson.

Suswandari. (2017). Incorporating beliefs, values and local wisdom of Betawi culture in a character-based education through a design-based research. *European Journal of Contemporary Education, 6*(3), 574–585. DOI: 10.13187/ejced.2017.3.574

Swalwell, K. (2015). Mind the civic empowerment gap: Economically elite students and critical civic education. *Curriculum Inquiry, 45*(5), 491–512.

Thein, A. H., Barbas, P., Carnevali, C., Fox, A., Mahoney, A., & Vensel, S. (2012). The affordances of design-based research for studying multicultural literature instruction: Reflections and insights from a teacher-researcher collaboration. *English Teaching: Practice and Critique, 11*(1), 121–135.

Tyson, C. A. (2003). A bridge over troubled water: Social studies, civic education, and critical race theory. In G. Ladson-Billings (Ed.), *Critical Race Theory: Perspectives on Social Studies* (pp. 15–25). Greenwich, CT: Information Age Publishing.

VanFossen, P. J. (2005). "Reading and math take so much of the time . . . ": An overview of social studies instruction in elementary classrooms in Indiana. *Theory & Research in Social Education, 33*(3), 376–403.

Van Maanen J. (1988). *Tales of the field: On writing ethnography.* Chicago, IL: University of Chicago Press.

Vogler, K. E., Lintner, T., Lipscomb, G. B., Knopf, H., Heafner, T. L., & Rock, T. C. (2007). Getting off the back burner: Impact of testing elementary social studies as part of a state-mandated accountability program. *Journal of Social Studies Research, 31*(2), 20–34.

Wang, F., & Hannafin, M. J. (2005). Design-based research and technology-enhanced learning environments. *Educational Technology Research and Development, 53*(4), 5–23.

Wang, S., & Hsu, H. (2017). A design-based research capturing science teachers' practices of information and communication technology (ICTs) integration using the new literacy framework. *Journal of Computers in Mathematics and Science Teaching, 36*(4), 387–396.

Westheimer, J., & Kahne, J. (2004). What kind of citizen? The politics of educating for democracy. *American Education Research Journal, 41*(2), 237–269. DOI: 10.3102/00028312041002237

Young, I. M. (1990). *Justice and the politics of difference.* Princeton, NJ: Princeton University Press.

8

DESIGN-BASED IMPLEMENTATION RESEARCH IN A GOVERNMENT CLASSROOM

A Teacher's Shifting Pedagogy over Four Years[1]

Jane C. Lo, Carol M. Adams, Alexandra Goodell, and Sara Nachtigal

Ann Brown's (1992) seminal work on design experiments showcases how engineering and studying learning processes simultaneously can produce more effective interventions in complex classroom settings. In Cobb, Confrey, diSessa, Lehrer, and Schauble's (2003) view, "design experiments are extended (iterative), interventionist (innovative and design-based), and theory-oriented enterprises whose 'theories' do real work in practical educational contexts" (p. 13). Of the many adaptations of Brown's model, design-based implementation research (DBIR) (Fishman, Penuel, Allen, Cheng, & Sabelli, 2013) works to address the scalability of DBR projects. This chapter shows, through the presentation and discussion of an empirical study, how DBIR: (a) extends the DBR framework; (b) helps bridge theory, research, and practice in scalable ways; and (c) can impact the future of teacher professional development (PD) and curriculum development in the social studies. Specifically, we argue that DBIR provides flexibility in curriculum design and professional development processes that allow changes in the curriculum to occur alongside changes in teacher beliefs and practices, which may lead to more robust forms of teacher growth.

As other chapters in this book suggest, DBR offers a way for researchers to design and test innovations within various learning contexts (Brown, 1992; Cobb et al., 2003). The iterative design process within DBR is particularly helpful in allowing researchers and practitioners to revisit, redesign, and improve upon particular innovations over time. By focusing on theory-driven practices, DBR also allows researchers to see how theories actually play out in real life situations.

Design-based *implementation* research (DBIR) shares these traits with one additional caveat: an eye for scalable implementation (Fishman et al., 2013). While DBR has focused on improving learning environments in particular contexts, it has had limited success in scaling up these innovations (Penuel, Fishman, Cheng, & Sabelli, 2011). DBIR seeks to address this issue of scalability. It draws from the implementation research literature to consider larger buy-in and success of innovations (Fishman et al., 2013). Effectively, DBIR researchers ask, "What works when, for whom, and under what conditions? And how can we make this innovation work under a wide range of conditions?" (Fishman et al., 2013, p. 146). Asking these questions allows researchers to better deliver innovations and supports that are sustainable over time. In this chapter, we provide an empirical example of how DBIR can work to support social studies teacher practice in ways that might lead to scalable professional development and curriculum design efforts. Furthermore, we argue that DBIR allows for teachers to contribute to curricular design changes, which may help amplify teacher learning as they reflect on the influence they have on personalizing a curriculum.

In this chapter, we report findings from a longitudinal study on the experiences of one teacher, Mr. Peterson, who implemented a project based learning (PBL) Advanced Placement Government (APGOV)[2] course in an urban high school situated in the Pacific Northwest of the United States. While APGOV was not a required course, all students were encouraged to sign up, making it sometimes the first (and only) AP course that many students took. Examining shifts in Mr. Peterson's practices provides an example of how the DBIR approach can help researchers better understand sustainable and scalable professional development and curriculum development in social studies classrooms.

DBIR in a Government Classroom

This study is part of the Knowledge in Action (KIA) project, which aimed to foster deep and transferable content learning through PBL principles within the context of AP high school coursework (Parker et al., 2013; see also Darling-Hammond, Bransford, LePage, Hammerness, & Duffy, 2007; National Research Council, 2000). By contrast, AP has a reputation for producing courses that offer "coverage" but not depth of learning—testing too many topics, rather than deeply investigating a few of them. Instead of viewing breadth and depth in opposition, the KIA project sought to diffuse this dichotomy through a PBL model that embedded the core concepts designated by the College Board into projects, thereby giving students a "need to know" the material (see Schwartz & Bransford, 1998).

The KIA project operated within the movement to "democratize" AP (Lacey, 2010, p. 34), where AP courses are offered and encouraged to as many students as possible. In some cases, AP courses are required for all students in a school, rather than just those students who choose to be a part of the AP program. Especially for these students who find themselves (perhaps unwittingly) in an AP class, the key aim of the KIA project was to provide a learning experience that is at the same time deep and broad, attending both to the breadth of content as dictated by the College Board and to the depth of learning touted by the learning sciences literature. Rather than to disregard the AP test, the KIA project team saw it as a valuable and practical constraint, as thousands of students take the test each year and many gain college credit through it. The KIA project took an innovative approach to social studies curriculum design by reorganizing content included on the test (e.g., three branches of government, separation of powers, etc.) into a series of projects. Rather than taking away the textbook or lectures, we leveraged PBL to help students learn from textbooks and lectures.

The PBL version of the APGOV course consists of five projects: Founder's Intent, Election, Supreme Court, Congress, and Government in Action (see Parker and Lo, 2016). Each project puts students into a role (e.g., delegate to the Constitutional Convention) and presents them with a challenge or problem to solve (e.g., convince my constituents to ratify/not ratify the Constitution). Each problem involves a series of tasks that require students to apply AP content to solve them (e.g. draft a letter to constituents arguing for or against ratification).

The KIA team designed the PBL course according to five core design principles: rigorous projects as the spine of the course; project cycles that embed important concepts multiple times from different perspectives; "engagement first" that provides students with a *need to know*, so that learning is purposeful and meaningful; teachers acting as collaborators with researchers; and an eye towards scalability across contexts (see Parker et al., 2013). The ultimate aim is for teachers to become not just co-designers of the curriculum, but also "flexible adapters" of it, making changes that embody the design principles while also meeting the specific needs of their students and contexts (Hammerness et al., 2005).

Theoretical Framework

The KIA project offers an opportunity to examine the thinking and practices of social studies teachers who teach rigorous content in secondary schools, and addresses calls for articulating the processes and mechanisms of professional learning in a complex learning environment (Kazemi & Hubbard, 2008; Wilson & Berne, 1999). In this chapter, we draw on Clarke and Hollingsworth's Interconnected Model of Professional Growth (2002) to examine the mechanisms of professional learning through a DBIR approach. This model recognizes "professional growth as an inevitable and continuing process of learning" (p. 950), which reflects KIA's emphasis on promoting teachers' flexible adaptation of design principles and curriculum to best suit their students' needs (see Hammerness et al., 2005; Penuel & Gallagher, 2009).

Designed to represent the "process by which teachers grow professionally and the conditions that support and promote that growth" (Clarke & Hollingsworth, 2002, p. 947), the Interconnected Model posits that the non-linear nature of each teacher's learning forms recognizable patterns of enactment and reflection among four change domains (Figure 8.1).

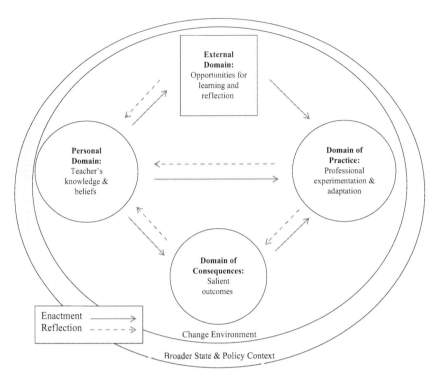

FIGURE 8.1 Clarke and Hollingsworth's (2002) Interconnected Model of Professional Growth.

The Interconnected Model views teacher learning as individually unique and interactive, operating through multiple recursive pathways across four change domains. Thus, the Interconnected Model arrays the domains in a circle (see Figure 8.1) to indicate the non-linear path of teacher learning. It describes the change domains as follows:

1. The *external domain* incorporates all resources that originate outside the teacher. In addition to the PBL-APGOV curriculum, the external domain in our case included professional development (PD), learning communities, and instructional resources.
2. The *domain of practice* is where teachers experiment and try out new ideas and resources in the unique context of their respective schools and classrooms. The conceptual and practical moves a teacher makes, and the practices and resources they discard, adapt, or appropriate, are considered in the domain of practice.
3. The *domain of consequences* refers to salient outcomes for teachers. "Outcomes" refers here to teachers' goals; thus, salient outcomes exert a strong influence on teacher thinking and decision-making. For example, one teacher might

view test scores as an important outcome and consequently emphasize activities he believes further that end, while another teacher might value vigorous student debate. Teachers select material, resources, and pedagogical moves that further the outcomes they deem valuable.

4. Finally, the *personal domain* accounts for teachers' subject matter knowledge, pedagogical knowledge, beliefs, and attitudes. Of particular interest to this study is the teacher's perception of how students learn, as well as his beliefs about the legitimacy of AP and PBL.

Clarke and Hollingsworth (2002) locate teacher learning in two mediating processes: *enactment* and *reflection* (see Figure 8.1). Enactment is the "putting into action of a new idea or a new belief or a newly encountered practice" (p. 953). In the Interconnected Model, all teacher actions (e.g., instructional moves, classroom talk, or assessments of learning) are seen as the "translation of a belief or pedagogical model into action" (p. 951). This sounds straightforward, but putting what one knows into action can lead to a "problem of enactment" (Kennedy, 1999), where teachers may know what to do, but find it difficult to apply that knowledge in practice (e.g., a teacher understands the importance of discussing a reading, but is not sure how to facilitate that discussion). This challenge begins with novice teachers (indeed, novices in all professions) and persists for teachers embarking on unfamiliar curricular approaches, such as PBL-APGOV (Ball & Cohen, 1999; Grossman, Hammerness, & McDonald, 2009; Hammerness et al., 2005).

In the case of PBL-APGOV, many teachers experience the approach as an unfamiliar array of pedagogical practices and theories of learning—not only in regard to more student-focused learning routines, but also to design principles such as *engagement-first*, which counters the practice of "frontloading" (i.e., teaching content before asking students to apply it in projects). Even though the KIA curriculum utilizes PBL pedagogy, it is important to note that PBL itself is not the focus of this study. Many strategies, of which PBL is one example, can present teachers with challenges and difficulties. What is of consequence in this study is how teachers effectively navigate challenging practices. It is challenging for teachers to learn and integrate such practices and conceptual understandings, in part because prior personal experience is known to strongly inform teachers' conceptions of what high school instruction should look like (Lortie, 1975). Additionally, school systems are well known for establishing expectations for teaching and learning that are not always conducive to approaches such as PBL-APGOV, which intentionally disrupt traditional roles of teachers and students (O'Brien, Stewart, & Moje, 1995; Tyack & Tobin, 1994).

Teacher change, as identified in the Interconnected Model, is described in one of two ways: A brief or momentary change in two or more domains, connected by reflection or enactment, is described as a "change sequence," whereas a more lasting change that occurs across multiple domains is described as a "growth network" (Clarke & Hollingsworth, 2002). For example, when we documented a shift in teaching practice (domain of practice) that subsequently led to changes in teacher thinking (personal domain) and teacher goals (domain of consequence), we considered those changes a "growth network." Data grounding this claim would entail observations of the changed practice over time (classroom observation data) as well as evidence of teacher reflection on those changes (interview and PD data).

The Interconnected Model helped us examine the ways in which teachers interacted with the curriculum, PD, and researchers (the external change domain) over time, and how those interactions contributed to changes in their beliefs and practices. While there were multiple teachers in the larger research study, we focus this longitudinal analysis on a single case of Mr. Peterson, a PBL-APGOV teacher, in order to gain a nuanced understanding of the processes that facilitated his growth.

Methods

At the outset of the broader research study, the KIA team chose a design-based implementation research (DBIR) approach because it fit our aim of fostering meaningful curricular reform over time. Drawing on Penuel et al.'s (2011) four guiding principles of DBIR, our project: (a) focused on a *persistent problem*—in our case, of AP courses being too broad—from multiple stakeholders' perspectives; (b) committed to *iterative, collaborative design*; (c) aimed at *developing theory* related to both classroom learning in the AP context; and (d) focused on *developing capacity* for sustaining Mr. Peterson's (and other teachers') practice in AP courses. Accordingly, researchers and practitioners worked collaboratively to identify joint problems of practice in the PBL-APGOV setting, asking questions about what works, when, how, and for whom, as well as how these practices might be scalable to other teachers in different contexts.

True to the spirit of DBIR, the design team made adjustments to the PBL-APGOV course and accompanying professional development (PD) in each implementation, based on teacher input, student experiences, and research analysis. As we learned through this project, this type of reciprocity between researcher, institution, and school is important for successful reform efforts, because it speaks to the need to "hybridize" such efforts to align with "local needs and knowledge" (Tyack & Tobin, 1994, p. 478). Given the challenges of disrupting traditional AP instruction, DBIR proved to be a fitting approach for this work, as it allowed systems and routines, through which researchers and teachers could learn and collaborate, to develop organically over time. This new space provided an opportunity where "existing research and understanding and knowledge of practice [could] inform the design of innovations that in turn enrich[ed] both practical knowledge and research understandings" (Russell, Jackson, Krumm, & Frank, 2013, p. 178).

To understand how teacher learning occurs within the complexity of research and practice, we deemed it important to examine particular teacher experiences, and specific moments of change, through the full trajectory of a DBIR process.

Thus, we selected a longitudinal case study approach to examine the processes that supported teacher growth over time. Case study, both as a process of inquiry and as a product, investigates a phenomenon in complex contexts and attempts to explore how those involved construct meaning (Merriam, 2009; Yin, 2013).

Mr. Peterson

We selected Mr. Peterson as the case for this study for two reasons. First, he was a vocal and constructive critic in the KIA team: He actively responded to the PBL-APGOV curriculum, articulating what he felt worked and did not work for his students, and candidly reflected on his challenges with enacting its design principles. Second, Mr. Peterson participated in the study for all four years, allowing us to examine how his pedagogy shifted over time. (Other teachers on the project participated for subsets of this time period due to changes in schedules or district constraints, making their datasets less complete.) These two criteria satisfied our aim to create a DBIR narrative of one teacher's journey with this curricular reform.

Mr. Peterson was also chosen because of his strong beliefs and opinions about the benefits of PBL, as well as his critiques of the superficial nature of standardized testing generally and AP tests specifically. Mr. Peterson believed that PBL is an effective way for students to learn, regardless of their performance on an arbitrary test of knowledge like the AP exam. He also believed that his job as a teacher is to help kids in urban settings learn practical skills for life through relevant pedagogy. This is one of the reasons he was drawn to PBL but disliked AP, because he saw AP as not relevant to most of his students. When Mr. Peterson joined the project, he had just started his second year of teaching social studies and his first teaching AP, and was well liked by his colleagues and students. As a mid-career changer, he was drawn to teaching because of its potential impact on young lives.

Data Collection and Analysis

Three main sources of data inform the present analysis: (a) interviews with Mr. Peterson, (b) video-recorded classroom observations, and (c) video-recorded professional development sessions. As part of the larger research study, our focal teacher participated in formal interviews at the beginning and end of each school year and impromptu interviews throughout each year. Questions on the semi-structured interview protocols were designed to elicit understanding of Mr. Peterson's teacher practices, pedagogy, and beliefs (Merriam, 2009).

The larger research team video-recorded Mr. Peterson implementing targeted segments of the curriculum, focusing on Project 1 (Founder's Intent) and Project 3 (Supreme Court, or SCOTUS), during the 2011–2012 and 2013–2014 school years.[3] The team also video-recorded all professional development (PD) sessions, including several feedback sessions devoted to curricular revisions based on teacher feedback. Prior to the start of each school year (except 2012–2013), the larger team held a four-day "Summer Institute" for both returning and new teachers. In 2011–2012 and 2013–2014, several PD sessions were held during the year, which were also videotaped.

Since this chapter draws on data collected by a number of researchers over the four years of the larger project, we (the authors) first catalogued all data that included Mr. Peterson from 2010–2014. Our initial goal was to generate a narrative from the interviews and film footage that would help us arrive at preliminary understandings of key shifts in Mr. Peterson's pedagogical decisions and beliefs. We then proceeded with two phases of coding. The first utilized a grounded theory approach to look for potential codes and themes (Glaser & Strauss, 1967). This inductive coding process surfaced patterns that we later mapped onto the Interconnected Model of Professional Growth. Year 1 interviews and observations served as a baseline, as the research team did not collect data in Mr. Peterson's classroom prior to his joining the project in 2010–2011 and cannot speak to his practices and beliefs before that.

To target specific classroom observations for analysis, we conducted a keyword search in a research-memo spreadsheet developed at the outset of the project and utilized by all of the researchers. The spreadsheet was intended to benefit the teams' different research strands (e.g., civic engagement, literacy) and allowed the larger team to collectively identify and highlight keywords to use when documenting classroom observations. The team periodically revisited the coding scheme to ensure inter-observer agreement. After identifying all observational notes that included Mr. Peterson, we then triangulated relevant data sources for understanding Mr. Peterson's pedagogical shifts.

Findings from these initial analyses surfaced two major themes of change, as described below. In a second phase of analysis, we utilized the Interconnected Model of Professional Growth (see Figure 8.1) to expound on these themes. We looked across the model's four domains to document shifts in Mr. Peterson's practice, drawing on data sources both within and across years. We analyzed all of Mr. Peterson's interviews spanning the four years and coded for "teacher's knowledge and beliefs" as they related to his practice (domain 2), salient outcomes (domain 3), and perceptions of the PBL-APGOV curriculum (domain 4). That coding led us to examine more closely segments of classroom instruction and PD sessions related to the instances we coded as shifts. We then worked out the directional relationships between domains until they accurately represented Mr. Peterson's learning and change over time. Findings about these relationships contribute to an expansion of the Interconnected Model that we discuss later in the chapter.

Findings

In the sections below, we focus on two key shifts in Mr. Peterson's practice: First, we examine how his practices and beliefs about learning from text changed over time, and then we explore changes in his perceptions about the relationship between PBL and AP. In looking closely at these two growth networks, we illuminate how the DBIR approach facilitated his growth.

Part I: "Throw Out the Worksheet! Throw out the Textbook!"

When Mr. Peterson first joined the project in 2010, the course was three years in the making, having been designed according to the principles described earlier and piloted by a small group of teachers in a suburban school district. The transition to urban schools such as Mr. Peterson's, however, exposed literacy issues not previously taken into account, particularly in "AP for all" classrooms where many students were underprepared to grapple with complex texts. These realizations, as well as a shift to working with Mr. Peterson and other urban teachers as collaborators rather than mere implementers, led to the development of an additional design principle: learning from text.

By the end of his first year, while Mr. Peterson expressed excitement about PBL in general, he talked at length about his frustration with the dense APGOV textbook, his students' resistance to reading, and his perceived inability to adequately support student learning from text. In Mr. Peterson's typically candid style, he described these challenges in an interview at the end of the 2010–2011 school year when he threw up his hands and declared, "Throw out the worksheet! Throw out the textbook!" Mr. Peterson talked about being at a loss for how to effectively teach the AP content with his available text-based materials; at this time, he believed there was no place in his classroom for textbooks or difficult texts.

Interview and classroom observation data collected across teachers, including Mr. Peterson, in 2010–2011 suggested that the urban PBL-APGOV teachers were "working around" text rather than supporting students to engage with text-based content or holding students accountable for learning from text (Valencia & Nachtigal, 2012). By "working around" text, we refer to teacher practices that avoided the need for students to read, such as lecturing on textbook content and providing videos, Internet sources, chapter summaries, and handouts in lieu of text.[4] This was problematic given that the goals of KIA were to promote not only "equity of access" (AP for all), but also "equity of outcomes" (all students could achieve success in the course). Thus, KIA researchers agreed to more directly address literacy in upcoming PD sessions.

The only literacy practices that were embedded in the curriculum at this time were reading guides. Researchers suggested several new pedagogical strategies, such as think-alouds, during the 2011 Summer Institute. Yet because Mr. Peterson missed that event,[5] his first exposure to a literacy-focused PD was at an after-school session held in October 2011, during which a literacy researcher gave a brief presentation and showed a video of a history teacher enacting a close-reading technique. Limited time in the session was devoted to teachers discussing how they might use this approach. Subsequent observations and interviews indicated that Mr. Peterson did not incorporate the strategy into his practice, as it was still easier for him to "work around the text."

"Widening the gap": Growth model before feedback. Mr. Peterson's beliefs about the use of textbooks and other difficult texts such as primary source material persisted through his second year of the project. He reported feeling that using the textbook with his diverse group of students was actually disadvantaging them. During the Fall 2012 Advisory Session, he lamented, "[The students] try and they would struggle *so* much with understanding what [the textbook was] saying and getting what they needed out of it, that it seemed like all it was doing was widening the gap in the class." Given his difficulty engaging students with texts, Mr. Peterson reported that he attempted to "take away the burden of the textbook" by creating one-page chapter summaries. In the end, he found little success with the strategy; his students were no more inclined to read the summaries, and Mr. Peterson came to believe that the one-pager did not support his students' learning of content.

This persistent frustration with texts on the part of Mr. Peterson and other teachers led the research team to make an important shift in the way we worked with teachers on literacy. At the Spring 2012 PD session, the team, attempting to provide more grounded and relevant support, spent nearly an hour modeling for teachers how to take students through one of the core Supreme Court cases embedded in the curriculum, *Roe v. Wade*. While the curriculum suggested that teachers have their students read the court case, it offered no guidance to help teachers structure that reading. During the PD, literacy experts modeled setting a clear purpose for reading the court case and thinking aloud about how and when to pause to make sense of the text, while teachers observed the modeling. Little time was spent discussing or critiquing this demonstration, however, thus diminishing its effectiveness.

Shortly thereafter, Mr. Peterson attempted to enact the approach with his students. His implementation was what we might call a "procedural" implementation, meaning he tried to mirror the process modeled in the PD, but without a deeper conceptual understanding of what it meant to support learning from text. He introduced the reading activity by telling students they were going to read *Roe v. Wade*, but did not set a purpose for reading that connected to their Supreme Court project or help students know what they ought to learn from the text. Rather than thinking aloud about *how* he made sense of the text and asking students to engage in similar close reading and sense-making, Mr. Peterson had a student read aloud and then, sensing confusion, he simply reread the sentence without further clarification:

Mr. Peterson:	Somebody read for us [looks around the room]. Lela, full voice, right?
Lela:	[reads from text] "At the time many states had outlawed abortion except in the cases where the mother's life was in danger. . ."
Mr. Peterson:	[Interjecting] Pause. . . [Mr. Peterson pauses for approximately 2.5 seconds, then begins to reread] "Many states had outlawed abortion except in the cases where the mother's life was in danger." OK, thanks. Can you continue to read for us?

(Classroom Observations, Spring 2012)

In the excerpt above, Mr. Peterson paused the student at an appropriate moment for sense-making, similar to the strategy modeled in the PD session.

However, he did not verbalize his thinking, leaving students without any support to understand the purpose for pausing and rereading.

Figure 8.2 depicts this exchange through the lens of the Interconnected Model of Professional Growth. The figure shows a momentary change in practice, where Mr. Peterson engaged somewhat with the external domain, in what Clarke and Hollingsworth (2002) call a "change sequence." He seemed willing to try out the strategy he learned, but perhaps only in performance and not in intent—going through the motions of the modeling, without fully understanding the intentions behind the strategic moves. At the end-of-year feedback session and in his individual interview, Mr. Peterson spoke without prompting about how his implementation of the close reading strategy did not reach its full potential and directly asked the research team for more literacy support. In addition, when a researcher asked what might have helped him in his implementation, he responded, "I was hoping for more literacy support and help this year. I really wanted to make a strong push on literacy this year and was only able to make a weaker one."

After observing Mr. Peterson's enactment of the *Roe v. Wade* lesson and reviewing his and other's reflections in PD and interviews, the team again re-envisioned ways to support teachers' conceptual understanding of integrated literacy, so they could enact strategies like close reading. This shift led to the formal adoption of *learning from text* as a new design principle for the

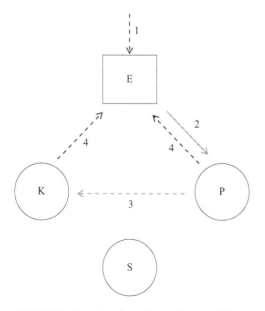

1 – PD: Based on previous DBIR reflection and observation, researchers demonstrate a literacy strategy.

2 – Mr. Peterson enacts the strategy.

3 – After the enactment, Mr. Peterson believes there is potential in the strategy but realizes he needs to know more in order to implement it successfully.

4 – Reflection through DBIR:
- K → E: Mr. Peterson conveys his limited understanding of the strategy to researchers.
- P → E: Mr. Peterson's perception of his enactment is supported by researchers' observations.

FIGURE 8.2 Learning from Text, Phase 1: Momentary Changes to Practice to Enact a "close reading" Strategy. E = External domain; P = Domain of Practice; S = Domain of consequences (Salient outcomes); K = Personal domain (Teacher's Knowledge and beliefs)

course. Figure 9.2 depicts this feedback and revision process through the two arrows labeled "4," in which the personal domain and domain of practice (Mr. Peterson's teaching and reflection) informed changes in the external domain (the APGOV curriculum and PD sessions).

"It's just time well-invested." After the DBIR feedback session, both the researchers' approach to PD and Mr. Peterson's literacy practice in the 2013–2014 school year looked markedly different. The researchers and teachers redesigned the curriculum to marry specific *learning from text* routines and strategies with content goals (see Valencia, Adams, & Nachtigal, 2016). This entailed incorporating a before-during-after approach to learning from text. To this end, the lesson plans provided a purpose to establish *before* reading that explicitly linked the content material to the project tasks, suggestions for how teachers could help support students' understanding *during* reading, and ways for students to clarify and extend their understanding *after* reading. At the 2013 Summer Institute, time was devoted to engage with and critique the approach. By this point, Mr. Peterson's attitude towards not working during the summer months shifted enough to allow him to attend the session, suggesting further buy-in to the project. During one of the PD sessions, Mr. Peterson remarked, "This is a really good use of my time right now to take really seriously how to use the reading and assign homework." Recollecting how he used to assign full chapters for homework, he said, "This is just vastly better." At each subsequent PD session during the school year, a portion was devoted to engaging with, trying out, and discussing *learning from text*. These experiences led to consistent changes in his practice; he used text and supported students to learn from text in nearly all observed classes in the 2013–2014 school year.

In addition, across all 2013–2014 interviews and professional development sessions, Mr. Peterson frequently remarked that devoting time and energy to learning from text was beneficial for his students. One representative example is when Mr. Peterson worked with students to make sense of two precedent cases for their upcoming affirmative action moot court. He began by setting a purpose for reading: "In preparation for your cases, read to find out: What kind of affirmative action is allowed and what kind is not?" After students read through the case individually, Mr. Peterson articulated his objective by saying: "Let's work through this together. If you feel uncertain along the way, ask so that you can feel confident. What does the Supreme Court say in the Grutter case about diversity in education?" As students responded to this opening question, Mr. Peterson repeatedly directed attention to the text, rereading segments aloud, probing student thinking with questions like, "Where in there do they say that and how do they word it?" and "What does it mean when it says, 'compelling state interest'?" At one point, a student misunderstood a key point, and rather than clarifying the idea for her, Mr. Peterson pressed her by saying, "Careful. Let's look at the second-to-last paragraph. It says 'institutions cannot establish quotas' and then what's the next sentence? They define quota for you in the next sentence. Let's read that." After working through the case, Mr. Peterson then engaged students in a conversation applying what they read to their own cases: "If you are trying to win a Supreme Court case next week in our class, how can you use this ruling in Grutter to win?"

In this example, Mr. Peterson gave students explicit reasons for engaging with the text. Not only were students reading to answer a specific question, they were also figuring out how the case related to their own mock cases. This gave them a purpose for needing to learn the information from the text. These pedagogical moves were significantly different from Mr. Peterson's approach to *Roe v. Wade* two years prior, where he provided students with much less support for learning from text.

The combination of embedded *learning from text* supports in the PBL-APGOV curriculum and the corresponding Summer Institute PD helped Mr. Peterson learn both the conceptual underpinnings of the *learning from text* design principle and how to translate them into practice. Figure 8.3 depicts his evolution in terms of the Interconnected Model, as a case of *durable change to practice, salient outcomes, and beliefs*, or what Clarke and Hollingsworth (2002) call a "growth network."

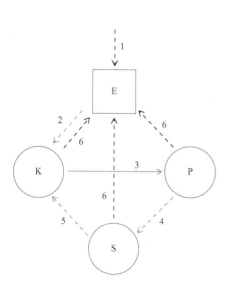

1 – Prior DBIR cycle leads to learning-from-text strategies being embedded in revised curriculum and addressed at length in PD.

2 – The retooled PD and curriculum help Mr. Peterson develop conceptual understanding of the learning-from-text approach.

3 – Mr. Peterson enacts the approach.

4 – Mr. Peterson perceives the approach helping his students learn important information from texts; this matches his content goals.

5 – Mr. Peterson comes to believes his students can and should learn information from texts.

6 – Reflection through DBIR:
- P→E: Mr. Peterson's enactment successfully engages students in close reading, which is supported by researcher observations.
- S→E: Mr. Peterson informs researchers that the emphasis on learning from text has shifted his salient outcomes to now include a goal for having students learn from.text
- K→E: Mr. Peterson believes this work is worthwhile for his students and that it will help them learn important content.

FIGURE 8.3   Learning from Text, Phase 2: Durable Changes to Practice, Salient Outcomes, and Beliefs.

In an interview at the end of the year, Mr. Peterson described his pedagogical shift in using text in the classroom:

Mr. Peterson:	[The] strategies that [Researcher] shared are I think totally valuable, and I'll absolutely do them again, both because, well . . . why? Because I felt like it helps the kids to read the hard stuff rather than give them a sanitized version. And because when we read it together—go figure!—there was buy-in and engagement reading what should've been dry text that's really difficult.
Researcher:	You said when you read it *together*?
Mr. Peterson:	When we did it, yeah. We did some really close scrutiny together in class. We spent an hour doing it. And they [students] were with us the whole time. And that was really impressive.

As this excerpt shows, Mr. Peterson no longer avoided using texts in the classroom, but instead leveraged them as an important site for learning. Although we present one specific example here in the *Grutter v. Bollinger* case, Figure 8.3 represents an enactment and reflection cycle that we saw beginning after the 2013 Summer Institute and continuing throughout the school year. The cycle impacted all teacher change domains: practice, salient outcomes, and beliefs, suggesting the DBIR process can support durable change. It is worth emphasizing that the DBIR iterative process changed not only the PD but also the curriculum as a result of the PD. This is where DBIR can be a particularly powerful tool when it comes to designing curriculum and PD in tandem.

Part II: Shifts in Mr. Peterson's Beliefs about AP over Time

The development of a collaborative relationship between Mr. Peterson and the research team led to shifts in his beliefs not only about text-based learning, but also about AP in general. At the beginning of the project, Mr. Peterson saw AP tests (and the courses) as a way for the College Board essentially to offer a different "credit by exam" option to students. However, over the four years, Mr. Peterson came to believe the AP program could help students learn college-level content in meaningful ways, especially through PBL.

A useful starter kit. As stated above, Mr. Peterson initially joined the project because he believed PBL made learning more meaningful. He articulated this sentiment during an interview several months after the August 2010 Onboarding Institute:

> [The projects] are designed to get students to sort of take an active role and play a part of somebody involved in this and understand it by being that person, playing that role, rather than just reading about it. You play at it or you be it, and then you discover, "Oh this is how it feels like and this is how I can use this and this and this to accomplish my goals."

In contrast to this sentiment about PBL are Mr. Peterson's comments during the same interview about his experiences at the Institute for AP Government & U.S. Politics in September of 2010. This institute was not part of the professional development provided by the KIA team, but rather a series of sessions provided by local AP teachers through the College Board. Peterson stated:

> Ugh horrible. I mean it was a very useful sort of window into, "what do you do if you just need to teach to the test," but I would not survive a semester teaching the way we saw recommended, and I know that my students would not make it through, either.

Mr. Peterson clearly distinguished between PBL as *doing* and a traditional approach to APGOV as *reading and testing*, positioning them in opposition to one another. His statement above that "his students would not make it" in a traditional AP classroom illustrates how Mr. Peterson felt about the strategy of covering what he perceived as irrelevant content in preparation for the AP exam. Additionally, he thought teaching AP in this traditional way would be detrimental to his students' success. Mapping Mr. Peterson's early experiences with the project onto the Interconnected Model of Teacher Growth shows that the underlying principles of the course design reaffirmed his own beliefs about good instruction being meaningful for his students (Figure 8.4, arrow 2). To him, the PBL design could potentially address the shortfalls of traditional AP instruction.

In his initial enactment of PBL-APGOV, Mr. Peterson incorporated aspects of it that most easily mapped onto his existing beliefs about PBL and AP. In an interview at the end of that year, he expressed that he was not convinced to incorporate parts of the course specifically designed to get students into the textbook and to prepare them for the AP exam, saying, for example, that "adding this [AP preparation tool] is not helping me." This appears mostly due to his perception that the AP test is just another way for students to get credits, not a way to viably measure what students actually know. Instead, Mr. Peterson gravitated towards the PBL components, calling the curriculum "a useful starter kit," but one that he felt compelled to ask himself at nearly every turn, "Do I even want to use this at all? Or would I skip this and replace it with something else?" (Figure 8.4, arrows 2 and 3). At this point, neither the curriculum nor the professional development had changed Mr. Peterson's goals for his students to learn deeply, rather than just to pass a test, or his beliefs about the dichotomy between AP and PBL (arrow 4).

When the course first migrated into urban schools, new teachers were positioned as adapters rather than collaborative design partners. This positioning of teachers changed over time as new problems of practice arose. As described in the section above on *learning from text*, the research team was interested in teachers' adaptations and feedback during the migration. However, the team was not yet engaged in collaborative problem solving about issues at the heart of the teachers' urban context. As a result, Mr. Peterson was not sure how to voice his

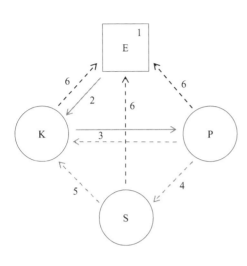

1 – Mr. Peterson joins the project and attends the Summer Institute.

2 – Mr. Peterson's belief that an alternative PBL approach is engaging is affirmed.

3 – Enactment Cycle: Over two years, Mr. Peterson selectively enacts portions of the curriculum; he develops his understanding of PBL but believes the more AP-like components of the course are detrimental to his students.

4 – Mr. Peterson perceives the PBL curriculum as too focused on AP; there is tension between his salient outcomes and AP goals.

5 – Mr. Peterson comes to believe that PBL can be an engaging curricular approach, but remains unconvinced about the importance of meeting AP goals.

6 – Reflection through DBIR:
- P → E: Mr. Peterson explains his selective enactment in interviews.
- S → E: Mr. Peterson shares that he still believes AP goals are not relevant for his students
- K → E: Mr. Peterson articulates that he still finds AP goals and PBL incompatible.

FIGURE 8.4 AP Beliefs, Phase 1: Enduring Dissonance with Salient Outcomes.

discomforts with the curriculum. The excerpt below shows Mr. Peterson asking about the feedback process during a subsequent November 2011 PD meeting:

Mr. Peterson: So I found myself editing the materials that we get. Like I revised the persona for the candidates and I revised the way the tasks are written because I think, "well that's not going to work." Should I ever feed those back to you guys? Like my modified versions?

Researcher: Well, yeah, that *was* the Summer Institute; those who attended the summer institute fed back the revisions they had made during the year, which became the new modifications.

Mr. Peterson: Are you telling me the ship has sailed? [laughs]

Researcher: No . . . that's sort of the current model such as it is, for working those revisions back into the curriculum.

In this exchange, both the researcher and Mr. Peterson recognized the feedback process as faulty. While "the ship had *not* really sailed," Mr. Peterson did not, in this first year, have adequate avenues to express the dissonance between his beliefs and the goals of the curriculum.

It is not surprising that in his second year with the project (2012–2013), when asked how he navigated certain aspects of the revised curriculum, Mr. Peterson explained that he deviated quite a bit, heavily revising away from AP preparation to better engage his students, whom he continued to believe were not motivated by the AP exam. The design team had asked teachers to follow the curriculum in order to see how the first year's urban-context revisions would play out[6], but Mr. Peterson reported abandoning an entire project that he described as "too AP" in order to "breathe some life into the class." Rather than working with the landmark court cases recommended by the AP exam, Mr. Peterson created his own fictional cases based on civil rights issues he felt more relevant for his students. For example, one of the cases focused on a college-readiness program predominantly serving African American students at the school. While students were encouraged to support their arguments with evidence, most students focused on building moral arguments rather than using constitutional reasoning that builds off legal precedent (Nolen, Tierney, Becherer, Cooper, Eng, & Ward, 2012). This may be due in part to students' perceptions that the "fake" cases did not hold merit, or in part to Mr. Peterson's limited attention to using precedent cases. Whatever the reason, the result was that students did not practice a skill central to the course: constitutional reasoning.

Through modifications like these, Mr. Peterson continued to enact aspects of the curriculum that aligned most closely with his prior beliefs and practices, while avoiding those that he felt disadvantaged his students. As he described it:

> They didn't learn all the abstract facts and concepts that the book wants them to learn. But they got into the project and that hooked them. They didn't really dive into the textbook reading and all of its million facts. They learned what we believed are the more important concepts than the minutiae of the AP test. I think that is a huge thing even though one of the central goals of the project is to have the kids do well on the AP test and prep them for it strongly.

Thus at the end of his second year, Mr. Peterson was still unconvinced that preparing for the AP exam ought to be a salient outcome for his students (see Figure 8.4, arrow 5).

Reflection through DBIR. By the third year of working in urban schools (2013–2014), the KIA team began to more intentionally reposition teachers as collaborators in the DBIR process, and thus redesigned the PD in several important ways. Rather than presenting the curriculum material to teachers and telling them about the design principles, researchers began to engage in problem solving with teachers that reflected issues at the heart of their practice.

A crucial aspect of this shift was the team's invitation for more open dialogue with teachers about both the underlying theories that informed the course and the practical challenges of classroom implementation. As a result, PDs took on a more collaborative and discursive structure, devoting substantial time for teachers to reflect on the strategies modeled by the research team, to consider how the pedagogical strategies aligned with their own practices, and to develop modifications with the support of the team. During this period, Mr. Peterson and the research team discussed, via multiple one-on-one conversations and small group feedback sessions, his concerns with what he perceived as AP prep work (Figure 8.4, arrow 6). In response, the KIA team more tightly embedded AP content within the project tasks so that "AP prep" was no longer distinguishable as a separate objective. For example, we incorporated campaign finance rules as an integral part of the Elections project so that students would have to know those rules to be successful in the project. This change came after other teachers prompted a need to teach more explicitly about campaign finance reforms, since it is always tested on the exam.

Once the curriculum more successfully integrated AP content goals with the PBL learning design, and PDs evolved toward a more dialogue-oriented space, Mr. Peterson's enactment began to incorporate more AP prep and content. For instance, in the 2013–2014 school year, classroom observations of the SCOTUS unit showed Mr. Peterson privileging several landmark cases suggested by AP, devoting significant time in class to working through precedent cases with his students and emphasizing how they might use the case in their own arguments. In his feedback to students following one round of SCOTUS arguments, he told students, "You guys did well pulling precedent cases—that's the key" (Classroom observation, March 2014). Similarly, whereas in previous years Mr. Peterson avoided terminology he deemed "too AP," such as "linkage institutions," in 2013–2014 he not only used this term numerous times across four different projects, but he also reflected in an interview that he felt the term helped students in their project work *and* prepared them for the AP exam.

As Figure 8.5 depicts, this enactment and reflection cycle led to a durable change in Mr. Peterson's salient outcomes and beliefs: He not only came to see his students as *able* to learn challenging content, but also that they ought to be given the opportunity to demonstrate their knowledge, as on the AP test (Figure 8.5, arrows 3, 4, 5 and 6). In an interview during the 2013–2014 school year, Mr. Peterson explained:

> This year I decided to give a final exam as a way to motivate the kids for AP review. So we had a final exam—like, the day after the AP test or something. And that way the studying for the two things is the same and we're all doing it together in case you decided to opt out of the [AP] test.

This shift suggests a departure from Mr. Peterson's earlier beliefs that AP prep "disadvantaged" his students by wasting their learning time on preparing for an arbitrary test that may or may not help them with college credit.

The conversations in these later PD sessions allowed both Mr. Peterson and the researchers to participate as learners, each contributing ideas and asking

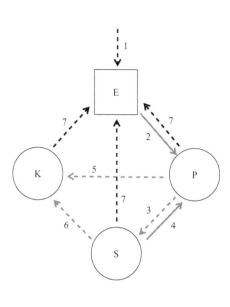

1 – Based on prior DBIR cycle, changes are made to curriculum and PD to address perceived conflict between PBL and AP goals.

2 – Mr. Peterson enacts the revised curriculum, including AP prep and content.

3 – Mr. Peterson perceives students are engaged in PBL even when challenging AP content is included.

4 – As his salient outcomes shift to include AP, Mr. Peterson presents AP goals as a valued opportunity for students in his class.

5 – Mr. Peterson rethinks his belief that an AP focus disadvantages his students when he sees their success with challenging material.

6 – Mr. Peterson believes that incorporating AP content and prep does not compromise the PBL approach.

7 – Reflection through DBIR:
• P → E: Mr. Peterson enacts both PBL and AP components of the curriculum
• S → E: Mr. Peterson reflects back to researchers that he sees value in engaging with AP content and preparing his students for the AP exam.
• K → E: Mr. Peterson reflects back to researchers that he understands how PBL and AP goals can work together.

FIGURE 8.5 AP Beliefs, Phase 2: Changes in Salient Outcomes and Beliefs.

questions that moved collective thinking forward. We attribute Mr. Peterson's shift in enduring beliefs and salient outcomes over time to the DBIR process, namely the opportunities for reflection and the responsiveness of KIA researchers to teacher feedback. When the DBIR feedback and revision process is incorporated into Mr. Peterson's growth model (see Figures 8.1–8.4), we see that his reflections back to the external domain (i.e., the curriculum design and PD models) provided important learning opportunities for both researchers and teachers.

Discussion

This chapter began by touting the possibilities of utilizing a DBIR approach to study curricular innovation and teacher growth. Findings from our study of Mr. Peterson suggest two important contributions of DBIR to social studies research, one methodological and the other theoretical. Methodologically, the study showed how DBIR can refocus researchers' attention on the *interaction* between teachers and curriculum, rather than fixating on one pole or the other. Theoretically, the study suggests an important addition to Clarke and Hollingsworth's Interconnected Model of Professional Growth (2002): a bidirectional pathway between the external domain and teacher practices and beliefs. This pathway can help researchers better understand teachers' professional growth contexts and investigate how teachers learn to incorporate complex social studies instructional strategies over time.

Focusing on the Relationship between Teachers and Curriculum

DBIR facilitates collaborative, iterative, and theoretically grounded innovations in curriculum and professional development. It thus allows researchers to observe and analyze the relationship between curricular changes and the teachers as agents of change over time, rather than just examining one implementation of a strategy after a stand-alone PD session (e.g., the Summer Institute). This method of conducting research on teacher learning treats the *relationship* between teachers and the curriculum as the unit of analysis instead of focusing on one pole or the other in isolation. Rather than simply looking at what the teacher is doing (or not) or what features of the curriculum are working (or not), DBIR allows researchers to tap into how teachers are manipulating or learning from the curriculum. Essentially, the relationship between the teacher and the curriculum (the arrows, rather than the boxes) become important.

In our case, the DBIR process allowed us to build a deep and lasting relationship with Mr. Peterson. Rather than positioning the research team as the "experts" who designed the external domain, the team partnered with Mr. Peterson to collaboratively refine the PBL-APGOV curriculum and accompanying professional development. Because of Mr. Peterson's candid reflections throughout the DBIR process, our PD shifted from being more presentation-oriented to being more relational and dialogic. By the end of Mr. Peterson's fourth year on the project, the PD sessions began to incorporate, and were responsive to, teachers' instructional knowledge and goals. It was also through this process that Mr. Peterson's beliefs about AP and salient outcomes for his course began to shift. As his input contributed to external domain changes, Mr. Peterson developed a deeper understanding of the design principles, which in turn became more clearly incorporated into his enactment of the PBL-APGOV course.

Interacting with the External Domain to Extend Professional Growth

This last point suggests how the DBIR process can extend Clarke and Hollingsworth's Interconnected Model of Professional Growth (2002) by establishing a bidirectional relationship between the teacher and the external domain. DBIR helps the curriculum adaptation process align with teacher learning, since teachers work as *principled adapters* (Penuel & Gallagher, 2009) of the curriculum, where their autonomy and agency are leveraged. In DBIR, the responsiveness of curricular changes to teachers' contributions may help facilitate and amplify teacher learning as they experience and reflect on the influence they have on the curriculum. In Mr. Peterson's case, seeing his input directly influence changes in the curriculum helped shift his teaching strategies around text and beliefs about AP.

Instead of seeing the external domain as *initiating* the process of professional growth, DBIR provides teachers with an opportunity to *modify* the external domain. Without the reciprocal nature of the DBIR process that served to bridge research and practice, Mr. Peterson's request for guidance on supporting student learning from text may have gone unspoken and unmet. He could have dropped the close-reading strategy after his first unsuccessful attempt or resisted all AP preparation-like aspects of the curriculum. On the contrary, the DBIR approach gave him a chance to provide feedback about points of dissonance, which fed into to a more substantial literacy-focused iteration of the curriculum and new PD strategies. This in turn led to Mr. Peterson's more successful iterations and an important shift in his belief about using text for learning. In summary, this DBIR project illuminates the benefits for professional growth when teachers are provided with opportunities not only to reflect on their enactment of curriculum, but also to influence its very design.

Limitations and Conclusion

While the case of Mr. Peterson is instructive, we acknowledge the limitations of generalizing from a single case study to other teachers in other contexts. Our selection of Mr. Peterson was both a strength and a limitation. His four years of consistent participation allowed us to study his growth pathways over time, but we acknowledge that he was a unique participant in two key ways: (a) His prior beliefs aligned well with PBL, and thus he was eager to disrupt the "grammar of schooling" (Tyack & Tobin, 1994), something that proved challenging for more traditional teachers; (b) Mr. Peterson was a reflective and particularly vocal participant, offering his ideas, concerns, and triumphs throughout his four years with the project. Nevertheless, the study's findings have theoretical and practical significance about how PD might be conducted in other curriculum development projects. While we know that DBIR studies are inherently context-specific, the fact that they *are* deeply contextualized allows for a much richer exploration of how social studies professional development may be implemented. In the future, we see benefits in examining similar uses of DBIR in other contexts.

Ultimately, DBIR provides a unique way for researchers to study the process of teacher professional growth over time, especially when teachers are incorporating complex instructional strategies such as PBL into their teaching. At the same time, the DBIR process supports teachers' long-term professional growth in important ways. We argue DBIR can help the field better understand and develop the kinds of curriculum and PD needed to sustain durable teacher learning for rigorous and meaningful instruction.

Acknowledgements

The authors would like to thank the KIA team for its data collection and curriculum development efforts, as well as the Spencer Foundation and the George Lucas Education Foundation for their support. We would also like to thank the editors and blind reviewers at *Teaching and Teacher Education*, where a previous version of this chapter was published, for their insights and suggestions on an earlier version of this manuscript.

Notes

1 An earlier version of this chapter was published in *Teaching and Teacher Education, 64,* pp. 79–92 (Adams, Lo, Goodell, & Nachtigal, 2017). It is published here, somewhat revised, by generous permission of the journal.
2 Advanced Placement (AP) is a curricular program of the College Board, where high school students can take college-level introductory coursework at their schools and potentially receive college credit upon successful passage of a subject-area AP test.
3 No data was collected during the 2012–2013 school year, since the project team was focused solely on rewriting the curriculum at that time.
4 See Valencia, Nachtigal, and Adams (2014) for further description of how "workarounds" impacted student learning, and how this research finding led to curricular revision.
5 Mr. Peterson missed the meeting due to his personal beliefs about not working during the summer months.
6 The revisions were intended to bridge a perceived gap between the PBL projects and preparation for the AP exam by more tightly marrying content instruction with project tasks and outcomes.

References

Adams, C. M., Lo, J. C., Goodell, A., & Nachtigal, S. (2017). Shifting pedagogy in an AP US government & politics classroom: A DBIR exploration of teacher growth. *Teaching and Teacher Education, 64,* 79–92. DOI: 10.1016/j.tate.2017.01.011

Ball, D. L., & Cohen, D. K. (1999). Developing practice, developing practitioners: Toward a practice-based theory of professional education. In L. Darling-Hammond & G. Sykes (Eds.), *Teaching as the learning profession: Handbook of teaching and policy* (pp. 3–32). San Francisco, CA: Jossey-Bass.

Brown, A. L. (1992). Design experiments: Theoretical and methodological challenges in creating complex interventions in classroom settings. *The Journal of the Learning Sciences, 2*(2), 141–178.

Clarke, D., & Hollingsworth, H. (2002). Elaborating a model of teacher professional growth. *Teaching and Teacher Education, 18*(8), 947–967. DOI:10.1016/S0742-051X(02)00053-7

Cobb, P., Confrey, J., diSessa, A., Lehrer, R., & Schauble, L. (2003). Design experiments in educational research. *Educational Researcher, 32*(1), 9–13. DOI: 10.3102/0013189X032001009

Darling-Hammond, L., Bransford, J., LePage, P., Hammerness, K., & Duffy, H. (Eds.). (2007). *Preparing teachers for a changing world: What teachers should learn and be able to do* (1st edition). San Francisco: Jossey-Bass.

Fishman, B. J., Penuel, W. R., Allen, A.-R., Cheng, B. H., & Sabelli, N. (2013). Design-based implementation research: An emerging model for transforming the relationship of research and practice. In B. J. Fishman & W. R. Penuel (Eds.), *National Society for the Study of Education: Vol. 112. Design Based Implementation Research* (pp. 136–156). New York: Teachers College Press.

Glaser, B., & Strauss, A. (1967). *The discovery of grounded theory: Strategies for qualitative research.* Chicago, IL: Aldine Transaction.

Graves, M. F., & Graves, B. B. (1995). The scaffolded reading experience: A flexible framework for helping students get the most out of text. *Reading, 29*(1), 29–34. DOI: 10.1111/j.1467-9345.1995.tb00135.x

Grossman, P., Hammerness, K., & McDonald, M. (2009). Redefining teaching, re-imagining teacher education. *Teachers and Teaching: Theory and Practice, 15*(2), 273–289.

Hammerness, K., Darling-Hammond, L., Bransford, J., Berliner, D., Cochran-Smith, M., McDonald, M., & Zeichner, K. (2005). How teachers learn and develop. In L. Darling-Hammond, & J. Bransford (Eds.), *Preparing Teachers for a Changing World: What Teachers Should Learn and Be Able to Do* (pp. 358–389). San Francisco, CA: Jossey-Bass.

Kazemi, E., & Hubbard, A. (2008). New directions for the design and study of professional development: Attending to the coevolution of teachers' participation across contexts. *Journal of Teacher Education, 59*(5), 428–441. DOI: 10.1177/0022487108324330

Kennedy, M. M. (1999). The role of preservice teacher education. In L. Darling-Hammond & G. Sykes (Eds.), *Teaching as the learning profession: Handbook of teaching and policy* (pp. 54–86). San Francisco, CA: Jossey-Bass.

Lacey, T. (2010). Access, rigor, and revenue in the history of the Advanced Placement program. In P. M. Sadler, G. Sonnert, R. H. Tai, & K. Klopfenstein (Eds.), *AP: A critical examination of the Advanced Placement program* (pp. 17–48). Cambridge, MA: Harvard Education Press.

Lortie, D. C. (1975). *Schoolteacher: A sociological study* (2nd ed.). Retrieved from http://www.press.uchicago.edu/ucp/books/book/chicago/S/bo3645184.html

Merriam, S. B. (2009). *Qualitative research: A guide to design and implementation* (3rd ed.). San Francisco, CA: Jossey-Bass.

National Research Council. (2000). *How people learn: Brain, mind, experience, and school.* Washington, DC: National Academies Press.

Nolen, S. B., Tierney, G., Becherer, K., Cooper, S. E., Eng, S., & Ward, C. J. (2012). Engagement in what? The negotiation of joint enterprise in project-based learning. Paper presented at the annual meeting of the American Educational Research Association, Vancouver, BC, April.

O'Brien, D. G., Stewart, R. A., & Moje, E. B. (1995). Why content literacy is difficult to infuse into the secondary school: Complexities of curriculum, pedagogy, and school culture. *Reading Research Quarterly, 30*(3), 442–463. DOI: 10.2307/747625

Parker, W. C., & Lo, J. C. (2016). Reinventing the high school government course: Rigor, simulations, and learning from text. *Democracy and Education, 24*(1). Retrieved from http://democracyeducationjournal.org/home/vol24/iss1/6

Parker, W. C., Lo, J., Yeo, A. J., Valencia, S. W., Nguyen, D., Abbott, R. D., Nolen, S. B., Bransford, J. D., &Vye, N. J. (2013). Beyond breadth-speed-test toward deeper knowing and engagement in an Advanced Placement course. *American Educational Research Journal, 50*(6), 1424–1459. DOI: 10.3102/0002831213504237

Penuel, W. R., Fishman, B. J., Cheng, B. H., & Sabelli, N. (2011). Organizing research and development at the intersection of learning, implementation, and design. *Educational Researcher, 40*(7), 331–337. DOI: 10.3102/0013189X11421826

Penuel, W. R., & Gallagher, L. P. (2009). Preparing teachers to design instruction for deep understanding in middle school earth science. *Journal of the Learning Sciences, 18*(4), 461–508. DOI: 10.1080/10508400903191904

Russell, J. L., Jackson, K., Krumm, A. E., & Frank, K. A. (2013). Theories and research methodologies for design-based implementation research: Examples from four cases. *Yearbook of the National Society for the Study of Education, 112*(2), 157–191.

Schwartz, D. L., & Bransford, J. D. (1998). A time for telling. *Cognition and Instruction, 16*(4), 475–522.

Smith, K. A., Sheppard, S. D., Johnson, D. W., & Johnson, R. T. (2005). Pedagogies of engagement: Classroom-based practices. *Journal of Engineering Education, 94*(1), 87–101. DOI: 10.1002/j.2168-9830.2005.tb00831.x

Tyack, D., & Tobin, W. (1994). The "grammar" of schooling: Why has it been so hard to change? *American Educational Research Journal, 31*(3), 453–479. DOI: 10.2307/1163222

Valencia, S. W., Adams, Carol M., S., & Nachtigal, S. (2016). *Rigorous content learning: Making text-based learning real.* Paper presented at the Annual Meeting of the American Educational Research Association, Washington, D.C.

Valencia, S. W., & Nachtigal, S. (2012). *Literacy challenges for teachers and students in rigorous courses in urban high schools.* Paper presented at the Annual Meeting of the American Educational Research Association, Vancouver, B.C.

Valencia, S. W., Nachtigal, S., & Adams, C. M. (2014). *The role of disciplinary literacy in a PBL APGOV course: Lessons learned.* Paper presented at the Annual Meeting of the American Educational Research Association, Philadelphia, PA.

Wilson, S. M., & Berne, J. (1999). Teacher learning and the acquisition of professional knowledge: An examination of research on contemporary professional development. *Review of Research in Education, 24*(1), 173–209. DOI: 10.3102/0091732X024001173

Yin, R. K. (2013). *Case study research: Design and methods* (5th edition). Los Angeles: SAGE Publications, Inc.

PART IV

Contextualizing DBR Historically, Socially, and Politically

9

THEORIZING CONTEXT IN DBR

Integrating Critical Civic Learning into the U.S. History Curriculum

Beth C. Rubin

> I don't think I have to pledge to a flag to show honor for my country when the words that we say are not true. One nation under God. Well, we are under God, but I don't feel like we are all one nation because some people still do segregate, and there's still not justice—liberty and justice—for all people.
>
> —*Zaria, an African American eighth grade student in*
> *an urban middle school*

Young peoples' experiences living and learning amid distinct community and school contexts in the United States inform how they make sense of traditional notions of citizenship and school-based civic education. As Zaria explains, historical and contemporary injustice toward African Americans, exemplified by continued segregation of her entirely Black and Latinx middle school, was the context in which she considered the truth of the Pledge's claim of "liberty and justice for all." During this classroom discussion about the Pledge of Allegiance, Zaria makes visible the need to attend to the larger historical and structural contexts within which we live and learn. For design-based research (DBR) projects in social studies, which aim to create theory-informed innovations and study them as they are implemented, it is particularly important to consider the full dimensions of context. If not, we risk recreating approaches that continue to sideline the issues of race and inequality that are central to a critical understanding of history and citizenship in the United States. These critical theorizations of context are absent from much of mainstream DBR, including DBR in social studies.

In this chapter, I reflect and draw upon the design-based project that was the basis for the book *Making citizens: Transforming civic learning for diverse social studies classrooms* (2012), elaborating on how a critical theorization of context that incorporates the country's enduring history of racialized inequality can both shape design-based efforts to restructure social studies education and also be a key analytical construct to help us learn from those efforts. In so doing, I argue that design-based work in the social studies should not proceed as though students from diverse communities process civic and historical learning through the same set of experiences—as though the historical and contextual dimensions of structural inequality aren't deeply relevant to social studies curriculum and pedagogy. Indeed, such understandings are foundational to history and the social sciences, and should be inseparable from research in social studies education.

Critically Theorizing Context for Design-Based Research on Civic Learning

Research on youth civic identity indicates that young people's sense of themselves as citizens takes shape amid the interconnected contexts of classroom, school, community and society (Nasir & Kirshner, 2003; Rubin, 2007; Youniss, McLellan & Yates, 1997). Young people from non-dominant communities experience challenges to their rights as citizens (e.g., Coates, 2015; Alexander, 2010) that school-based civic education rarely takes into account (Abu El-Haj, 2007; Cohen, Kahne & Marshall, 2018; Levinson, 2014; Rubin, 2007). Contemporary discourses of citizenship instantiated in texts and curricula largely exclude the critical and socioculturally embedded perspectives that connect to the civic concerns of youth from non-dominant communities (Abowitz & Harnish, 2006).

   With this critique in mind, this chapter considers one attempt to bring critical analyses of historical, political, economic, and social context into a design-based project that attempted to improve social studies learning. Drawing on the emerging field of transformative social design (Gutiérrez & Jurow, 2016; Gutiérrez, 2016; Gutiérrez & Vossoughi, 2010), I argue that context is neither interchangeable nor secondary to design projects, but rather must be fully and rigorously articulated throughout each stage and aspect of these projects: theorization, site and participant selection, development of the intervention, implementation, and analysis. The "context" of the intervention—the nested layers within which the proposed innovation is situated—include historical patterns of inequality that manifest in contemporary settings, disparities in the policies that shape peoples' lives (i.e. housing, education, criminal justice), local economic resources, and the social, cultural, and linguistic dimensions of the setting. The rest of this chapter will engage with this idea, describing how each aspect of "Teaching for Civic Learning in Diverse Social Studies Classrooms," a DBR project, was shaped by and benefited from a critically theorized understanding of context.

The Project

In this project, I collaborated with three high school social studies teachers to design a new approach to the traditional U.S. History course, one that would connect to and build upon students' civic experiences while attending to the larger social, economic, and political issues at play in their communities and beyond. An understanding of context rooted in critical theory— "the ways institutional power, social context, and history both manifest and maintain unequal power relations" (Brown & Au, 2014, p. 362) —shaped the way we structured the curriculum and designed instructional practice. At the same time, as we analyzed data from the project we became aware of the ways that school and community context molded students' engagement with the course, producing striking differences in how the intervention was enacted.

In this section, I describe how this critical consideration of context was threaded throughout the project, exploring its significance to the choice of school communities and classrooms for the project, the design principles, the curricular and pedagogical approach we developed, and the ways we chose to study the project's impact.

The Classrooms, Schools, and their Communities

While few DBR studies emphasize demography in their rationale for site selection, we foregrounded the racial, linguistic, and socioeconomic make-up of school and community settings in this methodological decision. As our aim was to study the implementation of a curricular and pedagogical intervention to create meaningful civic learning opportunities for students from non-dominant communities, the purposeful selection of schools and classrooms where there were large numbers of students from such groups was critical. It was equally important to select communities that varied racially, ethnically, linguistically, and socioeconomically; we wanted to understand how a design that emphasized critical civic learning would be enacted in a variety of diverse settings.

For these reasons, we chose classrooms within the sole large, public high school of each of three diverse communities, herein referred to as Allwood, Oak Knoll, and Surrey.[1] While these three communities were geographically within 65 miles of each other, each had a distinct profile and set of concerns, providing rich contexts for the implementation of a curriculum premised on the idea that for civic learning to be meaningful it should both be rooted in and critically explore students' lives and experiences.

Allwood was a middle-class suburb with a large and diverse immigrant population. A town of roughly 100,000 people, at the time of the study, the Allwood High school population was approximately[2] 48% White, 27% Asian American (with 18% of Allwood students reporting South Asian ancestry), 13% Latino, and 12% African American. Unemployment in Allwood as of 2007 was 4%, with a 6% poverty rate for individuals and a 3% rate for families. Statistically speaking, Allwood was a safe community, with a violent crime rate of 1.6 incidents per 1,000 residents, well below state and national averages. Allwood High School was one of two comprehensive high schools in Allwood. It served a less affluent segment of the Allwood population than the town's second high school. Indeed, although the median household income of Allwood families in 2007 was $81,000, the income of the families of Allwood High School students was about $60,000, and approximately 16% of Allwood High School students were eligible for free or reduced lunch.

Oak Knoll was a diverse suburban community, less affluent than Allwood and much smaller, with 44,000 residents. Oak Knoll High School's student population was 42% African American, 28% White, 22% Latino, and 8% Asian American. The unemployment rate in Oak Knoll as of 2007 was approximately 6%; the poverty rate for individuals was 5%, while for families with children under 18 was 7%. The crime rate in Oak Knoll fell well below the state and national averages, with a violent crime rate of 2 incidents per 1,000 residents. Although the median household income in Oak Knoll was $90,000, far surpassing both state and national figures, 27% of the student population at Oak Knoll High School qualified for free or reduced lunch, reflecting the difference in town and school population characteristics.

Surrey was a low-income, majority African American and Latino city. The student population of Surrey High School was 50% Latino, 46% African American, 2% Asian American, and 1% White. The median household income of this densely populated, declining post-industrial city of 80,000 was $23,000, well below the state average. The unemployment rate in Surrey, as of 2007, was 16%, with 41% of Surrey residents, and 49% of families with children under the age of 18, subsisting below the poverty line. Frequently cited on lists of the most dangerous places to live in the United States, Surrey's violent crime rate of 22 incidents per 1,000 residents was much higher than state and national averages. Surrey High School students dropped out of school at more than four times the rate of Allwood students and almost three times the rate of Oak Knoll students, had much lower graduation rates than students at the other two schools (with only one in ten students passing the state test to graduate), did poorly on the S.A.T., and seldom participated in A.P. courses.

In terms of academic achievement, as measured by students' performance on state proficiency exams, Allwood High School students exceeded state averages in both language arts literacy and mathematics. Oak Knoll students matched the state average in language arts literacy but struggled in mathematics, and fewer students reached advanced proficiency in either area than the state average. Surrey High School students' scores were consistently among the lowest in the state, with the majority of Surrey students not meeting proficiency levels. Indeed, according to the state's Department of Education, the school was third from the bottom of all public high schools in the state in academic achievement. In 2006–2007, the year before the study, all three schools failed to meet the annual yearly progress benchmarks set by the federal No Child Left Behind Act due to the performance of various subgroups on the state-wide assessment. While all three schools struggled to help their students with disabilities, students of color, and low-income students meet the proficiency threshold for state testing, Surrey's proficiency levels for students from these subgroups (which made up a major part of the Surrey student population) were dramatically lower than the other schools, with only a small fraction of the school's African American, Latino, and economically disadvantaged students meeting proficiency thresholds in mathematics, and close to two thirds of these groups failing to meet the threshold in language arts literacy.

As Table 9.1 presents, in two of these three high schools, we implemented the new curriculum within classrooms that were neither the highest nor the lowest track in the school. In all three high schools, we focused on classrooms with high levels of racial, ethnic and academic diversity, mirroring the demographics of the schools at large. The students in the classes in Allwood and Surrey High Schools more or less reflected the racial/ethnic breakdown of the rest of the school population, while the Oak Knoll classrooms, taught by Mr. Banks, reflected the demographics of this racially and socioeconomically polarized school's lowest track. The Allwood classes, taught by Ms. Tenney, were in the school's college preparatory track, which was neither the highest nor the lowest track in the school; the Surrey High students, taught by Mr. Brooks, were grouped together specifically because of their need for special education support in social studies.

This distribution provided us with an exciting opportunity to consider the possibilities and challenges of implementing the new approach in schools serving a wide variety of student populations. Allwood, Oak Knoll, and Surrey High Schools were good examples of how the term "diversity" does not begin to encompass the richly varied tapestry of the contemporary U.S. high school. As such, they were excellent sites within which to consider the enactment of a civic education intervention designed to build upon students' historically and structurally embedded experiences with civic life.

TABLE 9.1 Student Demographics and Tracks of Participating Classrooms

	Allwood HS	Oak Knoll HS	Surrey HS
# students	65	34	22
Track	2nd highest in 4 tier system	Lowest level in 3 tier system	Special education
Gender	26 male	19 male	18 male
	39 female	15 female	4 female
Race/ ethnicity	6 African American	19 African American	13 African American
	20 Asian American (East and South Asian)	1 Asian American	8 Latino
		10 Latino	1 Middle Eastern
	8 Latino	4 White	
	4 Middle Eastern		
	29 White		

Design Principles

Although we consciously selected schools serving large proportions of students from groups that are traditionally disenfranchised within the U.S. educational system, and we selected communities with varying dimensions of diversity, this methodological choice would only be meaningful if diversity and student experience were made central to the intervention being developed. While, in general, social studies classes are not structured to take into account or build upon students' varying experiences with civic life, and many educators choose to avoid controversial social issues in their classrooms, this intervention was rooted in a critical understanding of student experience. It also aimed to address the gap between the civic learning opportunities available to students in low-income communities and those available to their peers in higher income communities, including access to best practices such as open discussion of civic issues or issues of personal importance, service learning, and study of community problems (Kahne & Middaugh, 2008; Levinson, 2007).

Drawing upon research on youth civic learning, we developed four design principles, displayed in Figure 9.1, to capitalize upon students' daily experiences and social position and integrate high quality civic learning opportunities. The first two design principles in particular set the foundation for the development of a contextually embedded curricular and pedagogical approach that foregrounded students' experiences.

The Curricular and Pedagogical Approach

The inclusion of teachers from the three schools on the design team helped us to build attentiveness to context into the design of the new curricular and pedagogical approach. Two of the teachers, Mr. Brooks from Surrey and Ms. Tenney from Allwood, grew up in and resided within the school communities in which they taught, and thus brought deep contextual understanding to the project. The design team of three teachers, the principal investigator, and a research assistant met for two weeks during the summer preceding implementation to discuss the

1. Civic education should build upon students' own experiences with civic life, including daily experiences with civic institutions (e.g., schools, police).
2. Civic education should provide opportunities for students to consider and discuss key issues and controversies in civic life.
3. Civic education should build students' discussion, analysis, critique, and research skills.
4. Civic education should build students' knowledge of their rights and responsibilities as citizens in a way that connects directly to their own concerns.

FIGURE 9.1 Design Principles for Meaningful Civic Learning in Diverse Settings.

design principles and develop curricular and pedagogical approaches that integrated the principles into the required curriculum for the upcoming school year. We began by reorganizing the teachers' U.S. History II curricula into thematic segments undergirded by essential questions, described in more detail below. We then drew from the literature on best practices in civic education to develop four "civic skill building strands" designed to thread civic learning throughout the academic year: discussion, writing and expression, current events, and civic action research. After this summer of collaborative work by the study team, the teachers implemented the approach in their U.S. History II classes, as described below.

The Research Approach

The research aspect of this DBR project took a qualitative approach rooted in interpretive, critical sociocultural perspectives. This approach was able to capture ethnographically the ways that students engaged with the curriculum, which was vital to understanding how context shaped this engagement. To this end, the research team observed frequently in each class, taking field-notes full of "thick description" (Geertz, 1973) and seeking emic perspectives through interviews with youth. The entire project team met monthly to continue discussion and curriculum development. The principal investigator interviewed the teachers at the beginning and end of the school year. Students were also surveyed to learn about their experiences with the curriculum, and student work was collected throughout the year. This critical, interpretive approach allowed us to explore the ways that the intervention was enacted and experienced in the three distinct sites, as we explore later in this chapter. Results from this project are reported in Rubin (2012), Rubin and Hayes (2010), and Rubin, Hayes, and Benson (2009).

Integrating a Theorized Understanding of Context into a Design-Based Project

This theorized understanding of context was instantiated within the design of the new curricular approach in two major ways: (a) the restructured curriculum highlighted themes and questions that made room for students to grapple with issues directly related to their lives, communities, and contemporary events; and (b) the intervention emphasized pedagogical approaches centered around student discussion and engagement, thereby creating space for students to actively connect their own concerns and ideas to the curriculum and to critically explore the historical themes that impacted them daily.

Curricular Change

The thematic, question-based reframing of the United States history curriculum refocused the course from the coverage of a particular swath of time that is typical of such classes to an approach rooted in the "uncoverage" or "problematization" (Brown & Campione, 1994; Engle & Conant, 2002; Wiggins & McTighe, 2005) of meaningful issues and themes worth exploring (e.g., Brown & Brown, 2010; Chandler & McKnight, 2009; Freedman, 2007, 2015; Loewen, 2018). These issues and themes were those the team felt were most directly relevant to the students' experiences and most directly able to illuminate enduring critical issues in U.S. History, including racism, conflict, and immigration.

During a summer workshop, the teachers and researchers worked together to restructure the curriculum around central questions that link enduring civic issues to students' own lives. We began the summer workshop by examining how we could use our design principles to revise the U.S. History curriculum in a way that centered students' experiences amid larger nested contexts. Because the design principles emphasized drawing on students' own lives and experiences, the team realized that the traditional, chronologically organized curriculum was an impediment to making links between historical content, contemporary issues, and students' issues and concerns. A curriculum that would provide students the opportunity to grapple with big issues and questions would need to foreground the themes and questions that provide the links between students' nested levels of civic learning: classroom, school, community, and country.

To begin this redesign, each teacher brought his or her school's standard curriculum to the workshop and, with the help of a consulting historian and Wiggins and McTighe's (1998) "understanding by design" approach, we began to rethink how we would organize historical content. "Instead of 'covering' the 1920s merely because it's in the book," the historian advised, "try to think of ways to *use* the 1920s to teach about a particular theme." What began as a one-day effort to "pick some questions to thread throughout the curriculum" turned into a multi-day affair in which each teacher laid out his or her entire previous year's curriculum for collective reshaping. In a dynamic and energetic process, the teachers listed required content on butcher paper, and then we all highlighted, circled, and categorized this content thematically. Team members shared their categories, justified their choices, and with discussion and reconciliation, developed emerging themes supported by all.

In the end, we selected five themes to organize content (the first two sharing a marking period and the remaining three lasting one marking period each): *Government, Economics, Conflict and Resolution, Movement of People,* and *Social Change.* For each theme, we developed an essential question that would help students to make connections between contemporary issues and enduring civic questions. We hoped that these themes and questions would scaffold students' understandings of U.S. History so that after 180 school days, all students would be in a position to effectively grapple with the open-ended course question, "What is an American?"—a question with strong potential to bridge civics, history, and students' own lives and concerns. Table 9.2 displays the themes, questions, and content of the new curriculum.

TABLE 9.2 Themes and Essential Questions

Theme	Overarching Question	
	WHAT IS AN AMERICAN?	
	Essential Questions	*Content (not inclusive)*
Government	-What purpose does government serve? -What is a good American citizen? -Am I a good American citizen?	branches of government; democracy; federalism; political ideology; electoral politics
Economics	-What do Americans owe each other? -Why are some rich and some poor? - Is the American economy fair?	capitalism; stock market; Great Depression; industrialization; economic reforms; world economy
Conflict and Resolution	-What is America's role in the world? -Why does the U.S. go to war? When should it? -Can nations cooperate?	WWI; WWII; Cold War; Vietnam War; Korean War; Gulf War; Iraq War; war on terror; genocide
Movement of People	-Who is an American? -Why do people come to America? -Why do people move within the U.S.? -How do different groups define their American identities?	immigration; migration (various groups); Japanese internment; gentrification; globalization
Social change	-Are all Americans equal? -How do Americans make social change? -Who has the power to make change? Do you?	race/civil rights movement; Latino rights movement; gender/women's rights movement; social protest

These questions were intentionally crafted to connect to what the teachers knew (from personal experience) and what the researcher knew (from previous investigations and review of relevant empirical research) were relevant student concerns in the three communities, contexts within which questions of justice, immigration, identity, and racial equality were deeply relevant. While any of these questions could be pursued in ways that could be divorced from students' lives, the pedagogical aspects of the project, described below, were designed to pin the questions firmly to students' experiences by foregrounding voice, reflection, and communication.

Pedagogical Change

Along with reorganization, in order to tie the curriculum firmly to young peoples' ideas and experiences and to build their civic skills, we drew upon the best practices literature to weave particular pedagogical approaches throughout the year's instruction: discussion, creative written and oral expression, current events, and civic action research. We designed the pedagogical approach with an eye toward practices that facilitated students' direct engagement with the material and with each other on these critical issues, practices that centered on expression and engagement and that foregrounded youth-centered inquiry and action.

Discussion can be used to powerful effect in the U.S. History classroom to build students' speaking and listening capacities and promote an engaged orientation toward civic issues (Hess, 2009). We selected three distinct forms of discussion to integrate repeatedly—Socratic Seminar, civil conversation, and Take-a-Stand—as a way to build students' communicative abilities and to connect history to local and current civic issues in a meaningful and authentic manner.

We also used activities foregrounding creative written and oral expression in the study classrooms to build civic and literacy skills and more deeply engage students with civic questions. These included daily journal prompts, essays, persuasive speeches, debates, mock news conferences, and presentations, activities that meaningfully interweave the U.S. History curriculum and students' daily civic experiences.

Third, the team decided to integrate current events, a mainstay of traditional social studies classrooms, into every unit and topic throughout the year. We aimed to provide the opportunity for young people to consider what was occurring in that very moment in civic life from within the analytical framework of the redesigned U.S. History II classroom. In the three classrooms, essential questions were the pivot that connected the past to the present, allowing students to bring their own concerns and ideas to discussion of ongoing dilemmas in U.S. History, such as who is an American and when should America go to war.

Finally, we chose the ambitious goal of integrating civic action research—an approach in which students investigated civic problems they selected—into these U.S. History classrooms. This strand was designed to involve students in contextually relevant inquiry and action. Table 9.3 displays the civic skill-building strands, sample activities, and their purpose.

TABLE 9.3 Civic Skill-Building Strands

Strand	Activities	Purpose
Discussion	Seminar Take-a-stand Structured conversation	To center classroom discourse on students' ideas and opinions and cultivate their engagement with each other, and to build listening and speaking skills.
Writing/Expression	Social studies journals Persuasive letter Persuasive speech Newscast	To develop students' written and oral expression skills, and ability to work alone or in a group to prepare/present authentic tasks.
Current Events	Related to themes Related to questions Related to election	To weave students' consideration of current events into themes, events, and questions under study.
Civic Action Research	Problem identification Research Solutions presentation	To engage students in investigating and taking action on a student-selected concern.

Context Emerging through the Enactment of the Intervention

As the year unfolded, the curriculum and civic skill-building strands were taken up in the different classroom settings. The curriculum succeeded at connecting to students' personal experiences, effectively attending to local context. At the same time, the student-centeredness of the curriculum yielded very different kinds of discussions at each school, leading to insights about civic learning as illustrated in the examples below.

Discussing Morality and Violence in Surrey

In a Socratic Seminar led by Kevin Brooks at Surrey High School during the Conflict and Resolution theme, Mr. Brooks framed the seminar around the late eighteenth-century Edmund Burke quote "All that is necessary for the triumph of evil is that good men do nothing." The quote was a catalyst for students to discuss the violence in their community in relation to historical conflicts, pondering the obligation of individuals to stand up against evil.

> "What do you think Gustavo?" Mr. Brooks asks a boy. "Is Edmund Burke full of crap? Was there ever a time when you saw something wrong and you did nothing?" Gustavo doesn't reply. A second student walks into the classroom, Elliot. Mr. Brooks welcomes him to class and involves him in the seminar.

"Elliot, look at the quote. What do you think?"

"Oh yeah, yeah," Elliot responds, reading the quote from the board. "Because if they do nothing, it's just going to grow. I don't think anyone is good."

"What about you, Gustavo?" Mr. Brooks asks, probing the reluctant student. "Are you a good person?"

"No," Gustavo responds.

"Was there ever a time when you didn't do anything about a problem in your community?" asks Mr. Brooks.

"I was picking up my nephew," offers Elliot, "and some dudes were fighting and people called the cops and no one said anything. No one gave cops info about the fight."

"If I asked you that," Mr. Brooks persists, "what do you think it [the quote] means? For evil to happen, good people must sit back and do nothing."

"It's true," says Miguel loudly, with feeling. "Yes, there's a lot in this community that you see that you can't do something about—drugs."

"Suppose you thought something was right—is it always right to get involved?" pressed Mr. Brooks.

"You know drugs are bad but you can't fix it," responds Elliot.

"What about drug dealers," asks Mr. Brooks, bringing in a common local example, "you see them in the same spot, same day, all the time."

Elliot shifts responsibility for doing something about drug dealers to law enforcement, saying, "If they [cops] came every day, they'd move because they won't make money."

"What if you were to report them?" asks Mr. Brooks.

"You can't snitch in the hood," proclaims Manuel. "You get popped."

For a few minutes the students discuss whether or not one person can make a difference, then Mr. Brooks segues into the broader issue at hand, the essential question for the Conflict and Resolution theme.

"Should our country get involved in other countries' business?" he asks.

"NO!" exclaim all of the students in the class.

"We're at war now *because* of that," says Sandra.

"They trying to come here and kill us because we're over there killing people," adds Elliot.

In this seminar segment, Mr. Brooks began with a quotation for the students to consider, one which could be equally applicable to the students' own lives, events in history, and current happenings. Yet the Surrey students interpreted Burke's statement through the context of their daily lives, describing the impediments they felt they would face if they tried to "make a difference" in their own community. This sense of needing to mind one's own business, the futility or even danger of intervention, then appeared to influence the students' belief that the United States should stay out of the affairs of other countries.

Mr. Brooks reflected on the activity during one of our monthly design team meetings, saying,

> I mean from a student's standpoint, you know, especially the group of kids I have, learning about Reconstruction is not a priority to them, alright, but they see now, actually see these things happening in real life. The things we're discussing, they can see it and I think they can relate to it and are a lot more willing to make the connections.

Mr. Brooks, teaching special education social studies at an urban high school, indicated that his goals extended "far beyond the social studies domain." Reflecting on the problems his students grappled with, shaping the understandings they entered his classroom with each day, Mr. Brooks strove to teach in a way that validated these experiences, while also assisting his students as they navigated these dilemmas. This seminar allowed students to consider, in the midst of historical study, issues that had tremendous impact on their daily lives.

Studying Immigration in Allwood

Another example of how the curriculum created space for students to critically explore their contextually located concerns and experiences was the "Movement of People" theme at Allwood High School. In diverse Allwood, with students whose families had recently come to the United States from dozens of different countries, immigration was a vivid part of the community context; questions related to immigration had the potential to be a bridge between the civic and the personal. In an end-of-year interview, a student Vinnie, when asked if he could recall a particularly interesting discussion they had had in class, answered, "We had a class discussion on immigration. I have two parents that are immigrants, you know. It's something that. . . it's personal, it's personal. And you know, just hearing out the arguments, just understanding what my parents went through."

Allwood teacher Ms. Tenney described how her student-teacher, Kristi, approached the Movement of People theme, embedding current events within the study of U.S. history,

> . . . she did start out with Trail of Tears, and understanding that relocation. Japanese internment. And then Kristi posed the question that after 9/11, some people were calling for some kind of internment or some kind of questioning for Muslim Americans, and has the United States changed in 150 years? . . . [T]hey talked about immigration by choice, people moving to this country. And they talked about immigration that was happening with Ellis Island in the late 1800s into the early 1900s, and they talked about the Chinese Exclusion Act. And how immigration kind of slowed

down a bit in a certain period of time in our country and then picked up again after the 1950s. Different groups of people that came to the United States and why they came and then today, the largest group that comes to the United States, and she talked about our own community . . . our town and how it has changed and why do people come here.

Rather than chronologically separating significant episodes of movement into and within the United States, the design team had grouped these separate events together under the theme of Movement of People, framed by the questions "Who is an American? Why do people come to America? Why do people move within the United States? How do different groups define their American identities?" This organization allowed students to make connections across those events and to connect them to current and personally relevant concerns.

With this framing, Allwood students easily connected the historical study of immigration to current and personally significant issues. Ms. Tenney described how her students probed their own feelings about immigration during class activities and discussions:

> [T]hey understand the conflicts, they understand how hard it is to become a citizen. And they understand why they come here better than some other students would, and when they do discussions on this and structured conversations they brought a lot of their own personal situations and personal viewpoints into the situation. But it was interesting because the immigrants, the students that are immigrants, who came here legally, were very much opposed to people who came here illegally, and we have both in the classroom. We have illegal immigrants and we have legal immigrants. There's a very—there's almost a resentment among the students who came here legally, and those families that came here legally, versus those who came here illegally. I guess because of how much they had to fight to get here, sacrifice to get here. And people are coming here illegally, and they feel that it's just not fair, I guess.

She described how students directly engaged with each other on this topic, with legal immigrant students saying, "I'm an immigrant, and I came here legally, and I don't think that illegal immigrants should get amnesty or certain benefits and they should go through the process like everyone else," and undocumented immigrant students explaining, "In my home country, this is the way things are, and we had to get here any way we could and we contribute to the economy, we contribute to the society."

Thus, in this community, the theme of immigration allowed Ms. Tenney to connect the past to the present, embedding her students' consideration of current events in both their own experiences and within a larger critical framework. She reflected in a team meeting that, because we taught thematically, every day was current events. Because let's say we were talking about immigration. Well, the same problems are happening today that happened 100 years ago, so it's just a matter of pulling that theme through 100 years, and saying, you know, these are the same viewpoints today that people have for and against immigration that they had a hundred years ago. And that's your current event. And you can go on from there and talk about what Congress is planning to do on immigration and some of the viewpoints of immigrants and some of the viewpoints of people who are already citizens.

The curricular reform, in this case, provided space for students to make connections between the historical content, contemporary concerns, and their own lives throughout the entire year.

Researching Community Problems in Oak Knoll

In all three schools, the curricular reform included engaging their classes in a year-long participatory action research project on a topic selected by the students themselves. In Oak Knoll, this project gave students the opportunity to investigate injustices that they had experienced, of which their teacher was completely unaware. Emma, whose group had investigated police harassment of youth, explained:

> We did research in the county and also we tried to research in Oak Knoll. And go around and do surveys in Oak Knoll and give them to people from adults to kids. And ask them questions, if they have been [harassed], if they haven't been, if they know someone that has been, and how do you feel about the situation. And a good percent had been.

Their group produced a flyer titled "Racial Profiling in Oak Knoll." A descriptive article headed "Is it more of a problem than we thought?" shared the results of their survey on racial profiling ("Have you experienced racism personally? 49%—yes; 51%—no; When you enter certain establishments, do you feel you are being watched based on your physical appearance, race or color? 65%—yes; 35%—no"). The students included a data table of stops, searches, and arrests categorized by racial group in Oak Knoll. The flyer also described a program to end racial profiling that was instituted in Ontario and suggested it be adopted by Oak Knoll.

This student group's results were surprising to Mr. Banks who, unlike Mr. Brooks and Ms. Tenney, did not live in his school community. "I learned that they get hassled out in the real world more than I thought they would," he reflected. "By police officers, by authority figures. Two different groups did police harassment and racial profiling. I was like, 'really?'" This curriculum, embedded within a critical theorization of context that encouraged students to draw upon their daily experiences amid the racialized injustices of life as young African Americans and Latinos in a suburban community, opened up new areas of understanding for their teacher, who had previously not been aware of the level of harassment faced by his students.

In all three schools, the thematic, essential-question-focused curricular reorganization, meshed with the pedagogical approaches foregrounding critical inquiry and discussion, took shape most powerfully when school and community contexts were directly visible. Discussion and action research gave students critical entry points into considering relevant issues. At the study schools, almost 100% of the participating students (90–100% on each measure) agreed that they had had discussions during the year of the project in which they could freely offer their opinions and in which many different opinions were expressed; that they had talked about racism, sexism, and discrimination; that they had talked about current events; and that it was "OK" in the classrooms both to disagree with the teacher and to hold opinions that were different from those held by peers.

How a Theorized Understanding of Context Became Part of the Analysis

In this section, we will explore how attentiveness to social context was fundamental to data analysis during this DBR project. Indeed, if it had not been a key analytical construct, we would have failed to understand one of the most significant outcomes of the project: the differences in how students framed, carried out, and interpreted the significance of their civic action projects. This was particularly apparent when juxtaposing the civic action experience at Allwood and Surrey High Schools.

Contextually bound differences were apparent from the very beginning of the project, when students worked together to choose a school or community problem to investigate. Although students at both schools proposed a range of possible inquiries, the problems they ultimately settled on reflected differences between the two schools in students' immediate concerns. In Allwood, students decided to investigate a new school rule banning them from carrying their backpacks in the hallways. Intended as a safety precaution, the rule was very inconvenient for students, who had to struggle to get to their lockers through Allwood's very crowded hallways in the scant time between class periods. As one student noted, " . . . it's hard to get around because it's so crowded." In Surrey, on the other hand, students identified what they saw as the intertwined problems of rampant drug use in the community and the murder of young people that they had personally experienced. "It's basically like, if we would've chose murder, most of the murders here in Surrey are dealt with drugs, so basically if you stop drugs. . . you're stopping most of the murders," remarked one student.

Questions we posed to students to try to understand their perspectives on their own communities revealed the contextualized experiences that undergirded this problem selection. Allwood High students described their town as quiet, attractive, and a bit boring. "There's nothing great, like, nothing like, spectacular. You know, it's nice and mellow," said Daniel. Janet concurred, saying, "It's nice. . . I know that Allwood used to be a very highly looked-at community, like, back when. Now, I think it's just kind of one of those, like, whatever towns." Rebecca elaborated: "It's boring. No, it's not that boring. It's just, it's quiet. . . it's just very suburban. It's very. . . full of trees." She expanded further, describing how she experienced life in Allwood: "There's just, there's, I think there's a lot of a very nice feeling of community here. I think if you're in trouble, someone knows about it."

Surrey students, in contrast, described a town fraught with danger. As Narciso put it, "It's dirty. People always fighting. People always dying. If you just walk down the street you see drugs being handed out. It's the worst place to live." Tamika reflected the sense of insecurity she felt living in this context:

> Worst thing is the murders. Because you don't know like. . . like you don't know whether if you want to go to this place, go that place, because you don't know what's going to happen. You don't know what to look forward to when you go places.

Each student interviewed at Surrey High expressed concern about danger in the city, describing personal encounters with illegal drug use and murder. Interview questions about community context and rich field-notes from class discussions, coupled with open coding aimed at the elucidation of emic meanings, allowed for this analysis of the ways that this context permeated and shaped students' enactment of the civic action project.

The directions that these projects took can also only be understood through an analysis that takes context as a central fulcrum of meaning. In Allwood, as the year progressed, the civic action project became secondary to the other aspects of the new curriculum; students did not spend much time on it. However, when a new principal came in towards the end of the year and eliminated the no backpack rule, students felt they had made an impact. The effortless resolution of the Allwood problem was, on the one hand, empowering. As Tariq described proudly,

> We picked the backpack situation, [which] actually got done. We didn't even have to do anything. It just got done because of the new principal. Because I think he realized how nonsense that was, not to have backpacks. So what he did was he let us have string bags. Little sport bags. So we really, we won the battle.

Samara explained, "It was something we all wanted to do. It was a problem we all wanted to do so everyone got involved. . . It felt good because we got to make change."

In Surrey, by contrast, there could be no easy resolution to the problems of drugs and murder identified by the students. Indeed, Mr. Brooks was challenged to figure out a way for the students to productively engage with troubling problems that went far beyond their capacity to resolve. He developed the idea of having students create a "scrapbook," a compilation of writing, research, and photos on the problems of drugs and murder in the city of Surrey through which they could share their experiences with others. The students titled the scrapbook "Listen: An Anthology of Student Voices," and they worked hard on it. During the final quarter of the year, in inverse relation to the Allwood experience, the rest of the curriculum slipped away as students focused on writing and revising their pieces for the scrapbook. Surrey students cataloged their daily experiences. They used stories and photographs to effectively dramatize their chosen problems, creating an emotionally powerful document—a particularly impressive accomplishment for a special-needs social studies class in a school where very little writing was expected. Tamika spoke proudly of the project, saying, "We're talking about murders and stuff because we're writing a book. . . We're writing a book about the murders in the city of Surrey." In interviews, the students raved about the opportunity to work on a product like "Listen." "We've never done anything like this before in school," said Sara. "We've never written this much. I've gone through two whole notebooks this year!" Surrey students indicated that their work on the scrapbook and participation in the discussions and research gave them a sense that they were participating in meaningful action. Omar said he "loved" the project for that reason: This year's class was so different from previous years where "all we did was watch movies, hand out dittos, hand out ditto sheets."

Analysis of data from these projects led to deeper understandings of the ways that context shapes civic learning and the implications for school-based civic education. The data highlights how civic education is not a socially, historically, or politically neutral endeavor. In our democratic society, Junn (2004) notes, "inequality and barriers to action structure rather than pepper" the daily life of many young people, and "concepts such as freedom, fairness, equality, justice, and even democracy, are far from unambiguous" (p. 252). Civic action research, in this DBR project, facilitated the connection between the curriculum and students' lives and also laid bare the complexities of making such connections. A method that appeared simple and effective in Allwood's middle-class, suburban quiet brought Surrey students and their teacher face-to-face with the lived experience of a community suffering the consequences of long-term economic and political marginalization. For the latter, the learning was meaningful, but painful.

This DBR project dramatized how fundamentally civic identity development is embedded within particular historical, political, and economic contexts. Creating an intervention attentive to those dimensions of context both enabled and complicated meaningful civic learning. Without a critical theorization of context foregrounding the ways that unequal power relations shape the civic experiences of distinct U.S. communities, both historically and currently, this

DBR study would have missed an enormous part of what was significant in the implementation of a new curricular and pedagogical approach to civic learning.

Implications for Design Research in Social Studies

This chapter provided an example of the importance of a critically theorized understanding of context for design-based research projects in the social studies. For this particular project, which aimed to reconstruct a U.S. History course so as to foreground meaningful civic learning, it was essential that context be central to all of its components: the development of design principles, selection of the research team, choice of participating schools and classrooms, and collection and analysis of data. Attending to context was essential to the team's ability to develop a meaningful focus for the curriculum. It also informed an analysis that shed light on how to improve the quality and relevance of civic education for diverse, underserved youth.

The themes and concerns of the social studies are such that researchers developing design-based studies in our field need to consider the social, economic and historical locations of the intervention and its participants. Whether the topic be economic, political, or historical, young people make sense of the curricular and teaching practices they encounter by drawing upon the resources they have developed as members of particular communities. In this country, this means considering, in a nuanced, theorized, and critical manner, the racial, ethnic, and socioeconomic dimensions of the settings in which we hope to work.

Notes

1 The names of all people and places referenced in this chapter are pseudonyms.
2 Numbers are all approximations, to ensure anonymity.

References

Abowitz, K., & Harnish, J. (2006). Contemporary discourses of citizenship. *Review of Educational Research, 76*(4), 653–690.

Abu El-Haj, T. (2007). "I was born here, but my home, it's not here": Educating for democratic citizenship in an era of transnational migration and global conflict. *Harvard Educational Review, 77*(3), 285–316.

Alexander, M. (2010). *The new Jim Crow*. New York, NY: The New Press.

Brown, A. L., & Au, W. (2014). Race, memory, and master narratives: A critical essay on US curriculum history. *Curriculum Inquiry, 44*(3), 358–389.

Brown, A. L., & Brown, K. D. (2010). Strange fruit indeed: Interrogating contemporary textbook representations of racial violence toward African Americans. *Teachers College Record, 112*(1), 31–67.

Brown, A. L., & Campione, J. C. (1994). Guided discovery in a community of learners. In K. McGilly (Ed.), *Classroom lessons: Integrating cognitive theory and classroom practice.* Cambridge, MA: MIT Press/Bradford Books.

Chandler, P., & McKnight, D. (2009). The failure of social education in the United States: A critique of teaching the national story from "white" colourblind eyes. *Journal of Critical Education Policy Studies*, 7(2), 218–248.

Coates, T. (2015). *Between the world and me*. New York, NY: Spiegel & Grau.

Cohen, C., Kahne, J., & Marshall, J. (2018). *Let's go there: Race, ethnicity, and a lived civics approach to civic education*. Chicago, IL: GenForward at the University of Chicago.

Engle, R. A. & Conant, F. C. (2002). Guiding principles for fostering productive disciplinary engagement: Explaining an emergent argument in a community of learners classroom. *Cognition and Instruction*, 20(4), 399–483.

Freedman, E. B. (2007). Is teaching for social justice undemocratic? *Harvard Educational Review*, 77(4), 442–473.

Freedman, E. B. (2015). "What happened needs to be told": Fostering critical historical reasoning in the classroom. *Cognition and Instruction*, 33(4), 357–398.

Geertz, C. (1973). *The interpretation of cultures*. New York, NY: Basic Books.

Gutiérrez, K. (2016). Designing resilient ecologies: Social design experiments and a new social imagination. *Educational Researcher*, 45(3), 187–196.

Gutiérrez, K. & Jurow, S. (2016). Social design experiments: Toward equity by design. *Journal of the Learning Sciences*, 00, 1–34.

Gutiérrez, K. & Vossoughi, S. (2010). Lifting off the ground to return anew: Mediated praxis, transformative learning, and social design experiments. *Journal of Teacher Education*, 61, 100–117.

Hess, D. (2009). *Controversy in the classroom: The democratic power of discussion*. New York, NY: Routledge.

Junn, J. (2004). Diversity, immigration and the politics of civic education. *PS: Political Science and Politics*, 37(2), 253–255.

Kahne, J., & Middaugh, E. (2008). Democracy for some: The civic opportunity gap in high school. *Center for Information and Research on Civic Learning and Engagement*. Retrieved from http://www.civicyouth.org.

Levinson, M. (2007). The civic achievement gap. *CIRCLE* Working Paper 51.

Levinson, M. (2014). *No citizen left behind*. Cambridge, MA: Harvard University Press.

Loewen, J. (2018). *Teaching what really happened*. New York, NY: Teachers College Press.

Nasir, N., & Kirshner, B. (2003). The cultural construction of moral and civic identities. *Applied Developmental Science*, 7(3), 138–147.

Rubin, B. (2007). "There's still not justice": Youth civic identity development amid distinct school and community contexts. *Teachers College Record*, 109(2), 449–481.

Rubin, B. C. (2012). *Making citizens*. New York, NY: Routledge.

Rubin, B. C., & Hayes, B. (2010). "No backpacks" vs. "Drugs and murder": The promise and complexity of youth civic action research. *Harvard Educational Review*, 80(3),149–175.

Rubin, B. C., Hayes, B., & Benson, K. (2009). "It's the worst place to live": Urban youth and the challenge of school-based civic learning. *Theory Into Practice*, 48(3), 213–221.

Wiggins, G., & McTighe, J. (1998). *Understanding by design*. Alexandria, VA: Association for Supervision and Curriculum Development.

Wiggins, G., & McTighe, J. (2005). *Understanding by design*. Alexandria, VA: ASCD.

Youniss, J., McLellan, J. A., & Yates, M. (1997). "What we know about engendering civic identity." *American Behavioral Scientist*, 40(5), 620–631.

10

BEYOND NATIONAL DISCOURSES

South Korean and Japanese Students "Make a Better Social Studies Textbook"

Jongsung Kim

In 2015, the education department of South Korea announced a new task force to produce a state-issued history textbook. The department minister argued that some of the nation's textbooks contained "pro-North Korean bias," and proclaimed, "We cannot teach our children with biased history textbooks" (Agence France Presse, 2015). This announcement aroused fierce opposition, with many scholars, academic associations, teachers, parents, and students expressing anger at the idea. They were concerned that the so-called "*correct* history textbook" would reflect the government's historical viewpoint and might eliminate the space for free discussion. The textbook was published in 2017, but it came into disuse because no school adopted it.

As in the case of South Korea, most modern states have sought to educate their citizens in a certain way (Nakamura, 2008; Ulich, 1967). Public education has played an essential role in satisfying these intentions, with national curriculum, national standards, and state-authorized or state-issued textbook systems serving as the tools to achieve the state's goals (Apple & Christian-Smith, 1991; Apple, 2000). This tendency is even stronger in social studies education. Because this subject aims to educate for citizenship and involves political, geographical, and historical content deeply related to national identity (Hertzberg, 1981; Hursh & Ross, 2000), social studies has garnered substantial attention from modern state governments (Foster & Crawford, 2006; Nash, Crabtree, & Dunn, 1997). This relationship between a state and social studies education makes the "learning ecology" (Cobb, Confrey, diSessa, Lehrer, & Schauble, 2003, p. 9) of a social studies classroom somewhat different from that of other subjects.

I have studied how national discourses—or the ways a nation's people tend to organize knowledge and ideas—impact social studies classrooms and students' learning in South Korea and Japan. In 2016–2017, I conducted a design-based action research project that involved South Korean and Japanese students communicating with one another while co-creating a "better" social studies textbook. Through this intervention, students in each country were introduced to the other's historical and political discourses and asked to interrogate their own. Many did so enthusiastically, while others were more hesitant. To understand what students learned, I needed to consider the historical, social, and political context surrounding my intervention. This chapter describes this design-based action research project and shares my journey to grasp students' learning within the two countries' distinct contexts.

The Clash of National Discourses in International Settings

My interest in this topic dates back to an episode that I experienced as an elementary school teacher in South Korea. I was a sixth-grade homeroom teacher who taught most subjects, including social studies. One day, a new student came into my classroom who was Korean-Japanese. He had lived in Japan for most of his life but could speak Korean, so the language barrier was not a problem. What I worried about was a social studies lesson I had planned to teach about a part of Korean history in which Japan colonized Korea. The objective of the lesson was to understand why Japan changed the way it governed *Joseon* (Korea's name at that time) between 1910 and 1945. Until the student came into my classroom, I had no second thoughts about teaching the original lesson plan. But the presence of this Korean-Japanese student, who might have come from a different educational background and national discourse, made me nervous about my lesson plan. Eventually, however, this episode helped me to realize the existence of national discourses of which I only had superficial knowledge up to that day.

In many social studies classrooms, the national discourse has unquestionable power (Apple, 2000; Carretero, Asensio, & Rodríguez-Moneo, 2011). If there is no opportunity for exposure to other discourses, as when the Korean-Japanese student appeared in my class, it is difficult to think outside of one's own national discourse. Since this event, I have been interested in how each nation creates its interpretation of historical and social phenomena.

The current project involved comparing descriptions of the same historical and social phenomena in South Korean and Japanese social studies textbooks. Because both countries have an authorized-textbook system, these books can be seen as representations of each country's national discourse on these topics (Suh, Yurita, Lin, & Metzger, 2013). Not surprisingly, there were clear differences in how current issues that cause tension between South Korea and Japan were described in these textbooks (e.g., how to remember WWII). I also found unexpected differences hidden beneath a veil that I called "objective content knowledge."

For example, many teachers and students in South Korea and Japan regarded historical content about topics such as the Sino-Japanese War (1984–1985) and the Russo-Japanese War (1904–1905) as objective knowledge beyond all doubt

(Kim, 2017). However, the descriptions of these wars were quite different in the two countries' textbooks. The South Korean textbook depicted the Sino-Japanese War and the Russo-Japanese War as a "history of damage" (Kim, 2017, p. 9). A main cause of the wars, the book asserted, was a Japanese imperialist effort to place *Joseon* under their control. Many battles broke out on the Korean Peninsula, and many Koreans were killed by foreign militaries. The South Korean textbook emphasized the nation as victim. On the other hand, the Japanese textbook described the Sino-Japanese War and the Russo-Japanese War as a "history of victory" (Kim, 2017, p. 9). In this narrative, Japan won against China, a country that had wielded its power in Asia for a long time, and fought well against Russia, one of the strongest imperialist countries. The discourse of the Japanese textbook situated the wars as part of the process of Japan becoming a world power.

In today's globalized world, social studies educators are obligated to prepare students to be tolerant democratic citizens who pursue "associated living" (Dewey, 1916/1996, p. 31) with others in the global community. The mono-discourse of social studies classrooms in South Korea and Japan, however, insulate students from encountering, or even noticing the existence of, other national discourses. To tackle this problematic situation—in other words, to "cross the national border" (Nishikawa, 2001) with teachers and students—I decided to conduct a design-based action research study that would expose South Korean and Japanese students to each other's national discourses and prompt them to reevaluate their own.

Design-Based Action Research

Design-based research shares many of its epistemological, ontological, and methodological characteristics with action research (McKenney & Reeves, 2012; Cole, Purao, Rossi, & Sein, 2005). Wang and Hannafin (2005) have characterized design-based research as: (a) pragmatic, (b) grounded, (c) interactive, iterative, and flexible, (d) integrative, and (e) contextual. These five characteristics also apply to action research, which pursues improvements to practice through cycles of "planning, acting, observing, and analyzing and reflecting" (Lewin, 1946), bridging the gap between theory and practice, and generating contextual and practical knowledge (Whitehead, 1989).

Yet some differences do exist. First, the impetus for the project is different in the two methodologies. In the case of design-based research, researchers typically identify a problem and work with practitioners to devise a way to solve it (McKenney and Reeves, 2012). By contrast, action research starts with a problem a practitioner discovers in his or her local context. Second, the research process is different. A team of researchers and practitioners conduct design-based research together to create, evaluate, and improve a design (Plomp, 2007); a practitioner can conduct action research by oneself through reflecting one's own practice

(McNiff, 2013). Finally, the purpose of the research is different. Design-based research pursues generalizable theory such as domain theory, a design framework, or design methodology to make a broader impact beyond the site itself (Edelson, 2002). Action research places less emphasis on creating transferable knowledge (Nijhawan, 2017). It focuses rather on how practitioners create local knowledge in a specific context and grow as professionals (Carson, 1995; Stringer, 2013).

In the field of information systems, several researchers have suggested integrating design-based research and action research to compensate for the shortcomings of each method (Cole, Purao, Rossi, & Sein, 2005; Sein, Henfridsson, Purao, Rossi, & Lindgren, 2011). Applying this idea to education, Nijhawan (2017) proposes a hybrid methodology called "design-based action research" (p. 20). She argues that action research can enjoy the theory-driven characteristics of design-based research to generate "new theories from interventions into practice" (p. 20). Conversely, design-based research can benefit from insider knowledge, or in other words, teachers' practical knowledge that outside researchers cannot acquire.

The current project follows Nijhawan's suggestions. In order to bridge the discourse gap between South Korea and Japan, teachers in each country would need to introduce the other country's discourse into their classroom and help their students deconstruct their own country's discourse. However, many teachers might be uncomfortable with doing this, because it would mean problematizing their own government's actions. For this reason, in this design-based action research project, I acted as a researcher and a practitioner at the same time. I designed and taught a curriculum in one Japanese and one South Korean classroom that aimed to bridge the discourse gap between the two countries. This chapter shares the project's design narrative from my own "insider" perspective.

Authentic Communication as a Way to Cross the National Border

Critical Patriotism

Before describing my intervention, it is worth considering what constitutes a desirable relationship between a nation and its citizens. Social psychologists explain that there are two versions of this relationship: nationalism and patriotism. Nationalism concerns the "distinction between us and them" (Conversi, 1999, p. 564). According to Kosterman and Feshbach (1989), nationalism is the expression of "our" superiority over others who are outside the nation. It causes the exclusion of outsiders and a "competitive" atmosphere in the world (Druckman, 1994, p. 47). On the other hand, patriotism refers to a positive relationship between a nation and its citizens, and does not rely on the exclusion of outsiders (Bar-Tal, 1993). Patriotism thus could contribute to a "cooperative" atmosphere in the world (Druckman, 1994, p. 47).

Social studies education ought to promote patriotism, not nationalism. However, not all forms of patriotism are worth pursuing (Nussbaum, 2013).

Unconditional support for the nation is antithetical to the formation of a democratic mind (Engle & Ochoa, 1988; Parker, 1996). The form of patriotism that matches the aim of social studies, especially in the current globalized era, is a "critical patriotism" (Banks et al., 2003), which is based on awareness and appraisal of national discourses. To protect democratic values, citizens need to be aware of their in-group discourses and reject "blind" (Staub, 1997) and "authoritarian" (Westheimer, 2006) patriotism.

Authentic Communication in International Settings

Students need exposure to discourses from outside their national settings in order to promote critical patriotism in social studies education. Encountering discourses that are different from their own gives students the opportunity to reflect on their own nations' discourses (Allport, 1954; Brown & Hewstone, 2005). For students, hearing other national discourses challenges the myth that *our nation's discourse is the "right" one.*

Instead of being scared of the discourse gap, teachers can use it for initiating and continuing communication across national borders (Scollon, Scollon, & Jones, 2011). When students discover other possible interpretations, they think about how and why each is different. After comparing others' discourses with their own, students can begin to communicate with others, to exchange discourses, and to consider which is more persuasive. Through this process, students can deepen their understandings about their national discourses, deconstruct them, and reconstruct new discourses in collaboration with others (Habermas, 1984).

However, it is difficult to communicate with those who live abroad due to constraints of time, space, and language. Even though many educators in South Korea and Japan understand the importance of cross-national communication, they tend to settle with introducing other nations' discourses and letting students ponder them. This "intrapersonal communication," in which existing and novel discourses compete in the individual student's mind, is valuable for promoting critical self-reflection (Galinsky, Maddux, Gilin, & White, 2008).

For the purpose of building mutual understanding, however, intrapersonal communication falls short. The term "mutual" implies two directions: I (or we) to others and others to me (or us). To achieve intersubjectivity, speakers need to continuously express their own opinions in turn. With intrapersonal communication, students learn what and how others think, but they lack the opportunity to respond. To overcome this shortcoming and achieve mutual understanding in international settings, the results of intrapersonal communication need to be shared with people who operate within a different national discourse, forming an iterative cycle that I call "authentic communication" (Kim, 2016, 2017).

Authentic communication involves "(a) understanding others' discourses, (b) recognizing the perspectives behind these discourses, (c) analyzing and critiquing these perspectives and discourses, and (d) suggesting a new discourse"

(Kim, 2016, p. 51). Compared with intrapersonal communication, which ends up creating a comparison between others' discourses and one's own, authentic communication includes an additional step: sharing the resulting insights with others outside the national discourse. Authentic communication thus consists of multiple repetitions of the whole process from (a) to (d). It allows people to exchange opinions, discuss the discourse gap, and develop mutual understanding.

The media through which authentic communication can occur poses a challenge. With face-to-face communication, vocal and body languages are sufficient for exchanging opinions. However, these features are not realistic for cross-national interactions, especially in the case of South Korea and Japan, where students speak different languages. Additionally, as face-to-face communication can veer in many different directions, it can be difficult for teachers to ensure that it remains open and democratic. Thus, in international settings, "mediated communication" (Williams, 1977; Kiesler, Siegel, & McGuire, 1984) through documents, videos, and movies, can be more practical and beneficial than face-to-face communication.

In this design-based action research project, I focused on the social studies textbook as a medium for authentic communication. By deconstructing the textbook's representations of their national discourse and then collaboratively reconstructing a new one, students can develop their own understanding, rather than relying on what the government and publishers have provided (Kim, 2016). Furthermore, as textbooks in South Korea and Japan have bible-like status (Ryu, Choi, & Kim, 2014; Yamaue, 2010), rewriting a social studies textbook with others through authentic communication can change students' view of the textbook from that of a bible to that of a reference document (Kim, 2016, 2017).

Methods

Drawing on the principles of authentic communication, I created the intervention "Let's Make a Better Social Studies Textbook." This design-based action research project consisted of three phases, each dealing with a different social studies topic: South Korea (geography), the Sino-Japanese and the Russo-Japanese wars (history), and the Dokdo/Takeshima territorial issue (civics).

In this chapter, I focus on the civics topic, "Let's Make a Better Dokdo/Takeshima Textbook." Compared to the other two phases, it was more difficult to find schools in both countries that would allow me to conduct this project. I contacted several homeroom teachers at the elementary level and social studies teachers at the middle school level, but they were quite cautious about participating in the project. Although the teachers ultimately did agree to participate, the principals of some of the schools declined out of concern for potential problems that the project might cause within their schools. In this sense, Dokdo/Takeshima was the most controversial topic among the three. I thus determined that the phase of the project devoted to this territorial dispute would best fit the aim of this chapter: to illustrate how the historical, social, and political context affects design-based research and students' learning.

Study Context

"Dokdo" in Korean, or "Takeshima" in Japanese, is a 46-acre island between South Korea and Japan. It has been uninhabited for most of its history, but the issue of who would control it emerged in earnest with the appearance of modern nations. The history of Japan's colonial rule in *Joseon* made the issue still more complicated because, in the discourse of South Korea, the registering of Takeshima as Japanese territory during the Russo-Japanese war is regarded as a key moment in the history of Japanese colonization. Currently, South Korea maintains effective control over the island, while Japan argues that South Korea is staging an illegal occupation. (As of January 2019, one South Korean civilian and around 40 maritime police officers live on the island.)

According to a survey in 2018, many South Korean and Japanese citizens believe that Dokdo/Takeshima is a major cause of the high tension between the two countries (Genron NPO, 2018). The territorial dispute is one of the regular topics in mass-media reports of the South Korea–Japan relationship, and nationalistic voices in the media sometimes escalate the tension. However, the extent of the passion about the territorial dispute differs in South Korea and Japan. South Koreans tend to connect the issue to their history of being colonized by Japan. In general, South Koreans are eager to talk about the necessity of protecting Dokdo against Japan. On the other hand, people in Japan tend not to regard the issue as seriously as South Koreans do.

Each government has created its own national discourse on Dokdo/Takeshima and has educated students accordingly (Cho, Kim, & Choi, 2009). The South Korean government has conducted systemic Dokdo education. Most South Korean students can recite at least some parts of the song called "Dokdo is Our Territory," and they learn reasons why Dokdo is a South Korean territory from elementary to high school. Meanwhile, the Japanese government recently started adding the description "South Korea is illegally ruling Takeshima" to their state-authorized social studies textbook (e.g., Sakaue et al., 2016). Japanese students, though, do not have much knowledge about Takeshima, and they gain most it from mass media such as television or Internet articles (Bukh, 2015).

Project Overview

The project "Let's Make a Better Dokdo/Takeshima Textbook" consisted of four rounds and 13 hours total (Table 10.1). A class of 32 South Korean sixth graders (ages 11–12) at "KR Elementary School" and a class of 32 Japanese eighth graders (ages 13–14) at "JP Middle School" participated in the project. It was the first time the students had engaged in this kind of international project, and

TABLE 10.1 Outline of the Project "Let's Make a Better Dokdo/Takeshima Textbook"

Round	Direction	Activity	Date	Participants
1 (6 hours)	South Korea to Japan	(1) Understanding South Korean and Japanese discourses on Dokdo/Takeshima with multiple documents, including textbooks (2) Recognizing the perspectives of the discourses (3) Analyzing and criticizing them (4) Suggesting a better textbook to Japanese students	April, 2017	32 sixth graders at KR Elementary School in South Korea
2 (3 hours)	Japan to South Korea	(1) – (3): Same as Round 1 (4) Proposing ways South Korean students can make their suggested textbook better.	May, 2017	32 eighth graders at JP Middle School in Japan
3 (2 hours)	South Korea to Japan	(1): Omit (2) – (4): Same as Round 1	June, 2017	Same as Round 1
4 (2 hours)	Japan to South Korea	(1): Omit (2) – (4): Same as Round 2	June, 2017	Same as Round 2

the schools had no special connection to each other, such as sister-school status. The grade disparity was intentional, as Japanese students do not learn about Takeshima until the eighth grade.

In this design-based action research project, students were the agents of authentic communication and writers of a better Dokdo/Takeshima textbook. I played the role of researcher and practitioner simultaneously; I was not only a teacher, but also a translator and a facilitator of authentic communication. I went back and forth between South Korea and Japan and delivered the collective result of the intrapersonal communication among the students in each of the two countries.

The project began with a section from the Japanese textbook that describes Takeshima. In the first round, I translated this section into Korean and introduced it to the students at KR Elementary School. When those students objected to the Japanese version of events in the book, I explained the aim of the project and the need for them to suggest a better Dokdo/Takeshima textbook to their Japanese peers. By reading through documents that each government published and creating a timeline of events surrounding Dokdo/Takeshima, the South Korean students had opportunities to learn both countries' discourses. I then divided the class into small groups and asked each to create an outline for a better Dokdo/Takeshima textbook. After presenting and discussing the outlines, the class as a whole determined the contents for the new textbook. Each group then selected the part they wished to rewrite. After revising their section, each group gave a presentation in front of their classmates, received feedback, and made final modifications. After combing the manuscripts and fixing grammatical errors, I showed the final version to the students to confirm that it reflected their intentions.

In the second round, I translated the textbook suggested by the South Korean students into Japanese and introduced it to the students at JP Middle School. After giving the Japanese students sufficient time to share their thoughts about the book, I explained the aim of the project and the necessity of suggesting ways to make the textbook better. The Japanese students learned about both countries' discourses through the same learning activities as the South Korean students had, and then recorded their suggestions for how their Korean counterparts could improve the textbook further. Specifically, each student recorded their thoughts on a worksheet and shared them through a Take-a-Stand activity, in which students express their opinions on a continuum between two poles (e.g., acceptable versus non-acceptable). This process continued in the third and fourth round, as the South Korean students suggested a new, better Dokdo/Takeshima textbook that considered the Japanese students' opinions, and the Japanese students analyzed and critiqued the new textbook and conveyed their thoughts in turn.

Data Collection and Analysis

I utilized discourse analytic (Edwards & Potter, 1992) and grounded theory (Corbin & Strauss, 1990) approaches to answer two research questions: (a) "How did the project 'Let's Make a Better Dokdo/Takeshima Textbook' transform mono-discourse classrooms in South Korea and Japan?" and (b) "What did students in both countries learn in these new learning spaces?"

The altered textbooks suggested by the South Korean students in the first and third rounds and the Japanese students' suggestions in the second and fourth rounds form the substance of the authentic communication. By investigating how students in each country created their messages for students in the other country, and by examining how this exchange of opinion generated new classroom dynamics, I sought to explain the transformation that occurred throughout the project. I coded inductively the messages that students in each country tried to send to their peers, and then analyzed how this exchange created, escalated, or relieved tensions between the South Korean and the Japanese students. Additionally, I examined the learning materials, students' worksheets, video-recordings of the lessons, and my reflection notes in order to better understand the context within which this communication took place.

To capture what students in both countries learned through authentic communication, at the beginning of the intervention, I asked them to "write down what you know and what you think about Dokdo/Takeshima," and at the end of each round to "write down freely what you learned, felt, or rethought through this project." These prompts aimed to get at the meanings students gave to the authentic communication. After inductively coding these reaction essays, I conducted axial and selective coding focused on students' learning. I refined the codes after analyzing students' worksheets, their classroom discussion, and outside sources (e.g., news about Dokdo/Takeshima), to describe students' learning thoroughly and contextually. Additionally, to unearth and minimize validity problems that might arise from my identity as Korean, all analyses were independently conducted and peer-checked by several researchers and graduate students who identify as Japanese.

Authentic Communication Between South Korean and Japanese Students

"South Korea's Illegal Occupation": The Message of the Japanese Textbook

As the starting point of authentic communication, I utilized a middle-school geography textbook published by *Tokyo Syoseki*, one of the major textbook publishers in Japan. The Japanese students participating in this project were already using it in class, and it is also the most widely utilized middle-school geography textbook in the country.

Considering the authorized-textbook system in Japan, it is not difficult to imagine that the textbook reflects the government's voice. The book states that "Takeshima is Japan's indigenous island but it is occupied by South Korea illegally" (Sakaue et al., 2016, p. 133). Additionally, the book asserts that the

Japanese government not only "protests against the South Korean government" (p. 133), but also keeps trying to solve this problem in peaceful and legal ways, such as utilizing the U.N.'s International Court of Justice, with the South Korean government remaining unresponsive to these overtures. Interestingly, however, the textbook does not show any evidence to support the view that Takeshima is Japan's territory.

"You Are Wrong": The Process and Result of the First Round

At the beginning of the first round, I asked the students at the South Korean Elementary school to write down what they knew about Dokdo. The students' reactions affirmed their endorsement of the South Korean government's discourse, that Dokdo is "our territory." Some students expressed anger against Japan for trying to take Dokdo from South Korea, claiming that Japan was being "unreasonable" (South Korean student, from now on "KR," 15) and "obstinate" (KR 16). Others brought up evidence such as, "You can see Dokdo with the naked eye from South Korean island called Ullengdo" (KR 30), to support South Korea's national discourse on the topic, though most of this evidence was superficial.

In general, after reading the Japanese textbook, South Korean students found its description absurd, because their own understandings of Dokdo opposed the textbook's discourse. They problematized the textbook as having "just argument, no evidence" (KR 28). They also mentioned that "the textbook does not give Japanese students the opportunity to think of [the dominion of] the island critically" (KR 2). When the South Korean students realized the discourse gap between the two countries, I recommended making a better Dokdo/Takeshima textbook and presenting it to the middle-school students in Japan.

To create this new textbook, the South Korean students analyzed both countries' discourses. They read "Leaflet: Dokdo, beautiful island of Korea," published by the foreign office of South Korea; "Leaflet: Takeshima," published by the Japanese foreign office; and the Dokdo textbook for elementary school students authorized by the South Korean education department. Through these sources, the students learned how each government created that country's discourse, and they analyzed what kinds of historical events or documents each government preferred to use as evidence.

The South Korean students then sent their Japanese peers a new textbook that contained the underlying message of "You are wrong." The textbook they created had five parts:

(a) Preface
(b) What is Dokdo/Takeshima?
(c) Why do we fight for Dokdo/Takeshima?
(d) The arguments and evidence surrounding Dokdo/Takeshima
(e) Epilogue

In part (a), the South Korean students described their purpose for suggesting the textbook as "having opportunities to re-think Dokdo/Takeshima." In (b) and (c), they described the island's economic value and argued that this was the main reason for the territorial dispute. Part (d) was the centerpiece of the suggested textbook. The students divided it into four sections, based on the timeline they created while analyzing the discourse of the two countries: (1) 512–1600, (2) 1601–1887 (the latter date is when Japan published the *Dajyokan-Shirei* [Order of the Governor], which the South Korean government uses to prove their dominion over Dokdo), (3) 1888–1945, and (4) 1946–present day. Finally, in part (e) the Korean students concluded the textbook with the sentence, "What do you think about Dokdo/Takeshima?"

The suggested textbook made overtures towards acknowledging other interpretations of Dokdo/Takeshima's history. However, the South Korean student authors still only focused on their own county's discourse and intentionally excluded Japan's. One example is the way they wrote about "the reason why South Korea does not respond to Japan's demand of solving the territorial issue at the international court of justice." KR 18 researched the court and shared information about a Japanese judge in the institution. Based on this, the South Korean students added a description: "We are not afraid of losing the case. The reason why we do not bring the case to the court is because the judges are easily influenced by Japan." This discourse is quite common in South Korean online media. The South Korean students thought that this information supported their argument, that "Dokdo is ours," and so referred to it without critical analysis.

Another example of South Korean students' adherence to their country's discourse is the entirety of part (d), in which the students conducted intentional exclusion. In this first round of the project, the South Korean students saw Japan's discourse as akin to a foe they needed to defeat. Several students did mention that Japan also has its own logic for arguing that Dokdo/Takeshima is theirs (KR 3, 8, 10, 15, 25, 31). However, during whole-class discussion and feedback sessions on each group's presentation, these voices were silenced by more dominant students. Notwithstanding their exposure to both countries' discourses, the South Korean students only utilized in their suggested textbook the historical events and documents that supported their own national discourse, most likely because they felt their mission as representatives of South Korea was to persuade the Japanese students that the South Korean discourse was correct. For the South Korean students, the new textbook was a medium to deliver to their counterparts their own thoughts about the island.

"It Is not Fair!": The Process and Result of the Second Round

As I did with the South Korean students in the initial round, I began the second round by asking the Japanese students to write down what they knew about Takeshima. Through this activity, I affirmed that the Japanese government's discourse asserting that South Korea was occupying Takeshima illegally was dominant in the classroom. In contrast to the South Korean students, however, more than half of Japanese students said, "I don't know very much [about the island]." There were even some students who wanted either to "destroy Takeshima" (Japanese student, from now on "JP," 22), or to "divide it into two" (JP 21; JP 23) because territorial disputes worsen the relationship between South Korea and Japan. These differences between the South Korean and Japanese students most likely originated from discrepancies in the territorial education and social climate toward the issue in the two countries (Bukh, 2015; Cho, Kim, & Choi, 2009).

After reading the textbook suggested by their South Korean counterparts, the Japanese students said they could not accept it. They argued that the textbook was "biased" because it only presented South Korea's discourse. I recommended that they share their opinions about the textbook with the South Korean students in order to improve its content. Similar to the first round, the Japanese students learned about both countries' discourses through documents published by the foreign offices of South Korea and Japan, and through learning materials published by the Japanese city of Musashimurayama.

This inquiry resulted in the Japanese students sending the message, "It is not fair!" to their South Korean counterparts. They said they "could accept some of the South Korean discourse if the primary sources were true" (JP 19). However, like JP 8, who said, "It's all about South Korea," they found the balance of material problematic. They argued that Japanese viewpoints received short shrift, and that even the textbook's way of applying those viewpoints served ultimately to fortify South Korea's position. They objected, in other words, to the South Korean students' intentional exclusion of material that they (the Japanese students) deemed relevant.

"But. . . You Are still Wrong": The Process and Result of the Third Round

When the South Korean students first read the opinions sent by the Japanese students, they responded by asking "Why?" (KR 3) and by stating "I am disappointed" (KR 13). However, the reactions later shifted to "somewhat convinced" (KR 2) as they came to understand the cause of the Japanese students' remonstrance. The South Korean students realized that the textbook they had created did not adequately incorporate Japan's discourse. They decided to change the textbook's direction to deal with both countries' discourses, and suggested a new version to the Japanese students.

However, the message of this new textbook created in the third round essentially stated, "But. . . you are still wrong." The South Korean students said they "need to listen to the Japanese students' opinions" (KR 9) and that some of these opinions "can be accepted" (KR 11). Accordingly, in their revisions they expanded the amount of attention the textbook paid to Japan's discourse.

Yet at the same time, the South Korean students added refutations to the newly introduced Japanese discourse. The new textbook dealt with both countries' discourses; however, the South Korean students did not abandon their use of the textbook as a tool to persuade the Japanese students of their own point of view.

"Long Way Away": The Process and Result of the Fourth Round

When the Japanese students received the newly updated Dokdo/Takeshima textbook, they said, "This is better than the first one" (JP 26). They were somewhat satisfied with the degree of balance between the discourses of the two countries. However, they also said that "much [work] remained" (JP 11) to create a better Dokdo/Takeshima textbook together, arguing that the revised text did not reflect the Japanese students' opinions fully. Additionally, they mentioned that the sections containing Japan's arguments and evidence were still shorter than those containing South Korea's, and they objected to the section in which the South Korean students added their refutations to Japan's discourse. Finally, the Japanese students suggested adding more primary resources that people could utilize to think more critically about both countries' discourses.

What Students Learned

Seeing a Controversy as a Controversy

Even though the South Korean and Japanese students said that they could "listen to Japan's opinions" (KR 31) and "understand South Korea's arguments" (JP 3), not a single one changed positions on the Dokdo/Takeshima controversy. The South Korean students continued to assert that Dokdo was South Korea's territory, and the Japanese students that Takeshima belonged to Japan. However, the experience of having authentic communication with others versed in a different national discourse enabled the students, who originally thought that Dokdo/Takeshima was "unconditionally our territory" (KR 32, JP 19), to realize that *there is no such thing.*

Dokdo/Takeshima can be considered a controversial issue, which inherently causes "intellectual disagreement" (Evans, Newman, & Saxe, 1996, p. 2). However, the issue is presented as noncontroversial in South Korean and Japanese classrooms. Dokdo/Takeshima education mainly presents the given nation's official reasons why the island belongs to them (Akaha, 2008; Kozisek, 2016). For both the South Korean and Japanese students, Dokdo/Takeshima is an issue for which they know the *right* answer and is not considered open for discussion with others. These kinds of mono-discourse classrooms (and a mono-discourse societies) do not expose South Korean and Japanese students to differing views. At the outset of this project, students from both countries said that they needed to "keep the island from" (KR 2) the other country and could not "give it up" (JP 31).

By participating in authentic communication, however, the South Korean and Japanese students started to shift in their stance. As other research exploring the effect of encountering multiple discourses has found (Barton & McCully, 2010; Freedman, 2015; Goldberg, 2013; Parker, 2010), the students considered both points of view and deferred their judgment on the Dokdo/Takeshima controversy, rather than fixating only on the evidence supporting their side. For example, KR 16 said, "At first, I only wrote about South Korea's [discourse] because I did not know the other views well. But I started to feel that it is difficult to judge if Dokdo is ours or not," while JP 22 said, "I did not know Takeshima well, but now I understand this territorial dispute is very deep and complicated." These responses suggest that authentic communication not only provides an opportunity to learn about others' discourses, but also prompts students to consider that those discourses may hold merit. By bringing them into contact with others holding differing perspectives, the process transformed the mono-discourse classroom into a site for exploring legitimate points of controversy.

"Critical Understanding" versus "Selective Learning"

Once the South Korean and Japanese students saw the Dokdo/Takeshima dispute as a controversial issue, they were faced with the intellectual tension of considering which discourse was more persuasive than the other. This stimulus guided the students to think critically about both discourses. As mentioned above, before the intervention, most thought of Dokdo/Takeshima as their country's indigenous territory, but their evidence to support this claim was superficial and weak. At that time, they thought that the island was theirs *unconditionally*. By the end, however, 84% of the students mentioned that it was beneficial to know both sides, as this allowed them to reflect on their own point of view. For example, KR 1 said, "I thought Dokdo is ours unconditionally, but after listening to Japanese students' arguments, I thought that Dokdo being unconditionally ours might be wrong." The students also found "inconsistencies" (JP 20) and "incorrectness" (KR 12) in their own national discourse, and understood by the end of the project that the governments of both countries put forward only the evidence favorable to their side, such as JP 9 who said, "South Korea likes *Dajyokan-Shirei* and Japan likes Rusk documents."

Not all students achieved such critical understanding. As others have found in various contexts (Barton & Levstik, 1998; Epstein, 1998; Wertsch, 2000), the South Korean and Japanese students interpreted the information they encountered through their own cultural lens. By the end of the first and second rounds, 16% of the students still strongly believed that Dokdo/Takeshima was theirs, remarking solely that the intervention helped them "learn why" (KR 5; JP 30) it was theirs. The intense emotion associated with keeping the island from the other country may have hindered these students from considering their own discourses critically

(Porat, 2004; Goldberg, 2013). They used the intervention rather as a means of acquiring knowledge they could use to continue defending their national discourse. These students' selective learning may have arisen from the historical rivalry of the countries and from students' "win-or-lose" thinking (KR 28; JP 8)—issues to consider when revising this intervention for the next iteration.

Additionally, in comparing what students said in class to what they expressed in writing in each round (e.g., in the suggested textbooks), I noticed a gap between individual understanding and collective decision-making. The 84% of students who wrote about the benefits of critical understanding barely voiced these thoughts in front of their classmates, and sometimes, especially when giving a presentation, they defended their national discourse uncritically. When I asked the South Korean students if they were agreeable to suggesting a new textbook without including the Rusk documents (which support the Japanese discourse), they answered "yes." When I asked the Japanese students if they wanted to add the *Dajyokan-Shirei* (favored by the South Korean government), they avoided dealing with the topic. This tendency towards intentional exclusion caused me to realize that the process of authentic communication adopted in this project may not be a perfect way to move beyond national discourses. Supporting students to overcome peer-pressure (and societal pressure) in each country's classrooms should be factored into the design.

That said, the tendencies towards selective learning and intentional exclusion did grow weaker in the third and fourth rounds. The portion of students who said that they focused solely on information that supported their own national discourse dropped from 27% in rounds one and two to 2% in rounds three and four. Additionally, in the later rounds many students (especially South Koreans) began to realize they were practicing intentional exclusion in their suggestions for improving the Dokdo/Takeshima textbook. This indicates that iterative authentic communication may help to develop students' critical self-reflection.

Recognizing the Value of Authentic Communication

Through participating in the project, the South Korean and Japanese students came to realize the power of authentic communication. For example, KR 9 said, "Instead of just arguing that this is our territory, we need to listen to Japan's opinions and South Korea's opinions. Willingness to communicate with each other is necessary to solve the issue." Students from both countries mentioned that it was "helpful to deliver the opinions [on the island] to others" (KR 8; JP 31) through authentic communication. KR 10 said that "creating a textbook and suggesting it" to others caused him to feel like "a diplomat" (KR 10) working to bridge the gap between the two countries' discourses. Through their participation in the project, the students came to believe that communication that transcends national borders and "respects the counterpart's opinions" (JP 3) is important in finding a solution to the island dispute.

Like others have found in analogous projects (e.g., Goldberg, Schwarz, & Porat, 2011; Kolikant & Pollack, 2009), the students' experience with authentic communication convinced them of its value. They mentioned the need for it more enthusiastically in the project's later rounds. Additionally, in the first and second rounds, students mainly used collective nouns such as "South Korea" and "Japan" when they referred to others, whereas in the third and fourth rounds, they used more specific nouns such as "KR elementary school students" and "Japanese friends." The iterative exchange of opinions allowed the students to discover the individuals who lived inside the other nation and that they could enjoy communicating with "as a human" (JP 3). Dokdo/Takeshima was no longer a dispute between South Korea and Japan. It became "our [issue]" (KR 9; JP 16) between the South Korean and Japanese students.

Still, several students pointed out flaws in the project's procedure for encouraging authentic communication. They said both the South Korean and Japanese students remained too focused on "finding the others' weaknesses" (JP 1) and only talked about "their stories" (JP 6). To counter these win-or-lose attitudes, they suggested "setting a clear direction for the project of making a better textbook" (JP 1). As these students argued, the format of the project caused those involved to see the textbook improvement process as a rivalry between the two classes rather than a collaboration. These reactions to the intervention showed that there is still room for refinement.

Attending to Context in Design-Based Research

"Let's Make a Better Dokdo/Takeshima Textbook," an intervention based on authentic communication, reformed the mono-discourse classrooms of KR Elementary School in South Korea and JP Middle School in Japan. The students who participated had opportunities to think critically about their own and other people's discourses, and came to understand the complexity of the island dispute and the necessity of continuing to communicate with people from other nations. To achieve these results, I needed to attend to the socio-historical context surrounding the island dispute. Without considering current Dokdo/Takeshima education, Korean-Japanese history, the current relationship between the two countries, the schools' and communities' attitudes towards the dispute, and its portrayals in mass media, this design-based action research project might have adopted a dubious design that led to cursory findings.

Compared to other school subjects such as math and science, socio-historical context impinges on social studies instruction far more directly. More so than set, function, chemical reaction, or Pangaea, social studies content connects to students' lives, identities, and belief systems. When the South Korean and Japanese students participated in the project of making a better Dokdo/Takeshima textbook, they brought their own perspectives to the topic—perspectives framed by the context in which they lived. Numerous influences, from the mass media, friends and family, and prior in- or out-of-school learning, coalesced to form an intricate learning ecology.

For this reason, DBR in social studies can be more controversial than in other fields. As mentioned early on, the government of every state has sought to use social studies education to shape the consciousness of its citizenry. To advance the view that "Dokdo/Takeshima is unconditionally ours," the governments of South Korea and Japan have conducted territorial education that celebrates "our" discourse while excluding that of others. (Interestingly, the word "our" here has the opposite meaning from the one the South Korean and Japanese students used to characterize their relationship at the end of the project.)

DBR projects like this one work against this status quo (Wang & Hannafin, 2005). Design-based researchers therefore should anticipate pushback from families, schools, and regions invested in the current national discourse. In my case, giving students opportunities to challenge the dominant discourse by revising their textbook was difficult because of my own context, including the Dokdo education I received growing up, as well as my national identity as Korean. The principals and teachers who did not permit the project at their schools worried about the social pressure it might cause.

As this project illustrates, DBR can bring complexity and controversy into the classroom due to the historical, social, and political contexts in which these studies take place. Some may argue that conducting DBR in social studies is difficult and burdensome because of that. Yes, it is. However, we should not give up on creating innovative designs. DBR offers a means of reforming curriculum and instruction in meaningful ways that attend to the contextual factors at play. This chapter is a call for researchers and educators to plunge into the messiness of that endeavor.

Last but not least, projects like this one are not the exclusive provenance of those like me who can speak multiple languages and travel between two countries. With support from bicultural students, teachers, and parents cognizant of more than one national discourse, authentic communication is possible in many contexts. Teachers in different countries also could pair up and send materials and students' opinions back and forth electronically. Following the example described in this chapter, I hope many educators resolve to cross national borders with their students.

References

Agence France Presse (2015, November 3). South Korea accused of rewriting history in new school textbooks. *The Guardian*. Retrieved from www.theguardian.com/world/2015nov/03/south-korea-accused-rewriting-history-schoolbook-policy

Akaha, T. (2008). The nationalist discourse in contemporary Japan: The role of China and Korea in the last decade. *Pacific Focus*, *23*(2), 156–188.

Allport, G. W. (1954). *The nature of prejudice*. Cambridge, MA: Addison-Wesley.

Anderson, T., & Shattuck, J. (2012). Design-based research: A decade of progress in education research? *Educational researcher*, *41*(1), 16–25.

Apple M. W., & Christian-Smith, L. (Eds.). (1991). *The politics of the textbook*. New York, NY: Routledge.

Apple, M. W. (2000). *Official knowledge* (2nd ed.). New York, NY: Routledge.

Banks, J. A., McGee Banks C. A., Cortes C., Hahn, C. L., Merryfield, M., Moodley, K., Murphy-Shigematsu, S., Osler, A., Park, C., & Parker, W. C. (2003). *Democracy and diversity: Principles and concepts for educating citizens in a global age*. Seattle, WA: Center for Multicultural Education, University of Washington.

Bar-Tal, D. (1993). Patriotism as fundamental beliefs of group members. *Politics and the Individual, 3*, 45–62.

Barton, K. C., & McCully, A. W. (2010). "You can form your own point of view": Internally persuasive discourse in Northern Ireland students' encounters with history. *Teachers College Record, 112*(1), 142–181.

Barton, K. C., & Levstik, L. S. (1998). "It wasn't a good part of history": National identity and students' explanations of historical significance. *Teachers College Record, 90*(3), 478–513.

Brown, R., & Hewstone, M. (2005). An integrative theory of intergroup contact. *Advances in experimental social psychology, 37*, 255–343.

Bukh, A. (2015). Shimane Prefecture, Tokyo and the territorial dispute over Dokdo/Takeshima: regional and national identities in Japan. *The Pacific Review, 28*(1), 47–70.

Carretero, M., Asensio, M., & Rodríguez-Moneo, M. (2011). *History education and the construction of national identities*. Charlotte, NC: Information Age.

Carson, T. R. (1995). Reflective practice and a reconceptualization of teacher education. In M. F. Wideen & P. P. Grimmett (Eds.), *Changing times in teacher education: Reconstructing or reconceptualization?* (pp. 151–162). New York, NY: RoutledgeFalmer.

Cho, J., Kim, H., & Choi, J. Y. (2009). The Dokdo/Takeshima dispute between Korea and Japan: Understanding the whole picture. *Pacific Focus, 24*(3), 365–378.

Cobb, P., Confrey, J., diSessa, A., Lehrer, R., & Schauble, L. (2003). Design experiments in educational research. *Educational Researcher, 32*(1), 9–13.

Cole, R., Purao, S., Rossi, M., & Sein, M. (2005). Being proactive: Where action research meets design research. *ICIS 2005 Proceedings*, 27.

Conversi, D. (1999). Nationalism, boundaries, and violence. *Millennium, 28*(3), 553–584.

Corbin, J., & Strauss, A. (1990). Grounded theory research: Procedures, canons, and evaluative criteria. *Qualitative Sociology, 13*(1), 3–21.

Dewey, J. (1996). The democratic conception in education: John Dewey, 1916. In W. C. Parker (Ed.), *Educating the democratic mind* (pp. 25–43). Albany, NY: State University of New York Press. (Original work published 1916)

Druckman, D. (1994). Nationalism, patriotism, and group loyalty: A social psychological perspective. *Mershon International Studies Review, 38*(1), 43–68.

Edelson, D. C. (2002). Design research: What we learn when we engage in design. *The Journal of the Learning Sciences, 11*(1), 105–121.

Edwards, D., & Potter, J. (1992). *Discursive psychology*. London: Sage.

Engle, S. H., & Ochoa, A. S. (1988). *Education for democratic citizenship*. New York, NY: Teachers College Press.

Epstein, T. (1998). Deconstructing differences in African-American and European-American adolescents' perspectives on U.S. history. *Curriculum Inquiry, 28*(4), 397–423.

Evans, R. W., Newman, F. M., & Saxe, D. W. (1996). Defining issue-centered education. In R. W. Evans, & D. W. Saxe (Eds.), *Handbook on teaching social studies* (pp. 2–5). NW, Washington, DC: National Council for the Social Studies.

Foster, S. J., & Crawford, K. A. (Eds.) (2006). *What shall we tell the children? International perspectives on school history textbooks.* Greenwich, CT: Information Age.

Freedman, E. B. (2015). "What happened needs to be told": Fostering critical historical reasoning in the classroom. *Cognition and Instruction, 33*(4), 357–398.

Galinsky, A. D., Maddux, W. W., Gilin, D., & White, J. B. (2008). Why it pays to get inside the head of your opponent. *Psychological Science, 19*(4), 378–384.

Genron NPO (2018, July 20). The 5th Japan-South Korea joint public opinion poll: Analysis report on comparative data. Retrieved from www.genron-npo.net/en/opinion_polls/archives/5436.html

Goldberg, T. (2013). "It's in my veins": Identity and disciplinary practice in students' discussions of a historical issue. *Theory & Research in Social Education, 41*(1), 33–64.

Goldberg, T., Schwarz, B. B., & Porat, D. (2011). "Could they do it differently?": Narrative and argumentative changes in students' writing following discussion of "hot" historical issues. *Cognition and Instruction, 29*(2), 185–217.

Habermas, J. (1984) [1981]. *Theory of communicative action, volume one: Reason and the rationalization of society.* Translated by Thomas A. McCarthy. Boston, MA: Beacon Press.

Hertzberg, H. W. (1981). *Social studies reform, 1880–1980.* Boulder, CO: Social Science Education Consortium.

Hursh, D. W., & Ross, E. W. (2000). *Democratic social education: Social studies for social change.* New York, NY: Falmer Press.

Kiesler, S., Siegel, J., & McGuire, T. W. (1984). Social psychological aspects of computer-mediated communication. *American psychologist, 39*(10), 1123–1134.

Kim, J. (2016). "Taihwagata" kokusairikaikyouiku eno cyousen: Nikkan no kodomo o syutai tosita "Yoriyoi shakaika kyoukasyo zukuri" jissen o jireini (The challenge for "Communication-Based" international education: A case for "Making a Better Textbook" with South Korean and Japanese students as the main agents). *Shakaika Kennkyu (Journal of Educational Research on Social Studies), 84*, 49–60.

Kim, J. (2017). Jiko to tasha no "Sinseinataiwa" nimotozuku nikkan kankeisi kyouiku: Nikkan no kodomo o syutai tosita "Yoriyoi nissin/nichiro sensou no kyoukasyo zukuri" o jireini (Teaching history of Japan–Korea relations based on "Authentic Communication" between the self and others: A case for "Making a Better History Textbook as relates to the Sino-Japanese War and Russo-Japanese War" by Japanese and Korean students). *Shakaika Kyouiku Kennkyu (The Journal of Social Studies), 130*, 1–12.

Kolikant, Y. B.-D., & Pollack, S. (2009). The asymmetrical influence of identity: A triadic interaction among Israeli Jews, Israeli Arabs, and historical texts. *Journal of Curriculum Studies, 41*(5), 651–677.

Kosterman, R., & Feshbach, S. (1989). Toward a measure of patriotic and nationalistic attitudes. *Political Psychology, 10*, 257–274.

Kozisek, D. (2016). Us and them: Constructing South Korean national identity through the Liancourt Rocks dispute. *Culture Mandala: The Bulletin of the Centre for East–West Cultural and Economic Studies, 12*(1), Article 1. Retrieved from http://epublications.bond.edu.au/cm/vol12/issu1/1

Lewin, K. (1946). Action research and minority problems. *Journal of Social Issues, 2*(4), 34–46.

McKenney, S. E., & Reeves, T. C. (2012). *Conducting educational design research.* New York, NY: Routledge.

McNiff, J. (2013). *Action research: Principles and practice* (3rd ed.). Oxon: Routledge.

Nakamura, K. (2008). *Kokkyou o koeru koukyouiku: Sekaisiminkyouiku no kanousei (Public education that goes beyond the national border: The possibilities of global citizenship education).* Tokyo: Toyokan Press.

Nash, G. B., Crabtree, C. A., & Dunn, R. E. (1997). *History on trial: Culture wars and the teaching of the past.* New York, NY: Random House.

Nijhawan, S. (2017). Bridging the gap between theory and practice with design-based action research. *Studia paedagogica, 22*(4), 9–29.

Nishikawa, N. (2001). *Kokkyou no koekata (How to cross the national border)* (2nd ed.). Tokyo: Heibonsha.

Nussbaum, M. C. (2013). *Political emotions: Why love matters for justice.* Cambridge, MA: Harvard University Press.

Parker, W. C. (1996). Introduction: Schools as laboratories of democracy. In W. C. Parker (Ed.), *Educating the democratic mind* (pp. 1–22). Albany, NY: State University of New York Press.

Parker, W. C. (2010). Listening to strangers: Classroom discussion in democratic education. *Teachers College Record, 112*(11), 2815–2832.

Plomp, T. (2007). Educational design research: An introduction. In T. Plomp & N. Nieveen (Eds.), *An introduction to educational design research* (pp. 9–36). Enschede: SLO.

Porat, D. A. (2004). It's not written here, but this is what happened: Students' cultural comprehension of textbook narratives on the Israeli-Arab conflict. *American Educational Research Journal, 41*(4), 963–996.

Ryu Y., Choi, R., & Kim, D. (2014). Chodengkyosa suyeop hoikilhwa e daehan gungeoronjeok jeopgun (A study on the process of unified instructions in Korean elementary school based on grounded theory). *Yeolin Gyouyuk Yeongu (Open Education Research), 22*(4), 279–299.

Scollon, R., Scollon, S. W., & Jones, R. H. (2011). *Intercultural communication: A discourse approach* (3rd ed.). West Sussex: John Wiley & Sons.

Sein, M. K., Henfridsson, O., Purao, S., Rossi, M., & Lindgren, R. (2011). Action design research. *MIS quarterly, 35*(1), 37–56.

Suh, Y., Yurita, M., Lin, L., & Metzger, S. (2013). Collective memories of the Second World War in history textbooks from China, Japan, and South Korea. *Journal of International Social Studies, 3*(1), 34–60.

Staub, E. (1997). Blind versus constructive patriotism: Moving from embeddedness in the group to critical loyalty and action. In D. Bar-Tal & E. Staub (Eds.), *Nelson-Hall series in psychology. Patriotism: In the lives of individuals and nations* (pp. 213–228). Chicago, IL: Nelson-Hall.

Stringer, E. T. (2013). *Action research.* Thousand Oaks, CA: Sage.

Ulich, R. (1967). *The education of nation: A comparison in historical perspective* (2nd ed.). Cambridge, MA: Harvard University Press.

Wang, F. & Hannafin, M. J. (2005). Design-based research and technology: Enhanced learning environments. *Educational Technology Research and Development, 53*(4), 5–23.

Wertsch, J. V. (2000). Is it possible to teach beliefs, as well as knowledge about history? In P. N. Stearns, P. C. Seixas, & S. S. Wineburg (Eds.), *Knowing, teaching, and learning history: National and international perspectives* (pp. 38–50). New York, NY: New York University Press.

Westheimer, J. (2006). Politics and patriotism in education. *Phi Delta Kappan, 87*(8), 608–620.

Williams, E. (1977). Experimental comparisons of face-to-face and mediated communication: A review. *Psychological Bulletin, 84*(5), 963.

Whitehead, J. (1989). Creating a living educational theory from questions of the kind: How do I improve my practice? *Cambridge Journal of Education, 19*(1), 137–153.

Sakaue, Y., Tonami, K., Yagasaki, N., Arai, M., Ito, S., Ireko, S.,. . . Tokyosyoseki Kubushikikaisha (2016). *Atarashii shakai: Chiri (New Social studies: Geography)* (new ed.). Tokyo: Tokyoshoseki.

Yamaue, K. (2010). Kyoiku seisaku o yomu (4): kyoukasyo izon toiu zyubaku karano kaihou o (Reading Educational policy (4): For the liberation from the restriction called textbook dependence). *Gekkan Koukou Kyouiku (Monthly High School Education), 43*(8), 82–85.

Conclusion

11

TOWARD SOCIALLY TRANSFORMATIVE DESIGN RESEARCH FOR SOCIAL STUDIES

A Critical Epistemological Approach

Beth C. Rubin

In the past decade, researchers in the learning sciences have begun to grapple with the social, cultural, historical, and political dimensions of design research. The transformational aims of DBR, intended as they are to contribute to significant change in educational practice, call out for a grounding in the concerns of critical theory (i.e., Freire, Gramsci) so as not to replicate the inequalities that have marked educational settings. In her 2011 AERA Presidential address, Kris Gutiérrez proclaimed:

> in light of the demographic imperative and growing of inequity, we simply cannot continue to rely on efficiency and market-driven models for education that are certain to bankrupt the future of our nation's youth. We need models for educational intervention that are consequential—new systems that demand radical shifts in our views of learning and in our perceptions of youth from non-dominant communities so that they can become agents of newly imagined futures.
>
> *(2016, p. 187)*

This critical epistemological approach to design-based research foregrounds the transformative possibilities of education, seeking to put young people and their communities on equal footing with practitioners, scholars, and researchers "as knowledge producers and change agents for social justice" (Caraballo, Lozenski, Lyiscott, & Morrell, 2017, p. 312). A critical epistemology, in relation to design research, challenges traditional understandings of who holds and generates knowledge and centers the experiences and ideas of youth and adults from historically marginalized communities.

A variety of new terms have been used to describe such approaches: social design experimentation, participatory design research, critical design ethnography, and socially transformative design (see the 2016 special issue of *Cognition and Instruction* on this topic, 34, 3). Researchers in these areas ask questions about the ways that structural inequity and histories of colonialism and white supremacy shape the larger contexts within which DBR projects are enacted. They ask about how various dimensions of power and inequality figure into design researchers' collaborations with participants. They ask hard questions about the goals of design projects: Are they aimed at expanding transformative learning possibilities, or are they simply reproducing the status quo?

Such questions are particularly relevant for researchers in the social studies, a field long engaged with questions of justice and social transformation. Yet, perhaps due to the roots of DBR methodology in the learning sciences, DBR efforts focused on social studies, still small in number, have tended to follow a more traditional model. While these projects draw upon the method's unique conceptualization of theory-informed innovation to improve practice, they tend not to employ critical approaches that theorize the context within which the projects are taking place, they do not generally consider the ways that education has been employed as a tool of oppression in non-dominant communities, nor do they tend to take into account the complex power dynamics of researcher-participant-community relationships. This chapter considers the need for a critical epistemological approach to design-based research in social studies that attends to these issues of equity and power.

Socially Transformative DBR in Social Studies: Context, Purpose and Relationships

Socially transformative design projects, in contrast to more traditional forms of DBR, are "organized around a commitment to transforming the educational and social circumstances of members of non-dominant communities as a means of promoting social equity and learning" (Gutiérrez & Jurow, 2016, p. 2). Such projects aim to develop deep and sustainable intervention that impacts educators' beliefs and school-based norms of social interaction (Coburn, 2003). To do so, they consciously draw upon the "diverse forms of expertise" found in local communities (Gutiérrez & Jurow, 2016, p. 4). In the remainder of this chapter, I will map out a three-pronged approach to a socially transformative design research program in the social studies, focusing on three fundamental considerations for such projects: context, purpose, and relationships (Figure 11.1).

Critically Considering Context in Social Studies DBR

DBR began with the seemingly simple but apparently revolutionary notion that context matters: Educational interventions needed to be studied within real educational settings. But what is "context"? In the first wave of DBR projects, and many that followed, context was seen as consisting of the classroom and

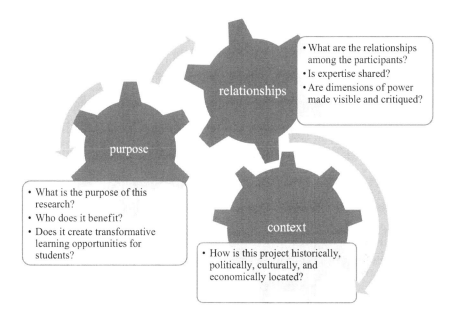

FIGURE 11.1 Transformative Design for Social Studies: A Three-pronged Approach.

those within. In this country, however, education takes place within settings and with people that diverge widely in their histories, access to cultural and material resources, and positioning within inequitable structures (Yosso, 2005). As Jurow and Shea (2015) write, "the possibilities of learning and development are deeply situated in unevenly developed historical, spatial, and social circumstances" (p. 4). These dimensions of context shape learning. As Gutiérrez & Vossoughi (2010) put it, "learning ecologies are co-created and grounded in the cultural historical practices of the communities involved" (p. 100).

One example of such an approach is Bang, Faber, Gurneau, Marin, and Soto's (2015) community-based design project in Indigenous communities in Chicago, in which "a long view of the relationships of schools to Indigenous communities and the colonization of North America" was essential to the endeavor (p. 7). In this project, the collaborators situated their research center within a community center, utilizing intergenerational learning and integrating a continued, critical focus on nature-culture relationships. This volume includes examples of a deeper theorization of and engagement with context as well. In Kim's work with elementary students in South Korea and Japan (this volume), the issues that his students grappled with were only controversial in relation to the historical and political context of those two nations. Rubin (this volume) describes an intervention that brought a critical theorization of context to bear on several of the study's components (from site selection, to design principles, to analysis of data), so as to foreground questions of history, power, and justice relevant to students. Stoddard and Rodriguez (this volume) designed their political-communications simulation in direct response to a contemporary political climate that makes the development of critical media literacy a pressing concern. Obenchain, Pennington and Bardem (this volume) describe how shifts in political context reshaped the work of their collaborating teacher, deeply impacting their project and leading the authors to conclude, "DBR is not a simple activity implemented in a static environment." For Day and Bae (this volume), a shifting policy context also shaped their work with teachers in developing authentic assessments. Monte-Sano (this volume) frames her study as an attempt to narrow the achievement gap in literacy.

In all of these projects, however—as in most design-based research—issues of race, social class, and other forms of inequity could be more fully theorized and addressed (Gutiérrez, Engeström, & Sannino, 2016). A consideration of context that goes beyond a depiction of classrooms and schools as interchangeable—one that attends to the historical, political, and structural dimensions of the multiple contexts that frame learning—is fundamental to socially transformative design. This would mean describing and factoring in the ways that communities, schools, classrooms, and students are located amid structures of power, as well as more deeply engaging with their strengths—strengths which are under-valued within our educational system and other social institutions (Yosso, 2005). Such considerations may also be essential for DBR that aims to improve social studies and civic learning. Projects that do not fully describe and theorize the contexts within which they are enacted may be missing the larger picture of education within real settings that is necessary for truly transformative design work.

Critically Conceptualizing Purpose

The purposes of social studies are broad, complex, situated, and political, resisting reduction to a cognitive model. This fact both complicates and enriches DBR in social studies. Given the ways that students are deeply impacted by inequitable contexts, how are we to think of the purpose of our projects? Gutiérrez and Jurow (2016) describe social design experimentation as "an approach to design research that is organized around a commitment to transforming the educational and social circumstances of members of nondominant communities as a means of promoting social equity and learning" (p. 2). They continue, "What sets social design experimentation apart as an approach is that it seeks a design process that strives to be a part of the process of fundamental social transformation" (p. 2).

Transformative purposes can be conceptualized in a variety of ways. McWilliams (2016) describes how "queering" participatory design research challenges the ways that "the heterosexual matrix permeates all aspects of culture," with the aim of "forging livable educational spaces for queer and gender diverse learners" (p. 270). Booker and Goldman (2016), aimed for a shift in epistemic authority from educators to parents that might begin to repair the "rift that repeatedly forms between experiences of formal mathematics education and parents' aspirations to help their children" (pp. 222–223). What is critical is that these projects aim to create transformative learning experiences.

In social studies, perhaps more powerfully than any other subject area, the very content of the field can be employed to either transform or sustain oppressive conceptualizations of society. As Anthony and Kefferlyn Brown (2015) note, "curriculum is about memory making, or the way a nation imagines and shapes what people come to know about the past and present" (p. 104). Curriculum, in social studies, is deeply political; the way that content is framed and presented can either upend or reinforce entrenched misconceptions of the country's past and present. Unfortunately, the social studies curriculum has traditionally played a role in upholding a Eurocentric view of U.S. history. In their review of social studies standards, Shear, Knowles, Soden, and Castro (2015) explain that, "despite recent movements to address social justice issues, and the one-sided nature of US history textbooks, social studies scholarship routinely finds that Euro-American voices dominate textbooks and content standards" (p. 69). Race and racism have not been fully or effectively engaged with in the frameworks created by the National Council for the Social Studies (Chandler & McKnight, 2011); even the latest version (the *C3 Framework*), which focuses on civic inquiry, "reflects the same raceless perspective as previous NCSS sanctioned documents" (King & Chandler, 2016, p. 9). Without critically and directly engaging with questions of race, the social studies curriculum cannot help students to understand the ways that white supremacy and racial violence undergird the country's past and present, understandings that are central to developing the forms of critical sociopolitical consciousness described below.

Providing access to transformative learning opportunities that result in sociopolitical development, and "historicity" is a central aim of civic education. Sociopolitical development is the "process of growth in a person's knowledge, analytical skills, emotional faculties, and capacity for action in political and social systems" (Watts, Williams, & Jagers, 2003, p. 185). Historicity is the development of an awareness of one's self as an historical subject with consciousness and agency. "Becoming historical actors," write Gutiérrez and Jurow (2016), "involves understanding one's self and one's cultural community in relation to their respective histories" (p. 7). Which school subject is more appropriate than social studies for helping youth develop "analytical tools to understand and write one's story into history" (p. 14)? These are highly relevant purposes for DBR in social studies.

Some of the work in this volume aligns with purposes like these. Burke built her study upon a transformational agenda for young children's understandings of race and gender. Kim proposes a "critical patriotism" that breaks down "the myth that our nation's discourse is the right one." Obenchain, Pennington, and Bardem aimed to develop children's critical civic literacy, while Stoddard and Rodriguez sought to cultivate young people's understanding of the ways that political media can shape discourses around social causes (e.g., environmentalism). Rubin's project placed critical civic learning at the center of the U.S. history curriculum, while Freedman's sought to help students understand the political stake in the past held by those in living in the present. Lo and her colleagues, in their project, aimed to make AP Government more relevant to the real world of politics. These projects employed DBR to aim at "developing an awareness of one's self as an historical subject rather than object" (Gutiérrez and Jurow, 2016, p. 14).

The purpose of socially transformative design projects can be directly linked to the purpose of social studies education: helping students to better understand themselves and the society around them so that they can be active civic participants who can write their own story into history. Social studies education has a unique capacity to contribute richly to socially transformative DBR aimed at the socio-political development, historicity, and transformative learning of young people.

Attending to Relationships

Finally, I want to draw attention to the relational aspect of DBR. A socially transformative approach assumes that designing interventions collaboratively with participants increases the likelihood that the designs will address their actual needs in a meaningful way. Thus, critical attention to the nature of these relationships is essential. Attending to dimensions of power, grappling with questions of authority and ownership, and taking an assets-based approach to relationships are common concerns for socially transformative design researchers.

Gutiérrez and Jurow (2016) write that social design experimentation requires "a shift from viewing schools, communities and other institutions as sites of study, as places in which empirical work is conducted, to viewing them as dynamic contexts for study that include partners who have agency for shifting their educational and life circumstances" (p. 5). Beyond conceptualizing students and educators as recipients of university-based researchers' new ideas or as marginal partners at best, this approach calls for an epistemological shift in which participants' knowledge is seen as central to the conceptualization of the project itself. Barab, Thomas, Dodge, Squire, & Newell, (2004) suggest "adopting a participatory posture, developing multi-tiered relationships, and having an evolving as opposed to an imposed agenda" (p. 265; see also McKenney & Reeves, 2012). Foregrounding the perspectives, agency, and voice of non-university participants can be difficult. Yet this idea of "making visible" participants' "practices that were once invisible brings forward the possibility for positive change" (Jurow, Teeters, Shea, and Van Steenis, 2016, p. 220).

Obenchain, Pennington, and Bardem (this volume) describe how their study began with their foregrounding of the teacher's goals for the project, but shifted over time because of political changes in the surrounding context. The collaborative relationship was fundamental to their choice of DBR as a methodology. "We chose a design-based research (DBR) approach for our collaboration," they explain, "as it allowed us to work with Maricela to bring CDL as an instructional model to the continually evolving context of her classroom in a flexible and responsive way." The opportunity to work collaboratively while remaining theoretically informed was critical, "because this level of collaboration opens up a space for the discussion of critical issues that potentially puts teachers and researchers in the position of challenging and potentially contradicting current curricula." Lo, Adams, Goodell, and Nachtigal (this volume) describe how a teacher's ability to influence the design of curriculum and professional development through his participation in a multi-year DBIR project shifted his practice and understandings. In reflecting on their project, Monte-Sano, Hughes, and Thomson (this volume) suggest that researchers using DBR ought to "learn from teachers and students in an iterative process that responds to their successes, expertise, and challenges."

The challenge posed by unequal power relationships among DBR project members related to age, race, gender, sexuality, educational level, and economic status can be particularly complex. Vakil, de Royston, Nasir, and Kirshner (2016), for example, acknowledge "the under-theorization of how race and power mediate researcher-researched relationships within DBR projects" (p. 196). Sometimes recognition of these power inequities does not come until after the end of the project. Burke (this volume) writes of her data collection activities during her DBR project investigating an anti-bias curriculum: "What I didn't account for when creating this study," she reflects, "is that by trying to get children to expand their thinking about gender, I was actually reifying the binary." Her thoughts demonstrate the critical reflexivity at the heart of any attempt to negotiate complex power relationships. Participation of historically marginalized people in design projects must go beyond superficial nods to inclusion, but rather be fundamental to project design, implementation, and analysis. Zavala (2016), reflecting on his design work with grassroots organizations, explains that full inclusion of these perspectives "has the potential to 'desettle' projects at a fundamental level," challenging traditional epistemologies (p. 236).

Making this shift is essential for truly transformative design work in social studies. Although civic participation is fundamental to democratic life, the voices and perspectives of young people, particularly those from non-dominant communities, are not often incorporated into the processes and practices of schools (Cohen, Kahne, & Marshall, 2018; Levinson, 2011; Rubin, 2007). Yet these youth can provide critical insights for school communities, helping to unearth and address problems that can be more clearly seen and understood from their vantage point (Gutiérrez & Jurow, 2016). Youth, for example, can be more apt to engage with difficult civic topics, such as race, equity, and social justice, which educators often overlook or avoid (Mitra, 2006). The studies in this volume reveal the utility of a design-based approach for blending research and instructional improvement in real classroom settings to improve social studies instruction. They also, in a variety of ways, suggest where DBR might be headed, hinting at how it might start to further encompass a more critical approach.

Generative Questions for a Socially Transformative Approach to DBR

In this chapter, I have argued that DBR in social studies research should aim to develop "equitable forms of learning and teaching that contribute to a socially just democracy" (Bang & Vossoughi, 2016, p. 173). I am advocating a critical epistemology for socially transformative design in social studies that attends to history and power and aspires toward transformative learning. An epistemological shift must occur in how knowledge is conceptualized and held within such projects (Booker & Goldman, 2016). To this end, I offer three questions for us to think about when initiating DBR studies:

1. *How are we thinking about context in this particular study—how is the project embedded in history, politics and structure?*
    This question will help design teams to create projects that are attentive to aspects of context that are often overlooked but are fundamental to learning—the dimensions of structural and historical inequality that shape students' school and classroom experiences.
2. *What is the purpose of the study—does it create opportunities for transformative learning, sociopolitical development, and historicity?*
    This question will help design teams to consider whether the aims of their projects are truly relevant and liberatory, particularly for students from historically marginalized communities for whom civic and social studies education has, more often than not, failed to incorporate or illuminate their civic experiences and those of their communities.
3. *What will the relationships be among the participants—are we taking an assets-based approach that gives authority to participants and attends to varying dimensions of power?*
    This question will help design teams to re-envision who holds and creates knowledge, encouraging projects built on multiple perspectives and centering marginalized voices.

Using these, or similar, critical questions will help us to play a part in the development of "transformative forms of learning in which people can become designers of their own futures" (Gutiérrez, Engeström, & Sannino, 2016, p. 276), projects that live up to the potential of both social studies and socially transformative design.

References

Bang, M., Faber, L., Gurneau, J., Marin, A., & Soto, C. (2015). Community-based design research: Learning across generations and strategic transformations of institutional relations toward axiological innovations, *Mind, Culture, and Activity*, DOI: 10.1080/10749039.2015.1087572

Bang, M., & Vossoughi, S. (2016). Participatory design research and educational justice: Studying learning and relations within social change making. *Cognition and Instruction, 34*(3), 173–193.

Barab, S. A., Thomas, M. K., Dodge, T., Squire, K., & Newell, M. (2004). Critical design ethnography: Designing for change. *Anthropology & Education Quarterly*, *35*(2), 254–268.

Booker, A., & Goldman, S. (2016) Participatory design research as a practice for systemic repair: Doing hand-in-hand math research with families. *Cognition and Instruction*, *34*(3), 222–235.

Brown, A. L. (1992). Design experiments: Theoretical and methodological challenges in complex interventions in classroom settings. *The Journal of the Learning Sciences*, *2*(2), 141–178.

Brown, A., and Brown, K. (2015). The more things change, the more they stay the same: Excavating race and the *enduring racisms* in U.S. curriculum. *Teachers College Record*, *117*(14), 103–130.

Caraballo, L., Lozenski, B., Lyiscott, J., & Morrel, E. (2017). YPAR and critical epistemologies: Rethinking education research. *Review of Research in Education March 2017*, *41*, 311–336.

Chandler, P., & McKnight, D. (2011). Race and the social studies. In W. Russell (Ed.), *Contemporary social studies: An essential reader* (pp. 215–242). Greenwich: Information Age Publishing.

Coburn, C. (2003). Rethinking scale: Moving beyond numbers to deep and lasting change. *Educational Researcher*, *32*(5), 3–12.

Cohen, C., Kahne, J., & Marshall, J. (2018). *Let's go there: Race, ethnicity, and a lived civics approach to civic education*. Chicago, IL: GenForward at the University of Chicago.

Gutiérrez, K. (2016). Designing resilient ecologies: Social design experiments and a new social imagination. *Educational Researcher*, *45*(3), 187–196.

Gutiérrez, K., Engeström, Y., & Sannino, A. (2016). Expanding educational research and interventionist methodologies, *Cognition and Instruction*, *34*(3), 275–284.

Gutiérrez, K., & Jurow, A. S. (2016). Social design experiments: Toward equity by design. *Journal of the Learning Sciences*, *00*, 1–34.

Gutiérrez, K., & Vossoughi, S. (2010). Lifting off the ground to return anew: Mediated praxis, transformative learning, and social design experiments. *Journal of Teacher Education*, *61*, 100–117.

Jurow, A. S., Teeters, L., Shea, M., & Van Steenis, E. (2016). Extending the consequentiality of "invisible work" in the food justice movement. *Cognition and Instruction*, *34*(3), 210–221.

Jurow, A. S., & Shea, M. (2015). Learning in equity-oriented scale-making projects. *Journal of the Learning Sciences*, *24*, 286–307.

King, L., & Chandler, P. (2016). From non-racism to anti-racism in social studies teacher education: Social studies and racial pedagogical content knowledge. In A. R. Crowe & A. Cuenca (Eds.), *Rethinking social studies teacher education in the Twenty-First Century* (pp. 3–21). Switzerland: Springer International Publishing.

Levinson, M. (2011). *No citizen left behind*. Cambridge, MA: Harvard University Press.

McKenney, S. E., & Reeves, T. C. (2012). *Conducting educational design research*. New York, NY: Routledge.

McWilliams, J. (2016). Queering participatory design research. *Cognition and Instruction*, *34*(3), 259–274.

Mitra, D. (2006). Student voice or empowerment? Examining the role of school-based youth-adult partnerships as an avenue toward focusing on social justice. *International Electronic Journal for Leadership in Learning*, *10*(22), 1–12. Downloaded on 1/21/18 from http://iejll.journalhosting.ucalgary.ca/iejll/index.php/ijll/article/view/622/284

Rubin, B. C. (2007). "There's still not justice: Youth civic identity development amid distinct school and community contexts." *Teachers College Record*, *109*(7), 449–481.

Shear, S., Knowles, R. T., Soden, G. J., & Castro, A. (2015). Manifesting destiny: Re/presentations of indigenous peoples in K–12 U.S. history standards. *Theory & Research in Social Education, 43*(1), 68–101.

Vakil, S., de Royston, M., Nasir, N., & Kirshner, B. (2016). Rethinking race and power in design-based research: Reflections from the field. *Cognition and Instruction, 34*, 194–209.

Watts, R., Williams, N., & Jagers, R. (2003). Sociopolitical development. *American Journal of Community Psychology, 31*, 185–191.

Yosso, T. (2005). Whose culture has capital? A critical race theory discussion of community cultural wealth. *Race Ethnicity and Education, 8*(1), 69–91.

Zavala, M. (2016). Design, participation, and social change: What design in grassroots spaces can teach learning scientists. *Cognition and Instruction, 34*(3), 236–249.

INDEX

Page numbers for figures are given in *italics*, and for tables they are given in **bold**. Notes are given as: [page number] n [note number].